CHARACTERISTICS Black bears aren't always black. They can be brown, cinnamon, blond, or even blue-grey.

MOVEMENT Black bears are good fishers and swimmers.

YOUNG Cubs usually weigh less than one pound when they are born in January or February, but can weigh up to 125 pounds by their first autumn.

CHARACTERISTICS Bears, like dogs, can hear higher-pitched sounds than people can.

California
Science

Harcourt
SCHOOL PUBLISHERS

Visit *The Learning Site!*
www.harcourtschool.com

California Science

California black bears

Series Consulting Authors

Michael J. Bell, Ph.D.
Assistant Professor of Early
 Childhood Education
College of Education
West Chester University of
 Pennsylvania
West Chester, Pennsylvania

Michael A. DiSpezio
Curriculum Architect
JASON Academy
Cape Cod, Massachusetts

Marjorie Frank
Former Adjunct, Science
 Education
Hunter College
New York, New York

Gerald H. Krockover, Ph.D.
Professor of Earth and
 Atmospheric Science
 Education
Purdue University
West Lafayette, Indiana

Joyce C. McLeod
Adjunct Professor
Rollins College
Winter Park, Florida

Barbara ten Brink, Ph.D.
Science Specialist
Austin Independent School
 District
Austin, Texas

Carol J. Valenta
Senior Vice President
St. Louis Science Center
St. Louis, Missouri
Former teacher, principal, and
 Coordinator of Science Center
 Instructional Programs
Los Angeles Unified School
 District
Los Angeles, California

Barry A. Van Deman
President and CEO
Museum of Life and Science
Durham, North Carolina

Series Consultants

Catherine Banker
Curriculum Consultant
Alta Loma, California

Robin C. Scarcella, Ph.D.
Professor and Director, Program
of Academic English and ESL
University of California, Irvine
Irvine, California

Series Content Reviewers

Paul Asimow, Ph.D.
Associate Professor, Geology
and Geochemistry
California Institute of
Technology
Pasadena, California

Larry Baresi, Ph.D.
Associate Professor
California State University,
Northridge
Northridge, California

John Brockhaus, Ph.D.
Department of Geography and
Environmental Engineering
United States Military Academy
West Point, New York

Mapi Cuevas, Ph.D.
Professor of Chemistry
Santa Fe Community College
Gainesville, Florida

William Guggino, Ph.D.
Professor of Physiology and
Pediatrics
Johns Hopkins University,
School of Medicine
Baltimore, Maryland

V. Arthur Hammon
Pre-College Education Specialist
Jet Propulsion Laboratory
Pasadena, California

Steven A. Jennings, Ph.D.
Associate Professor in
Geography
University of Colorado at
Colorado Springs
Colorado Springs, Colorado

James E. Marshall, Ph.D.
Professor and Chair,
Department of Curriculum
and Instruction
California State University,
Fresno
Fresno, California

Joseph McClure, Ph.D.
Associate Professor Emeritus
Department of Physics
Georgetown University
Washington, D.C.

Dork Sahagian, Ph.D.
Professor of Earth and
Environmental Science
Lehigh University
Bethlehem, Pennsylvania

Curriculum and Classroom Reviewers

Elizabeth Bundschu-Mooney
Teacher
Grant Elementary School
Richmond, California

Juanita Fast
Science Coordinator
Santa Ana Unified School District
Santa Ana, California

Lisa B. Friedberg
Teacher
Alderwood Basics Plus School
Irvine, California

Michael Lebda
Science Specialist
Fresno Unified School District
Fresno, California

Daniel Lee
Teacher
Creekside Elementary School
Salinas, California

Ana G. Lopez
Science Specialist
Fresno Unified School District
Fresno, California

Cristie McCabe
Resource Specialist
Franklin Elementary School
Riverside, California

SCHOOL PUBLISHERS

Science and Technology features
provided by

*Science Content Standards for
California Public Schools* reproduced by
permission, California Department of
Education, CDE Press, 1430 N Street,
Suite 3207, Sacramento, CA 95814.

Printed in the United States of America

ISBN 13: 978-0-15-347120-9
ISBN 10: 0-15-347120-4

5 6 7 8 9 0914 14 13 12 11 10 09

Introductory Unit
Getting Ready for Science

Big Idea You can answer your science questions by carrying out careful investigations.

Essential Questions

PHYSICAL SCIENCE

UNIT 1
Electricity and Magnetism

Big Idea Electricity and magnetism are related. They are part of things you use every day.

Essential Questions

People in Science

California On Location

Technology

LIFE SCIENCE

UNIT 2 — Energy for Life and Growth   150

Big Idea All living things need energy and matter to live and grow.

Essential Questions

Pacific sea otter

v

LIFE SCIENCE

UNIT 3 — Ecosystems — 206

Big Idea Living things depend on one another and on their environment for survival.

Essential Questions

EARTH SCIENCE

UNIT 4 — Rocks and Minerals — 268

Big Idea You can tell a lot about how a rock or mineral formed by studying its properties.

Essential Questions

EARTH SCIENCE

UNIT 5 — Waves, Wind, Water, and Ice 318

Big Idea Waves, wind, water, and ice shape and reshape Earth's land surface.

Essential Questions

References

Cliff at Big Sur

Getting Ready for Science

California Standards in This Unit

6 Scientific progress is made by asking meaningful questions and conducting careful investigations. As a basis for understanding this concept:

6.a *Students will* differentiate observation from inference (interpretation) and know scientists' explanations come partly from what they observe and partly from how they interpret their observations.

6.b *Students will* measure and estimate the weight, length, or volume of objects.

6.c *Students will* formulate and justify predictions based on cause-and-effect relationships.

6.d *Students will* conduct multiple trials to test a prediction and draw conclusions about the relationships between predictions and results.

6.e *Students will* construct and interpret graphs from measurements.

6.f *Students will* follow a set of written instructions for a scientific investigation.

What's the Big Idea?

You can answer your science questions by carrying out careful investigations.

Essential Questions

Hi, Angel!

We're having a great time camping. Today, we hiked through the park—we saw lots of interesting plants and even a marmot!

Our guide taught us how to measure how far we walked by counting our steps. For me, every 20 steps is about 100 feet. I lost count after 2,000 feet—almost half a mile—but it seemed like we walked for miles and miles after that!

I'll see you when we get back on Sunday.

Your friend,
Kyle

How far do you walk every day? How could you find out? What tools could you use to measure the distance? How do you think that relates to the **Big Idea?**

Investigation and Experimentation

6.b *Students will* measure and estimate the weight, length, or volume of objects.

LESSON 1

Essential Question

What Are Investigation Tools?

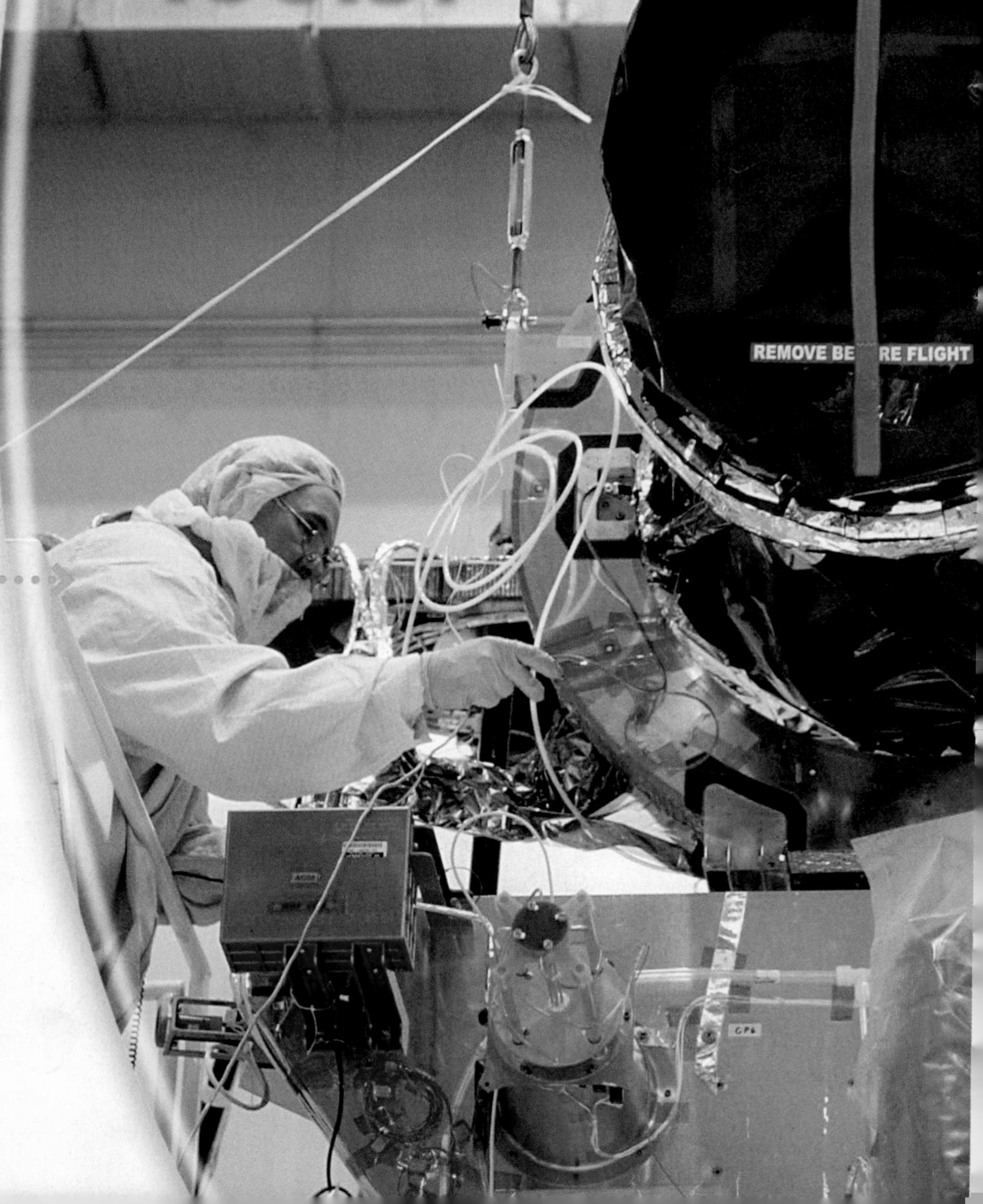

California Fast Fact

Eyes on the Planet

The *Mars Reconnaissance Orbiter* was developed and built at the Jet Propulsion Laboratory (JPL) of the California Institute of Technology in Pasadena, California. Its cameras will send back the most detailed pictures so far of Mars's surface.

REMOVE BEFORE FLIGHT

2

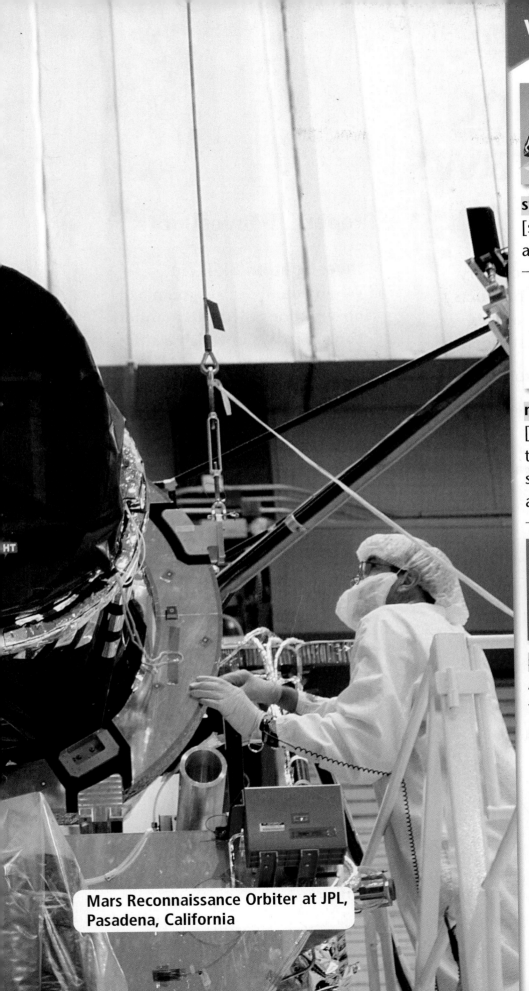

Mars Reconnaissance Orbiter at JPL, Pasadena, California

standard measure
[STAN•derd MEZH•er] An accepted measurement (p. 6)

microscope
[MY•kruh•skohp] A tool that makes an object look several times bigger than it actually is (p. 8)

spring scale [SPRING SKAYL]
A tool that measures forces, such as weight

(p. 11)

Measuring with Straws

Start with Questions

Suppose you go to the grocery store. There, all of the products have been carefully measured based on government standards.

- What exactly is measuring?

- What are some different ways to measure objects?

- Are there standard ways to measure the same objects?

Investigate to find out. Then read to learn more.

Prepare to Investigate

Investigation Skill Tip

When you measure, you make observations by using numbers. Look for ways in which a straw can be used to measure things. Then think about other ways you might measure the same things.

Materials

- plastic straws
- classroom objects
- 2 different-size cups
- water
- marker

Make a Data Table

Object	Measurement(s)

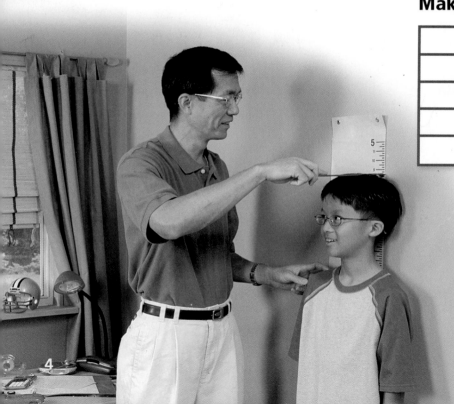

Follow This Procedure

1. Use straws to **measure** the length and width (distance along and across) of several objects. For example, you might begin with this textbook. **Record** your measurements.

2. Now use straws to **measure** the distance around a round object (its circumference). (Hint: Flatten the straws before you start.) **Record** your measurements.

3. Next, work with a partner to find a way to use straws to **measure** the amount (volume) of water in one of the cups. **Record** your measurements.

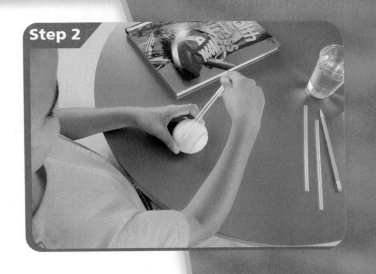

Step 2

Step 3

Draw Conclusions

1. Compare your measurements with those of other students. What can you conclude?

2. **Standards Link** Which of the objects you measured was the longest? Which cup held the greater volume of water? How can you tell? **6.b**

3. **Investigation Skill** Scientists **measure** carefully and record numbers accurately. Why do all scientists need to use the same unit of measurement when working on the same problem? **6.b**

Independent Inquiry   **Measure**

How could you use straws to measure weight? What other tools would you need? Plan and carry out a simple investigation to find out. **6.b**

VOCABULARY
standard measure p. 6
microscope p. 8
spring scale p. 11

SCIENCE CONCEPTS
▶ how scientist use tools to measure, observe, and manipulate
▶ how to use tools properly and safely

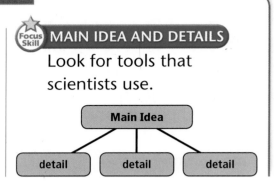

MAIN IDEA AND DETAILS
Look for tools that scientists use.

Main Idea

detail   detail   detail

Tools for Measuring Distance

Long ago, people sometimes used body parts to measure distance. For example, in the early 1100s, King Henry I of England had several identical iron bars made. The bars supposedly equalled the distance from his nose to his fingertips. They became a standard length—one yard. A **standard measure** is an accepted amount that is used to measure other things.

When it was introduced, the meter, another unit of length, was not based on a body part. It was defined as $\frac{1}{10,000,000}$ of the distance from the North Pole to the equator. Imagine measuring that distance!

These units of measurement may seem strange. Yet they helped people agree on the lengths of objects and the distances between places.

 **MAIN IDEA AND DETAILS** Why do we use standard units of measure?

▼ A flexible tape measure can measure circumference.

Geologists and surveyors use this tool to measure large distances.

◀ A ruler measures length. Place the first line of the ruler at one end of the object. The line closest to the other end of the object shows its length.

Tools for Measuring Volume

Cooks measure ingredients for recipes with cups and spoons. Scientists also measure volume with tools. To find the volume of a liquid, you pour it into a container, such as a measuring cup, beaker, or graduate. The numbers on the side of the container show the volume of the liquid. Never use tools from your science lab for measuring food or medicine!

To measure the volume of a solid, multiply its length by its width by its height. For example, a box has a length of 4 centimeters and a width of 2 centimeters. Its height is 2 centimeters. The volume is 4 centimeters × 2 centimeters × 2 centimeters = 16 cubic centimeters.

Insta-Lab

Personal Measuring Tools

Think of ways that you could measure distance or volume by using items you have at home or in the classroom. Test your new measuring tools, and exchange ideas with your classmates.

This is sometimes abbreviated 16 cm^3. All volumes are given in cubic units. So you may see cubic meters (m^3), as well.

Focus Skill **MAIN IDEA AND DETAILS** How do you measure the volume of a solid? Of a liquid?

Droppers are used to measure small amounts of liquid.

To measure a liquid, place a graduate on a flat surface. Your eyes should be even with the flat top of the liquid. The volume is the marking that is closest to the top of the liquid.

Tools for Observing and Handling

Sometimes scientists need to observe objects closely. Certain tools can help them observe details they might not be able to see with just their eyes.

A hand lens makes things look larger than they are. It magnifies them. Hold the lens a few centimeters in front of your eye. Then move the object closer to the lens until you can see it clearly. Never let the lens touch your eye. Never use it to look at the sun!

Forceps let you pick up sharp or prickly objects without getting hurt. You can also use them to hold delicate objects without handling those objects too much. However, you must squeeze the forceps gently.

A magnifying box is sometimes called a bug box. Students often use it to observe live insects. An insect can move around in the box while you watch.

A **microscope** makes objects look several times bigger than they are. The microscope shown on the next page has one big lens. Two knobs enable the user to adjust the image until he or she can see it clearly.

Focus Skill — MAIN IDEA AND DETAILS How do the tools on these pages help scientists?

A magnifying box lets you watch an insect move around but keeps it from getting away.

A hand lens helps you see many details. When you use forceps to hold an object, you can observe the object without having your fingers in the way. ▶

8

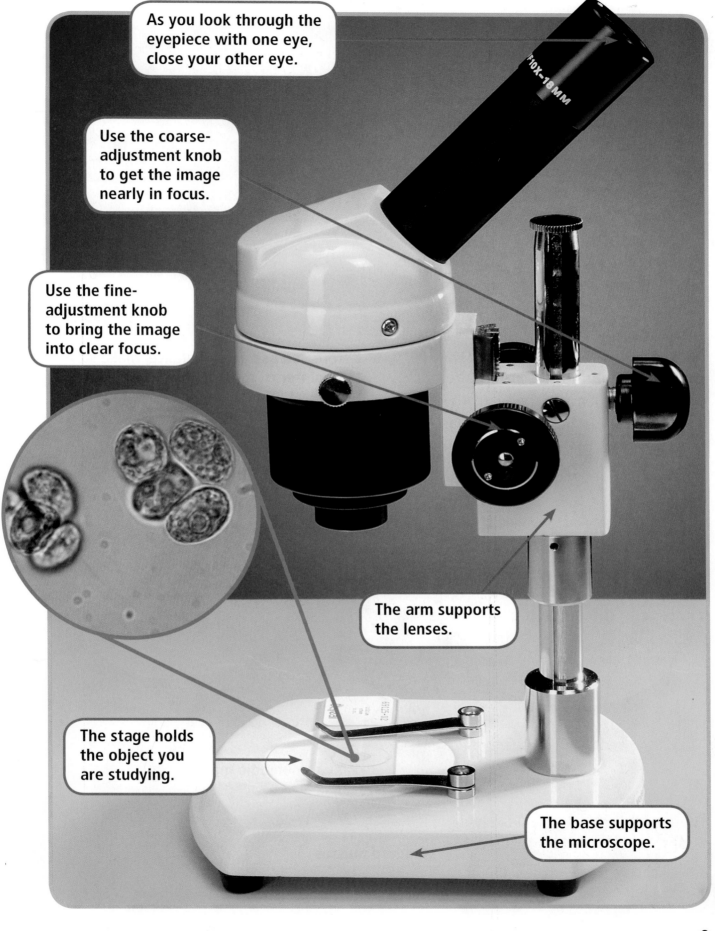

As you look through the eyepiece with one eye, close your other eye.

Use the coarse-adjustment knob to get the image nearly in focus.

Use the fine-adjustment knob to bring the image into clear focus.

The arm supports the lenses.

The stage holds the object you are studying.

The base supports the microscope.

Other Tools

Many other tools can help you measure. For example, a thermometer measures the temperature of the air or of a liquid. A thermometer is a hollow glass tube that has a bulb at one end. The bulb contains a liquid. The air or liquid around the bulb warms or cools the liquid inside the bulb. As the liquid inside the thermometer gets warmer, it expands and rises up the tube. Numbers on the thermometer tell how warm the air or liquid being measured is.

When you are using a thermometer, be sure to touch the bulb as little as possible. If your fingers are on the bulb, you will just measure the warmth of your fingers! Also, be careful—glass thermometers break easily. If one breaks,

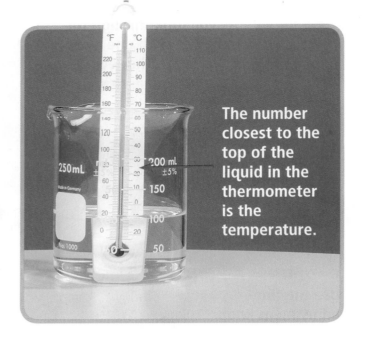

The number closest to the top of the liquid in the thermometer is the temperature.

▼ Before you use a pan balance, make sure the pointer is at the middle mark. Place the object in one pan, and add standard masses to the other pan. When the pointer is at the middle mark again, add the numbers on the standard masses. The total is the mass of the object.

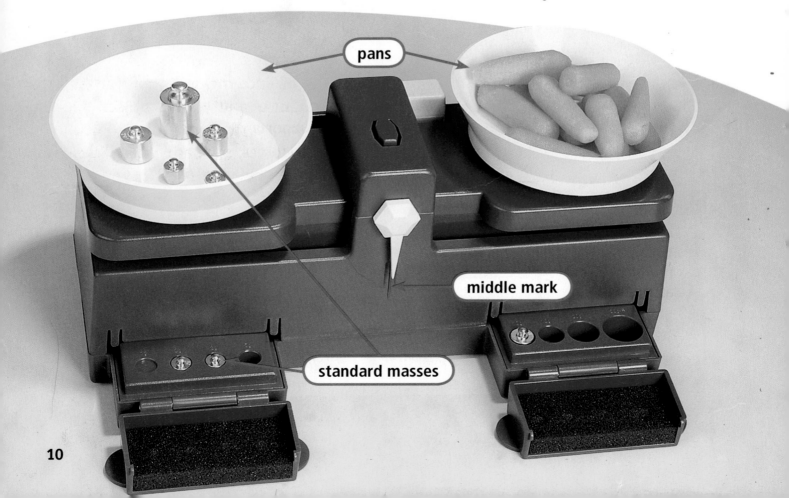

pans

middle mark

standard masses

This girl is using a spring scale to measure the rabbit's weight. ▶

A rock hammer can chip away smaller samples from a large rock. How might you observe these samples?

tell your teacher or another adult right away.

A pan balance measures mass. Mass is the amount of matter in an object. It is measured in grams (g). A **spring scale** measures forces, such as weight. Force is measured in newtons (N).

Other tools help scientists as well. The rock hammer shown on this page can help scientists gather samples from larger rocks. The scientists then identify the rocks by using other tools, such as hand lenses, to observe the patterns of crystals and other properties.

MAIN IDEA AND DETAILS What properties do a pan balance and a spring scale measure?

Essential Question

What are investigation tools?

In this lesson, you measured length and volume and learned about the tools used to measure weight, length, and volume.

Investigation and Experimentation Standard in This Lesson

6.b *Students will* measure and estimate the weight, length, or volume of objects.

1. **MAIN IDEA AND DETAILS** Draw and complete a graphic organizer to summarize the main idea and list details that support it. **6.b**

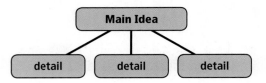

Main Idea

detail   detail   detail

2. **SUMMARIZE** Write two sentences that tell what this lesson is mostly about. **6.b**

3. **DRAW CONCLUSIONS** How would scientific experiments be different if scientists had no tools to use? **6.b**

4. **VOCABULARY** Write a fill-in-the-blank sentence for each vocabulary word. Trade sentences with a partner. **6.b**

5. **Critical Thinking** How do mass and weight differ? **6.b**

6. **Investigate and Experiment** How can you decide which tool to use in a certain experiment? **6.b**

7. Which tool measures length?
   A beaker
   B thermometer
   C pan balance
   D tape measure **6.b**

8. Which tool measures volume?
   A meterstick
   B pan balance
   C graduate
   D spring scale **6.b**

The **Big Idea**

 Writing ELA—W 1.2

Persuasive Writing

You are a scientist, but you can afford only two of the tools described in this lesson. Choose two tools, and write a persuasive paragraph explaining why they are the most important.

 Math NS 3.0

Solve a Problem

You are using a measuring wheel to determine the width of a street. A rotation of the wheel is 1 meter (3.3 ft). The wheel rotates $9\frac{1}{2}$ times. About how wide is the street?

bee stinger and sewing needle

 Art VPA—VA 2.5

Looking Closer

Draw an object as you would see it with your eyes. Then draw the same object as you think it would look under a hand lens. Now draw it as though it were under the highest-power microscope lens.

 For more links and activities, go to **www.hspscience.com**

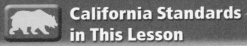
Investigation and Experimentation

6.a *Students will* differentiate observation from inference (interpretation) and know scientists' explanations come partly from what they observe and partly from how they interpret their observations.

6.b *Students will* measure and estimate the weight, length, or volume of an object.

6.c *Students will* formulate and justify predictions based on cause-and-effect relationships.

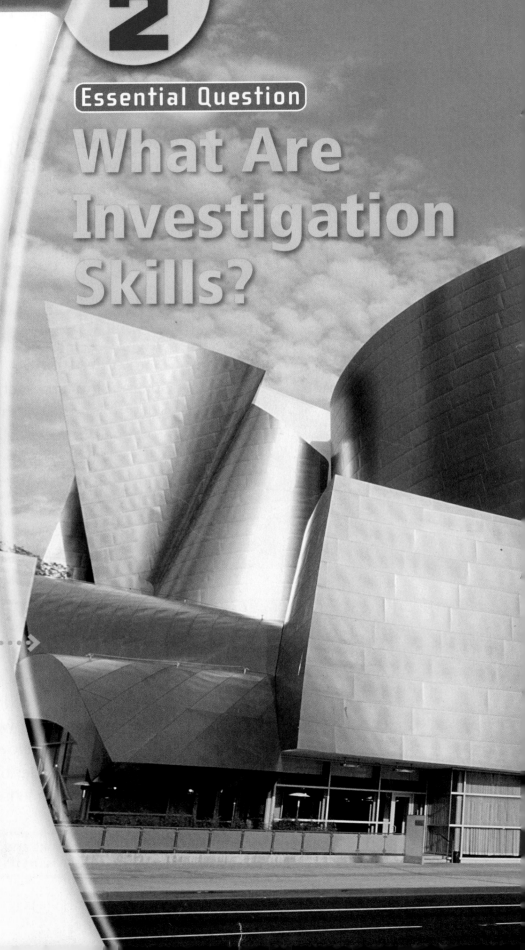

LESSON 2

Essential Question

What Are Investigation Skills?

California Fast Fact

Disney Design

Disney Hall in Los Angeles was a long science experiment! It took a team 12 years to plan and test models before the building could be made. The team worked hard to make a design that was interesting, safe, and had excellent sound quality.

14

observation [ahb•zuhr•VAY•shuhn] Information that you gather with your senses (p. 18)

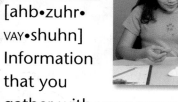

---

inference [IN•fuhr•uhns] An untested interpretation of observations (p. 18)

---

prediction [pree•DIK•shuhn] A statement of what will happen, justified by observations and knowledge of cause-and-effect relationships (p. 19)

---

estimate [ES•tuh•mit] An educated guess about a measurement (p. 22)

---

hypothesis [hy•PAHTH•uh•sis] A scientific explanation that can be tested (p. 23)

---

experiment [ek•SPER•uh•muhnt] A controlled test of a hypothesis (p. 23)

Disney Hall in Los Angeles

Build a Straw Model

Directed Inquiry

Start with Questions

You use investigation skills every day. You observe the world around you. You predict what will happen. You compare objects and ideas. You also build models.

- What is a model?

- How can using models help you answer questions about science?

Investigate to find out. Then read to learn more.

Prepare to Investigate

Investigation Skill Tip
A model is an object that looks or acts like the thing you are studying. Every model has limits. It can never be exactly the same as the thing you are studying.

Materials

- 16 plastic straws
- 30 paper clips
- 30-cm piece of masking tape

Make an Observation Chart

Step Number	Ideas and Observations

Follow This Procedure

1 Work with a group to construct a model of a building. First, discuss questions such as these: What should the building look like? What are some ways to use the paper clips and the tape with the straws? What will keep the building from falling down?

2 Have one group member record all the ideas. Be sure to respect each other's suggestions.

3 **Predict** which building methods will work best, and try them. **Observe** what works, **draw conclusions**, and **record** them.

4 **Plan** how to use your building methods to construct a model building. Then carry out the plan.

Draw Conclusions

1. Why was it important to share ideas before you began construction?

2. **Standards Link** How did your observations affect your conclusions?　6.a

3. **Investigation Skill** Scientists and engineers often **use models** to see how parts work together. What did you learn about building by making the model?

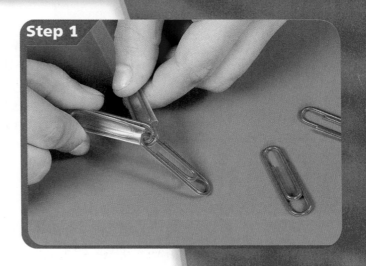
Step 1

Step 3

Independent Inquiry ▸ **Justify Predictions**

Choose one additional material or building method to use in making your model. Predict how it will improve your model. Justify your prediction, then test it.　6.c

VOCABULARY
observation p. 18
inference p. 18
prediction p. 19
estimate p. 22
hypothesis p. 23
experiment p. 23

SCIENCE CONCEPTS
► how scientists think
► how asking questions helps scientists learn and understand

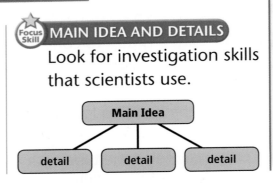

MAIN IDEA AND DETAILS
Look for investigation skills that scientists use.

Observe and Infer

Scientists practice certain ways of thinking, or *investigation skills*. You can use these skills, too. Learning them will help you think like a scientist.

Did you notice the clouds when you woke up today? If so, you made an observation. An **observation** is information from your senses. You can *observe* how tall a tree is and the color of its leaves.

Did you ever try to explain why a tree's leaves are green or why its bark is rough? You were not observing. You were inferring. An **inference** is an untested interpretation based on your observations and what you know. Scientists might observe that one star looks brighter than others. They could *infer* that the brightest star is bigger, hotter, or closer to Earth.

MAIN IDEA AND DETAILS Why do scientists use investigation skills?

An observation is information from your senses. You can record your observations with notes or drawings. ▼

Predict

You often use your knowledge to guess what will happen next. When you do this, you are predicting. A **prediction** is a statement of what is likely to happen, justified by what you know about cause-and-effect relationships.

A scientific prediction isn't just a wild guess. It is an educated guess. Scientists justify their predictions by their observations, their experience, and what they already know.

When you *predict*, you figure out patterns of events. Then you suggest what is likely to happen next. For example, scientists might observe a series of small earthquakes. They might use that information to predict a volcanic eruption.

Focus Skill **MAIN IDEA AND DETAILS** How are predictions different from guesses?

You use investigation skills to predict that a flower's buds will open. You might even predict what color they will be. ▼

▲ How are these plants the same and different? What words and numbers can be used to describe them?

Compare, Classify, and Use Numbers

How would you describe the plants in the picture above? Scientists—and you—often compare objects and ideas. When you compare, you identify how two or more things are alike and different. You can learn about plants, for example, by comparing their leaves and flowers.

Suppose you want to find a book in the library. How would you find it? Books in libraries are organized. They are sorted based on an observation.

For example, fiction is organized alphabetically by the author's name.

Scientists classify, or sort, objects, too. For example, they group plants by the types of flowers they have. Classifying helps you see patterns.

Using numbers helps scientists—and you—experiment and learn. Scientists use exact numbers to measure the mass of a seed. How might you use numbers to learn about the plants in the picture?

Focus Skill **MAIN IDEA AND DETAILS** Name a way in which you use each investigation skill on this page in your daily life.

Time/Space Relationships and Models

How do the orbits of the planets relate to one another? How does a pulley work? How does a seed grow into a plant? To answer these questions, you need to understand *time/space relationships*.

Space relationships tell where things belong in relation to each other. Time relationships tell the order of events.

Look at the pictures of the plant at the right. How has the plant changed? If you know the order of the events in its life cycle, you can infer that the plant has grown over time.

Have you ever used a little ball and a big ball to show Earth orbiting the sun? You were *using a model*. Models help you understand how things work. Scientists often use models to understand things that are too big, small, fast, slow, or dangerous to observe in person.

(Focus Skill) **MAIN IDEA AND DETAILS** How would you use time/space relationships when building a model of an ecosystem?

Knowing the order in which events happen over time can help you understand the life cycle of this plant. You could find out more by recording how long it takes the plant to grow and change. ▶

Measure and Estimate

When you investigate, you usually need to *measure* your results. Measuring allows you to compare your results to those of others. Scientists use the measurements of the International System of Units (SI), also called the *metric system.*

Measuring is one way of using numbers. Sometimes, scientists make exact measurements. They use tools such as metersticks to measure distance, and they use thermometers to measure temperature. They use graduates to measure volume of liquids, pan balances to measure mass, and spring scales to measure forces such as weight. Each tool gives a measurement as an exact number.

Sometimes, it's not possible to measure exactly. If something is too big, small, fast, slow, or dangerous to investigate up close, scientists may use their observations to make an estimate. An **estimate** is an educated guess about a measurement.

Focus Skill **MAIN IDEA AND DETAILS** How is measuring related to using numbers?

▲ This girl is estimating a length of about 75 cm.

▼ Careful measurements help these boys collect accurate data about distance and time.

◀ **What is a possible hypothesis for an investigation that uses these materials?**

Plan and Conduct an Investigation

Your CD player will not work. You think of several possible causes, such as dead batteries. Then you plan and conduct a simple investigation. You find and fix the problem. Scientists also solve problems in this way.

Suppose you have a more complex problem. For the school fair, your class is designing a large board with holes cut in it for a beanbag toss. You already have the beanbags. They measure 6 centimeters ($2\frac{1}{2}$ in.) around. You must decide how large to make the holes in the board.

You decide that the holes in the board should also measure 6 centimeters in diameter. This idea becomes your **hypothesis**, or scientific explanation that you can test. Next, you test your hypothesis.

You plan an **experiment** to test your hypothesis. Your teacher cuts

different-size holes in a board, and you toss the beanbags through them. You find that the beanbags go through an 8-centimeter hole more easily. But is it really the larger hole that makes the difference? Could the difference be your distance from the board? Could it be how high or low the hole is? How can you find out?

Focus Skill **MAIN IDEA AND DETAILS** **What is a hypothesis?**

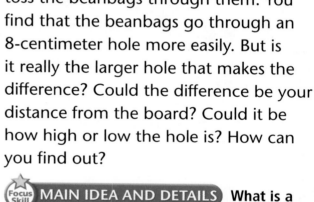

Insta-Lab

Full Measure

Choose an object in the classroom. Measure it in as many ways as you can. Record the measurements. Give them to your teacher. You will be given another list. Try to find the object that the new list describes.

These students are measuring how fast loaded and unloaded toys move. What variables are they controlling? What variable changes? What variable are they observing?

Identify Variables and Gather/Display Data

In an experiment, you must identify the variables—things that can change. In the beanbag experiment, the variables are the size of the holes, the distance of the player to the board, and the height from the ground to the holes.

To make a test fair, keep all of the variables the same except the one you are testing. In the first trial of the experiment, you change only the size of the holes. In the next trial, you change only the height from the ground to the holes. By controlling variables, you can make sure your results are due only to the thing you changed.

As you do your experiment, you write down your results. Then you display them in a graph or table.

MAIN IDEA AND DETAILS Why is it important to control variables?

24

Draw Conclusions and Communicate

During your beanbag experiment, you recorded your results for each size hole. Next, you need to interpret your data, or draw a conclusion about it.

After you study your data, you find that the results do not support your hypothesis. But that's OK! Remember, a hypothesis is just one possible explanation. The purpose of an experiment is to test a hypothesis. You still got the information you needed!

You can share the results of your experiment by discussing with your classmates how to build the game for the school fair. If the experiment were for a science fair, you would use other tools—writing, pictures, and graphs—to communicate the information. You might even display the beanbag board that you used to test your hypothesis.

Focus Skill **MAIN IDEA AND DETAILS** Why is communication an important skill?

▼ These students are using words, objects, and pictures to communicate. They are sharing how they conducted their experiment and what conclusions they drew.

Essential Question

What are investigation skills?

In this lesson, you learned about important skills scientists use to explain the world around them. These skills include observing, inferring, predicting, measuring, and estimating. Scientists use these skills and others when they experiment to test a hypothesis.

Investigation and Experimentation Standards in This Lesson

6.a *Students will* differentiate observation from inference (interpretation) and know scientists' explanations come partly from what they observe and partly from how they interpret their observations.

6.b *Students will* measure and estimate the weight, length, or volume of an object.

6.c *Students will* formulate and justify predictions based on cause-and-effect relationships.

---

1. **Focus Skill** **MAIN IDEA AND DETAILS** Draw and complete a graphic organizer to summarize the main idea and details that support it. **6.a** **6.b** **6.c**

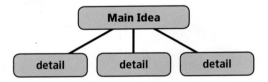

Main Idea

detail   detail   detail

2. **SUMMARIZE** Use your completed graphic organizer to write a lesson summary. **6.a** **6.b** **6.c**

3. **DRAW CONCLUSIONS** You cannot understand a classmate's science project. What investigation skill or skills does your classmate probably need to improve? **6.a**

4. **VOCABULARY** Create a word puzzle with the vocabulary terms. **6.a** **6.b** **6.c**

5. **Critical Thinking** How is an estimate like a prediction? **6.c**

6. **Investigation Skill** Which skills could you use to help you find out what kind of muscle tissue is shown on a microscope slide? **6.a**

7. Which investigation skill helps you notice a change in something?
 A hypothesize
 B communicate
 C observe
 D predict **6.a**

8. In an experiment, how can you make sure your results are due only to what you've tested?
 A by forming a hypothesis
 B by controlling variables
 C by drawing conclusions
 D by making a prediction **6.a**

The **Big** Idea

 Writing ELA—W 2.1

Narrative Writing

Write a story about how you or an imaginary person your age uses several investigation skills to solve a problem. At the end of the story, name the skills used.

$9 \div 3$ **Math** MG 1.1

SI Units

Find out more about the International System of Units (SI). What SI unit is used in place of the inch? The yard? The mile? What are the SI units of area that are most similar to the squares of these units?

 Health

Get Moving

What do you think is the main reason some people do not like to exercise? Think of a way to find out whether this reason—your hypothesis—is supported. Write the steps you would take.

  For more links and activities, go to **www.hspscience.com**

Investigation and Experimentation

6.e *Students will* construct and interpret graphs from measurements.

Essential Question

How Do Scientists Use Graphs?

Modern seismogram

California Fast Fact

Shake and Quake

A seismograph measures earthquakes and records the data on graphs. The strength, or magnitude, of an earthquake is measured using the Richter scale. Earthquakes with a Richter magnitude of less than 3.5 are mild. Quakes with a magnitude of 7.0 can cause serious damage. In this lesson, you'll learn how scientists—and you—display data like this on graphs.

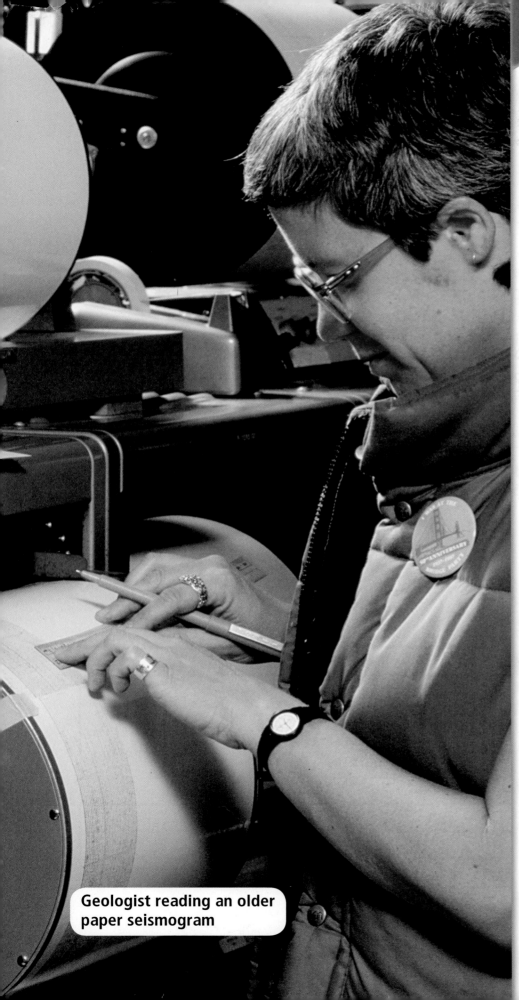

Geologist reading an older paper seismogram

interpret [ihn•TER•pruht] To analyze data, such as a graph (p. 32)

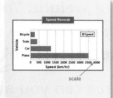

scale [SKAYL] One of the lines on a graph that show the sizes of the units on the graph (p. 33)

axis [AK•sis] The line at the side or bottom of a graph (p. 34)

Beam Strength Testing

Directed Inquiry **Start with Questions**

Big boards and steel beams can hold a lot of weight. You will do an investigation of the strength of smaller "beams"—drinking straws.

- What force can you apply to the straws to test their strength?

- How will you display your data?

Investigate to learn about using data, then read to find out more.

Prepare to Investigate

Investigation Skill Tip

Graphing is one way to display data from an investigation. Graphing makes it easier for you to see patterns and draw conclusions.

Materials

- 10 plastic drinking straws
- masking tape
- large paper clip
- paper cup
- pennies

Make a Data Table

Predictions and Results		
Number of Straws	Predicted Number of Pennies That Will Be Supported	Actual Number of Pennies That Were Supported
1		
2		
3		
4		

Follow This Procedure

1 Work with a partner. Use tape to make straw bundles. Make one bundle of 2 straws, one of 3 straws, and one of 4 straws. You will have one straw left.

2 Use the paper clip to make a hanger for the paper cup.

3 As your partner holds the single straw at each end, hang the cup from the middle of the straw. **Predict** how many pennies the straw can support. **Record** your prediction. Then add one penny at a time to the cup. Add pennies until the straw bends sharply. Then **record** the number of pennies in the cup.

4 Do Step 3 with each bundle of straws.

5 Use the data to make a graph.

Draw Conclusions

1. How are the bundles different from each other?

2. **Standards Link** Which number of straws was strongest? `6.e`

3. **Investigation Skill** Scientists **graph** information to help them interpret data and draw conclusions. What conclusion can you draw from your graph? `6.e`

Step 3

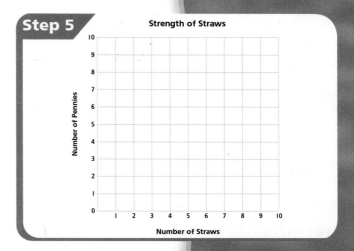

Step 5 — Strength of Straws

Number of Pennies (y-axis, 0 to 10)
Number of Straws (x-axis, 1 to 10)

Independent Inquiry — **Measure Mass**

Use a pan balance to record the mass of the pennies in the Investigate. What mass bent the single straw? What mass bent each bundle? Record your results, and display them in a graph. `6.e`

31

VOCABULARY

interpret p. 32
scale p. 33
axis p. 34

SCIENCE CONCEPTS

▶ how to use data to construct graphs

▶ how to interpret graphs

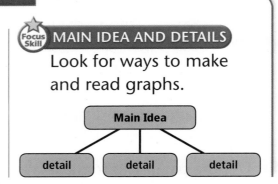

MAIN IDEA AND DETAILS

Look for ways to make and read graphs.

Getting Ready to Graph

When you do a science investigation, you must record your results. A table is a good way to record data in an organized way. Others can read your table easily to get useful information. You can read others' tables easily, too.

When you **interpret**, you analyze data to draw conclusions. To interpret the information in a table, first read the title. It tells you what the table is about. The table on this page shows the amount of rain in Carmel Valley, California.

Next, read the headings. They tell you what information is given in each part of the table. In the table on this page, the number of centimeters of rain is given for each month of the year.

Study the data, looking for patterns. You might notice here that the amount of rain increases in the winter and decreases in the summer.

Finally, draw conclusions. What is your interpretation of the data? One possible conclusion is that in Carmel Valley, January is the rainiest month.

MAIN IDEA AND DETAILS How are tables helpful?

▼ By studying the table, you can see how much rain fell during each month. A scientist might also display the data in a graph to look for patterns.

Average Monthly Rainfall in Carmel Valley, California						
Month	January	February	March	April	May	June
Average rainfall (cm)	8.9	6.8	8.3	4.2	1.0	0.7
Month	July	August	September	October	November	December
Average rainfall (cm)	0.2	0.2	0.7	2.2	7.1	7.1

Using a Bar Graph

A bar graph can show the same data as a table. It can be used to compare, at a glance, the data about different events or groups.

Bar graphs can help you interpret results. You don't have to read all the data as you do in a table. Instead, a quick look at a bar graph can give you important information. From the bar graph on this page, it's easy to see that in Carmel Valley, the most rain falls during January.

MAIN IDEA AND DETAILS In what way is a bar graph better than a table?

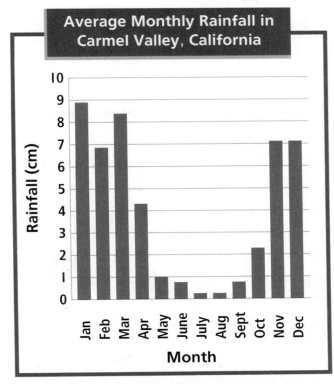

▲ The data in this bar graph is the same as in the table. A bar graph can be used to easily compare the data about different events or groups.

A **scale** on a graph shows you the size of the units. The scale at the left of this graph is marked in centimeters.

Carmel Valley, California

Using a Line Graph

In some investigations, data is collected over time. The data can be recorded in a table and displayed in a line graph. Line graphs often show changes over time.

The line at the side or bottom of a graph is called an **axis**. Numbers or labels are along each axis. The middle of a line graph shows points connected by lines. For each point, look down or left to see its value on an axis. Look for patterns. Then draw conclusions. On this page, what can you conclude from the dark orange points and lines?

 MAIN IDEA AND DETAILS What information do line graphs often show?

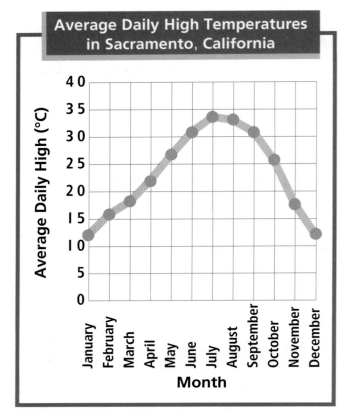

▲ A line graph often shows changes over time. The numbers along the *y*-axis of this graph tell you what temperatures are shown. The labels on the *x*-axis tell you the months when temperatures were measured. What patterns do you see?

A scientist collected this information about average high temperatures in Sacramento, California. ▼

Average Daily High Temperatures in Sacramento, California	
Month	Temperature (°C)
January	12.1
February	15.8
March	18.2
April	21.9
May	26.7
June	30.8
July	33.6
August	33.0
September	30.8
October	25.7
November	17.06
December	12.2

Using a Circle Graph

Some scientists wanted to classify the animals at a park. They wanted to find out which animal group had the most members. They counted 100 animals in all and recorded their data in a table.

Then they displayed their data in a circle graph to easily compare the animal groups. A circle graph shows data as a whole made up of parts. To read a circle graph, look at the label of each section to find out what is shown. Compare the sizes of the sections, and then draw conclusions.

Focus Skill **MAIN IDEA AND DETAILS** What conclusion can you draw from the circle graph on this page?

The circle graph shows the same data as the table. ▼

Animal Groups Observed at the Park

Reptiles 5%
Amphibians 3%
Mammals 7%
Birds 22%
Insects 63%

Insta-Lab

Make a Pie!
Circle graphs are sometimes called pie charts. You can make your own pie! With your classmates, find a way to classify all your shoes. You might classify them by color, size, or style. Display your data in a circle graph (a pie chart).

Animal Groups Observed at the Park	
Animal Group	Number Observed
Mammals	7
Insects	63
Birds	22
Reptiles	5
Amphibians	3

▲ The table shows how animals in a park were classified.

katydid

35

Essential Question

How do scientists use graphs?

In this lesson, you learned how to use graphs to organize and display measurements and other data. Graphs make it easier to interpret patterns in data and to draw conclusions.

Investigation and Experimentation Standard in This Lesson

6.e *Students will* construct and interpret graphs from measurements.

1. **MAIN IDEA AND DETAILS** Draw and complete a graphic organizer to summarize the main idea and details that support it. **6.e**

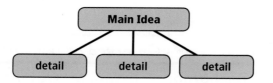

Main Idea

detail   detail   detail

2. **SUMMARIZE** Use the graphic organizer to write a lesson summary. **6.e**

3. **DRAW CONCLUSIONS** Why is a line graph a good way to display average temperatures in a city by month? **6.e**

4. **VOCABULARY** Write a definition in your own words for each vocabulary term. **6.e**

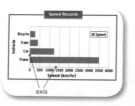

5. **Critical Thinking** What is the relationship between tables and graphs? **6.e**

6. **Investigation Skill** A fourth-grade class is studying the growth of plants. Over several weeks, the students have measured and recorded the growth of one plant. What would be a good way for them to display their data? Why? **6.e**

7. Which of the following **best** displays the relationships between the parts of a whole?
   A table
   B line graph
   C bar graph
   D circle graph **6.e**

8. How do graphs help you find answers to your science questions?
   A Graphs display data at a glance.
   B Graphs measure data.
   C Graphs test hypotheses.
   D Graphs control variables. **6.e**

The **Big** Idea

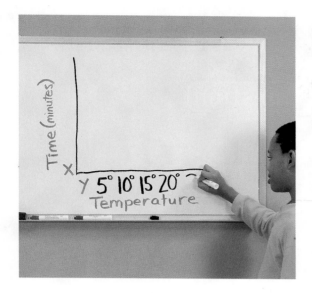

 Writing ELA—W 2.3

Write a Report

Suppose you're a scientist who has studied insects. Write a report that tells what kind of data you collected. Show how you recorded your data and how you used graphs.

 Math SDAP 1.1

Label Graphs

Find at least three graphs in newspapers or magazines. Identify and label the major parts of each graph.

 Social Studies HSS 4.4

Population Explosion

Use library resources to gather data about population changes in Los Angeles between 1980 and 2000. You might focus on how population has grown or what caused growth. Display your findings in a graph.

 For more links and activities, go to **www.hspscience.com**

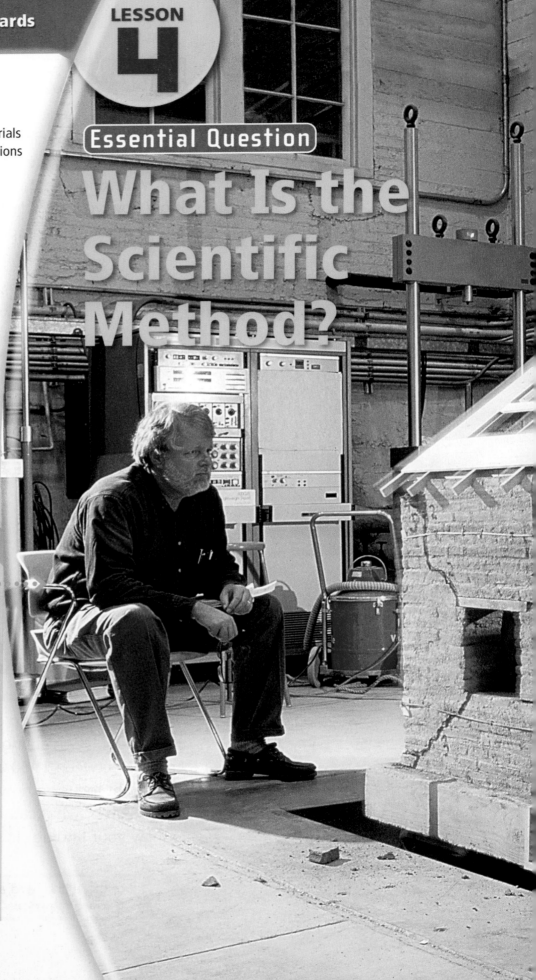

![bear] **California Standards in This Lesson**

Investigation and Experimentation

6.d *Students will* conduct multiple trials to test a prediction and draw conclusions about the relationships between predictions and results.

6.f *Students will* follow a set of written instructions for a scientific investigation.

Essential Question

What Is the Scientific Method?

California Fast Fact

Shake, Rattle, and Roll

This earthquake "shake table" at the University of California, Berkeley, was the first of its kind in the world. Scientists use it to model the strength of buildings in earthquakes. They gather and analyze data in experiments to learn how to make buildings stronger. In this lesson, you'll learn the steps scientists follow in an experiment.

scientific method
[sy•uhn•TIF•ik METH•uhd]
A series of steps that scientists follow to test hypotheses and to find out answers to their science questions (p. 42)

Earthquake "shake table" at the University of California—Berkeley

Model 7
Test 8
South

Model 7
Test 8
East

Testing a Straw Model

Directed Inquiry ## Start with Questions

You probably have questions about the world around you. For example, you might wonder what causes the weather to change. Scientists ask questions, too.

- How do scientists form their questions?

- What steps do scientists follow to answer their questions?

Prepare to Investigate

Investigation Skill Tip
When you experiment, you test a hypothesis. You answer science questions by using controlled procedures to gather data. You then analyze the data and draw conclusions.

Materials
- large paper clips
- straw model from Lesson 2
- paper cups
- pennies

Make a Data Table

Number of Pennies	Result

Follow This Procedure

① Bend a paper clip to make a hanger.

② **Predict** how many pennies your straw model can support. Hang your cup on the model. Add one penny at a time. Was your prediction accurate?

③ With your group, think of ways to strengthen your model. You might also look for other places on your model to hang the cup. **Record** your ideas.

④ **Form a hypothesis** about what will make the model stronger. Then **experiment** to see if the results support the hypothesis. Use multiple trials.

⑤ Discuss what made your straw model stronger, and **draw conclusions**. **Communicate** your findings.

Step 1

Step 2

Draw Conclusions

1. Were you able to increase the strength of your model? How?

2. **Standards Link** Why is it important to follow the procedure as it is described? **6.f**

3. **Investigation Skill** Scientists **experiment** to test their hypotheses. What did you learn from your experiments in this activity?

Independent Inquiry

Follow Written Instructions

Will your model support more pennies if their weight is spread across it? Plan and conduct an experiment, following written instructions, to find out. **6.f**

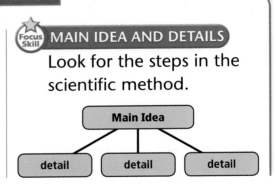

6.d, 6.f

VOCABULARY
scientific method p. 42

SCIENCE CONCEPTS
▶ what the steps in the scientific method are
▶ how the scientific method helps scientists learn

Focus Skill **MAIN IDEA AND DETAILS**
Look for the steps in the scientific method.

Observe and Ask Questions

The **scientific method** is a way that scientists find out how things work and affect each other. The five steps of this method help scientists test ideas. The steps describe how scientists—and you—can find answers to questions.

Observe and Ask Questions After observing the straw models your class built, you might ask these questions:

- Is a cube stronger than a pyramid?
- Are straws more likely to bend if they are placed at an angle?

- Is a shorter straw stronger than a longer one?
- Why do buildings use triangles?

Focus Skill **MAIN IDEA AND DETAILS** What is the scientific method?

You can find triangle shapes on bridges and other structures. Why is that? ▼

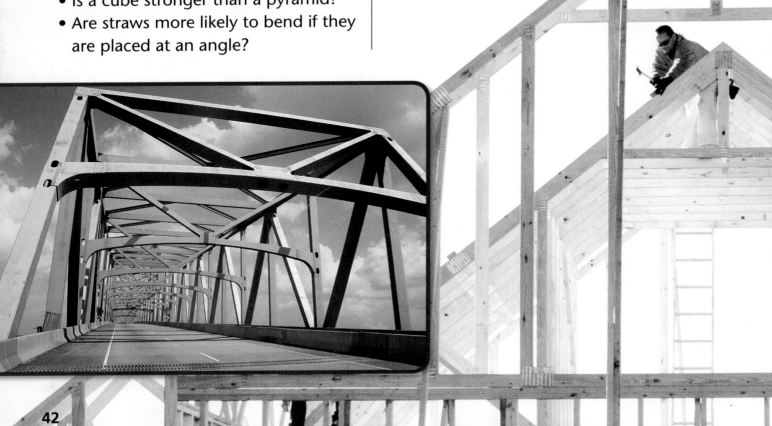

Hypothesize and Experiment

Form a Hypothesis Suppose you want to know whether a pyramid or a cube is stronger. You can form a hypothesis. A *hypothesis* is a scientific explanation that you can test. Here is one hypothesis: Pyramids hold more weight than cubes because triangles are stronger than squares.

Plan an Experiment How can you test your hypothesis? You can think of a plan and write it down as a set of steps. For example, you might hang a cup on each of two models and then add one penny at a time to each cup.

Next, you need to think about all the variables. Make sure you change only one variable on the trials of your test.

In this experiment, both models are made of straws. They are made the same way. The cups will be the same. Only one variable will be tested—the shape of the models.

The complete plan should list all the materials. Then it should list what to do in order. You should plan to conduct several trials. They help make your data more reliable. If you get about the same result for each trial, your measurements were done well.

Conduct an Experiment Now it's time to conduct, or carry out, your experiment. You should follow the steps in the correct order. In each step, you should record everything you observe, especially any results you didn't expect.

 **MAIN IDEA AND DETAILS** How do you plan an experiment?

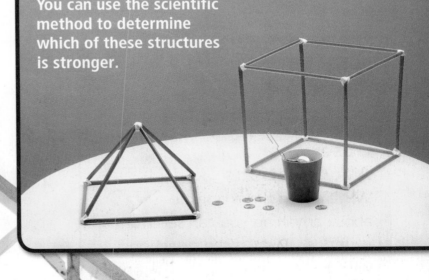

You can use the scientific method to determine which of these structures is stronger.

Share Your Findings

Draw Conclusions and Communicate Results The final step in the scientific method begins with drawing conclusions. Look at your hypothesis again. Then analyze the observations you recorded. Do the results support your hypothesis? Did the pyramid hold more pennies than the cube?

In this experiment, you could give the results in numbers. You recorded the number of pennies each model supported. Other times, you might describe the results in other ways. For example, you might explain that a liquid turned blue or a plant wilted.

Scientists share their results. This allows others to double-check the work. Other scientists should be able to repeat the investigation. If the results aren't the same, they can find and fix any mistakes. This allows scientists to build new ideas with knowledge that is reliable.

Sharing findings of an investigation allows others to learn as well. You can share your findings in a written or oral report. Your report should state your hypothesis, list your materials, and describe your procedure. It should include the details of your setup and a diagram. It should end with your results and conclusions. You should tell whether the results supported your

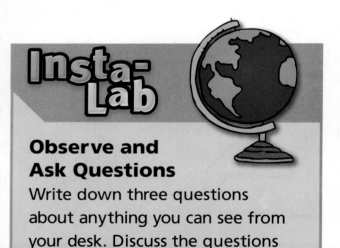

Observe and Ask Questions

Write down three questions about anything you can see from your desk. Discuss the questions with two classmates. Choose one question that none of you can answer. Then plan a way to find an answer.

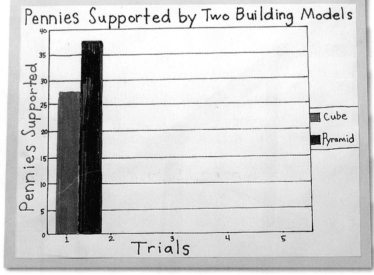

▲ **You can display your results in charts, graphs, or diagrams.**

▲ Your report should describe your hypothesis, materials, procedure, results, and conclusion. Another person should be able to read your report, repeat your investigation, and get similar results.

hypothesis or not. *Supported* means that the results matched your prediction. The hypothesis was *disproved* if the results were the exact opposite of your prediction.

Your results may not be clear. Maybe they don't support your hypothesis, but they also don't disprove it. That's OK! You should be curious about unusual data. It may show you a new question to investigate.

Unclear results may also lead you to improvements. You may need to measure more carefully. You may not have controlled variables well enough.

Charts, graphs, and diagrams can help you explain your results and conclusions clearly. Each graph should have a title, a key, and clear labels.

Focus Skill MAIN IDEA AND DETAILS Why should a report on an investigation be clear and detailed?

Essential Question

What is the scientific method?

In this lesson, you learned that the scientific method is a way that scientists find answers to their questions. The five steps of the scientific method help scientists find the correct answers. Repeated trials help show that results are reliable.

Investigation and Experimentation Standards in This Lesson

6.d *Students will* conduct multiple trials to test a prediction and draw conclusions about the relationships between predictions and results.

6.f *Students will* follow a set of written instructions for a scientific investigation.

1. **Focus Skill MAIN IDEA AND DETAILS** Draw and complete a graphic organizer to summarize the main idea and the details that support it. **6.f**

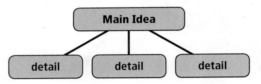

2. **SUMMARIZE** Write a summary of the lesson, beginning with this sentence: The scientific method helps us gain new knowledge. **6.d 6.f**

3. **DRAW CONCLUSIONS** Will the scientific method be different 100 years from now? Explain your answer. **6.f**

4. **VOCABULARY** Write a fill-in-the-blank sentence for the vocabulary term. **6.f**

5. **Critical Thinking** State an everyday problem a young person might have that could be solved with the scientific method. **6.f**

6. **Investigation Skill** Suppose you need to know whether short triangles or long ones are stronger. You predict that short ones are stronger, and your results support this. How can you make sure the results are accurate? **6.d**

7. When you use the scientific method, what are you testing?
   A instruments
   B experiments
   C hypotheses
   D observations **6.f**

8. List the five steps used to answer science questions. **6.f**

The **Big** Idea

Writing ELA—W 2.3

Write a Report

Choose an investigation you have conducted or observed. Then write a report about it. Describe how each step of the scientific method was followed—or how it should have been followed.

9÷3 Math NS 1.2

Solve a Problem

A pyramid supports 10 pennies, which weigh 28 grams (1 oz.) total. How much does one penny weigh?

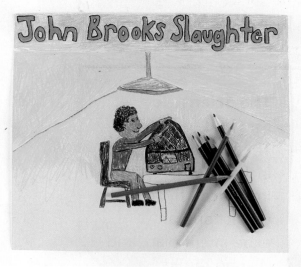

John Brooks Slaughter

Social Studies HSS 4.4

Super Scientists

Choose a California scientist who interests you. Research his or her life, challenges, and accomplishments. Then make a poster to share interesting facts about this scientist.

  For more links and activities, go to **www.hspscience.com**

Wrap-Up

▶ Visual Summary

Tell how each picture helps explain the **Big Idea**.

The Big Idea You can answer your science questions by carrying out careful investigations.

6.b

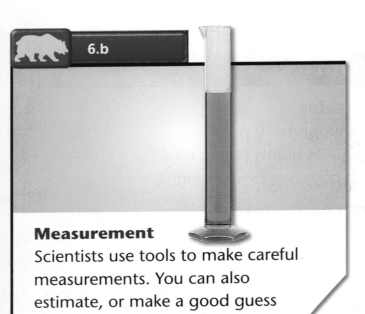

Measurement
Scientists use tools to make careful measurements. You can also estimate, or make a good guess about a measurement.

6.e

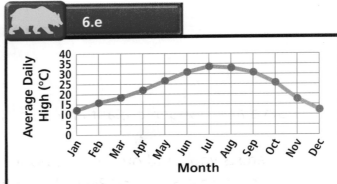

Display Your Data
You can organize measurements in a table and then display them on a graph. Graphs help you interpret data.

6.f

The Scientific Method
The scientific method includes observations, inferences, hypotheses, predictions, an experiment plan, and sharing results.

Show What You Know

Unit Writing Activity

Research and Report

The inventor of one of the earliest microscopes was Dutch scientist Anton van Leeuwenhoek. Use reference materials to learn about van Leeuwenhoek's life. Write a report that says what he is famous for and what kinds of things he observed with his microscope. How did van Leeuwenhoek apply the scientific method?

Unit Project

Interpret Information

Several endangered plant and animal species live in California. Use library resources to identify one species that interests you. Find out how its population has changed over the past 30 years. Record your findings. Then make a poster that communicates the data in a way that others will understand easily.

Vocabulary Review

Use the terms below to complete the sentences. The page numbers tell you where to look in the unit if you need help.

microscope p. 8

spring scale p. 11

inference p. 18

hypothesis p. 23

experiment p. 23

scientific method p. 42

1. Forces are measured by a _____. `6.b`

2. A _____ is a testable explanation of observations. `6.f`

3. When you make an observation and then draw a conclusion, you make an _____. `6.a`

4. To observe very small details, you might use a _____. `6.b`

5. Scientists find out how things work and how they affect other things by using the _____. `6.d`

6. A scientific test in which variables are controlled is an _____. `6.d`

Check Understanding

Choose the best answer.

7. What information can you get from the tool shown here? `6.b`
   A balance **B** weight
   C mass **D** volume

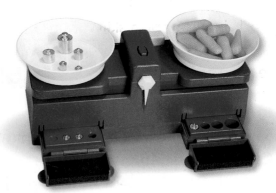

8. **MAIN IDEA AND DETAILS** Which is the main purpose of the scientific method? `6.f`
   A to ask questions
   B to share information
   C to test ideas
   D to plan an experiment

9. Why is it important to list enough details in reports about investigations? `6.f`
   A so that scientists can observe and ask questions
   B so that scientists can build new ideas on reliable results
   C so that scientists can form a hypothesis
   D so that scientists can plan and conduct a simple experiment

10. **SEQUENCE** Which letter below lists the steps of the scientific method in order? `6.f`
    1. Form a hypothesis.
    2. Ask questions.
    3. Conduct an experiment.
    4. Draw conclusions and communicate.
    5. Plan an experiment.
    A 2, 1, 5, 3, 4   **B** 1, 2, 3, 4, 5
    C 1, 2, 5, 3, 4   **D** 5, 4, 3, 2, 1

11. Which investigation skill is based on describing the ways in which things are alike and different? `6.a`
    A measuring   **B** sequencing
    C summarizing   **D** comparing

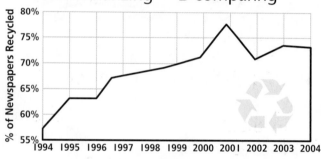

12. Use the graph above to decide what prediction you would make for recycling in 2010. `6.e`
    A It will increase a lot.
    B It will increase a little.
    C It will decrease a little.
    D It will decrease a lot.

13. Some students want to classify and compare the plants growing on the forest floor. They identify 100 plants and record their data. How can they best display their data? `6.e`
    A in a table   **B** in a line graph
    C in a report   **D** in a circle graph

14. Why do you control variables? `6.f`
    A to know what questions to ask
    B to know what caused the results
    C to form a hypothesis
    D to plan your investigation

15. Which characteristic must a hypothesis have? `6.f`
    A It must be a testable statement.
    B It must be a short prediction.
    C It must predict and plan.
    D It must predict and measure.

16. How would scientific experiments be different without tools? `6.b`
    A Measuring would be easier.
    B Information could be gathered.
    C The results would not be precise.
    D There would be no change.

Investigation Skills

17. A model is not the real thing. Why, then, do scientists use models? `6.f`

18. Which tool is used to measure the mass of water? `6.b`

Critical Thinking

19. An experiment is repeated, but the result is different. What are some possible causes? `6.f`

20. You want to find out how water temperature affects the movement of goldfish. Write a hypothesis. Then identify the variables you will control, change, and measure or observe.

The **Big** Idea

51

Electricity and Magnetism

California Standards in this Unit

1 Electricity and magnetism are related effects that have many useful applications in everyday life. As a basis for understanding this concept:

1.a *Students know* how to design and build simple series and parallel circuits by using components such as wires, batteries, and bulbs.

1.b *Students know* how to build a simple compass and use it to detect magnetic effects, including Earth's magnetic field.

1.c *Students know* electric currents produce magnetic fields and know how to build a simple electromagnet.

1.d *Students know* the role of electromagnets in the construction of electric motors, electric generators, and simple devices, such as doorbells and earphones.

1.e *Students know* electrically charged objects attract or repel each other.

1.f *Students know* that magnets have two poles (north and south) and that like poles repel each other while unlike poles attract each other.

1.g *Students know* electrical energy can be converted to heat, light, and motion.

This unit also includes these Investigation and Experimentation Standards: **6.a** **6.c** **6.d** **6.e** **6.f**

What's the Big Idea?

Electricity and magnetism are related. They are part of things you use every day.

Essential Questions

O'Shaughnessy Dam

Dear Jamie,

Today we visited the O'Shaughnessy Dam. It uses the energy of falling water to produce electricity. Workers have to be VERY careful around power lines, because they could get a REALLY BIG SHOCK. The guide said that sparks can heat the air around the insulators to 3000°C (5400°F)!

I'll tell you more about it when I get home.

Your friend,
Samantha

What did Samantha see that's related to electricity and magnetism? How do you think that relates to the **Big Idea?**

Unit Inquiry

Reducing Static Cling
What affects the amount of static cling? To answer this question, plan and carry out an investigation that uses a model.

Science Content

1.e *Students know* electrically charged objects attract or repel each other.

Investigation and Experimentation

6.a Differentiate observations from inference (interpretation) and know scientists' explanations come partly from what they observe and partly from how they interpret their observations.

6.c Formulate and justify predictions based on cause-and-effect relationships.

6.d Conduct multiple trials to test a prediction and draw conclusions about the relationships between predictions and results.

California Fast Fact

Lightning Is a Killer

Lightning is the result of static electricity. Every year in the United States, lightning hits the ground about 25 million times! Between 1995 and 2002, only three people in California were killed by lightning. During that same time, however, Florida had the most lightning deaths—70.

LESSON 1

Essential Question

What Is Static Electricity?

Lightning over Angel Island in San Francisco Bay

Vocabulary Preview

electric charge [ee•LEK•trik CHARJ] A basic property of the tiny particles that make up matter. Electric charges can be positive or negative (p. 58)

static electricity [STAT•ik ee•lek•TRIS•ih•tee] The buildup of electric charges in one place (p. 59)

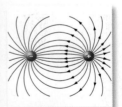

electric field [ee•LEK•trik FEELD] The area around electric charges, where electric forces can act (p. 62)

Rub a Balloon

Start with Questions

It's not the wind that's making this boy's hair stand on end. It's static electricity!

- Did your hair ever stick out like this when you took off a sweater?

- Why do you think that happened?

Investigate to find out. Then read to find out more.

Prepare to Investigate

Investigation Skill Tip
An inference is a conclusion based on observations and what you already know.

Materials

- 2 small, round balloons
- string
- marker
- masking tape
- scraps of silk and wool cloth
- plastic wrap
- paper towel

Make an Observation Chart

Material	Observations
silk	
wool cloth	
plastic wrap	
paper towel	
silk and wool	

Follow This Procedure

① Blow up the balloons, and tie them closed. Use string and tape to hang one balloon from a shelf or table.

② Rub the silk all over each balloon. Slowly bring the free balloon near the hanging balloon. **Observe** the balloons. **Record** your observations.

③ Again rub the silk all over the hanging balloon. Move the silk away. Then slowly bring it close to the balloon. **Observe** the balloon, and **record** your observations.

④ Repeat Steps 2 and 3 with wool, plastic wrap, and the paper towel.

⑤ Rub the silk all over the hanging balloon. Rub the wool all over the free balloon. Slowly bring the free balloon near the hanging balloon. **Observe** the balloons. **Record** your observations.

Step 2

Step 3

Draw Conclusions

1. Compare your observations in Steps 2 and 3.

2. **Standards Link** Think about how the balloons and materials acted. Compare that to what sometimes happens when clothes are taken from a dryer. `1.e`

3. **Investigation Skill** Which of your observations support the **inference** that a force acted on the balloons and the materials? `6.a`

> **Independent Inquiry** — **Make and Test Predictions**
>
> Think about how the materials affected the balloons. Then predict how a different kind of material might affect the balloons.
>
> Write a plan for an investigation to test your prediction. Be sure to include the materials, the steps of the procedure, and the data you will collect. `6.c` `6.d`

VOCABULARY
electric charge p. 58
static electricity p. 59
electric field p. 62

SCIENCE CONCEPTS
▶ what causes electric charges to build up
▶ why objects attract and repel one another

(Focus Skill) CAUSE AND EFFECT
Look for the causes of static electricity.

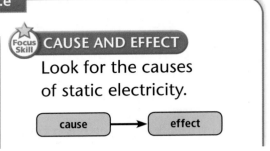

Two Kinds of Charge

You know the word *electricity*. It's used to describe some kinds of energy. You may have experience with them but not know how they are related. This lesson will explain how electricity works.

In the Investigate, you produced one kind of electricity. Rubbing the two balloons caused a change. They either pulled toward each other or pushed away from each other. These two results come from a single property of matter—*electric charge*.

An **electric charge** is a basic property of the tiny particles that make up matter. Electric charge can be positive or negative.

Positive and negative charges cancel each other out. As a result, matter usually has a balance of the two kinds of charge. This is called *neutral*. In the Investigate, you changed this balance

A positive charge is labeled ⊕. A negative charge is labeled ⊖.
When an object has more ⊕s than ⊖s, it has a ⊕ electric charge.
When it has more ⊖s than ⊕s, it has a ⊖ electric charge.

Positive Charge

Negative Charge

by rubbing. That moved some negative charges from the material to the balloon.

When an object has more particles with a negative charge than particles with a positive charge, it is *negatively charged.* If it has more particles with a positive charge, it is *positively charged.*

Positively and negatively charged objects affect each other. Opposite charges *attract*—or pull toward—each other. Charges that are the same *repel*—or push away from—each other.

Rubbing two balloons with wool makes each balloon negatively charged.

The kind of charge on each balloon is the same. As a result, the balloons repel each other.

The buildup of charges in one place is called **static electricity**. When clothes are taken out of a dryer, they crackle and stick together. The rubbing of the clothes against each other in the dryer causes static electricity.

Focus Skill **CAUSE AND EFFECT** What would happen if you combed your hair, then moved the charged comb close to your hair? Why?

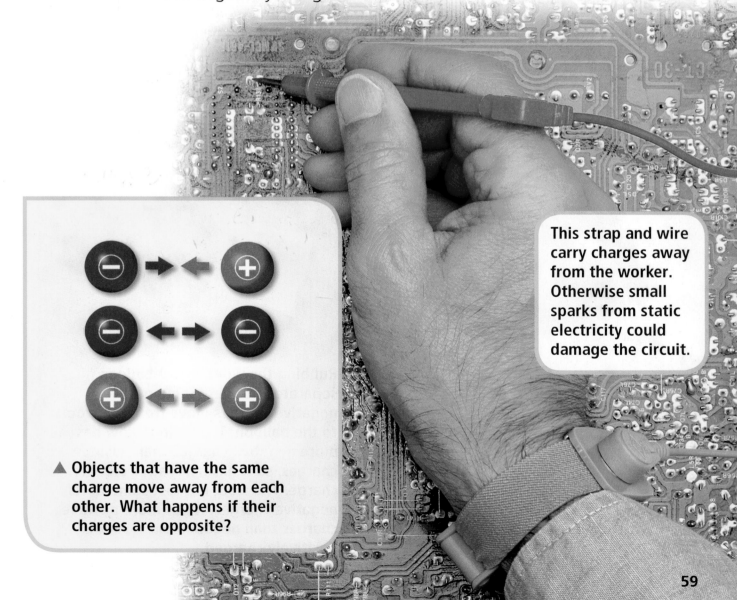

▲ Objects that have the same charge move away from each other. What happens if their charges are opposite?

This strap and wire carry charges away from the worker. Otherwise small sparks from static electricity could damage the circuit.

Separating Charges

Most of the time, you, a balloon, and a doorknob are neutral. You and the objects each have the same number of positive and negative charges, and you don't see their effects. To see the effects of forces between charges, you must separate negative charges from positive charges.

As you've observed, you can separate charges on some objects by rubbing them together. Rubbing pulls negative particles off one object and onto the other. Only negative charges move in this way. Positive charges don't move.

As clothes tumble in a dryer, different fabrics rub against each other. Negative charges move from one piece of clothing to another. When this happens, the clothes stick together. ▼

If a piece of wool is next to a balloon, usually nothing happens. You can infer that neither object has an electric charge. The numbers of positive and negative charges on the balloon are equal. The charges are also equal on the wool. Both objects are neutral.

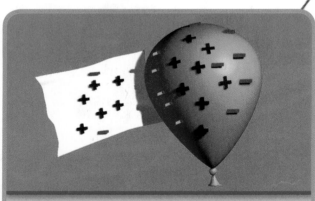

Rubbing the wool on the balloon separates charges. Some of the negative charges move from the wool to the balloon. The balloon now has more negative charges than positive charges, so it has a negative electric charge. The wool has lost some of its negative charges. It has more positive charges than negative ones, so it is positively charged.

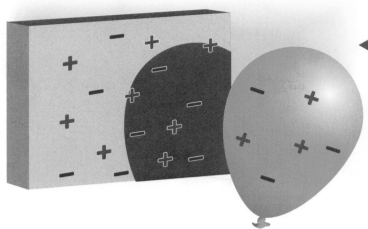

◀ The balloon and the wall each have the same number of positive and negative charges. Both objects are neutral. They are neither positively nor negatively charged.

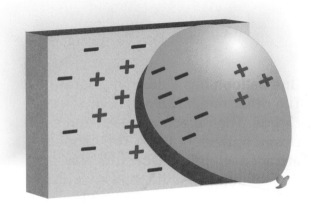

◀ After rubbing the balloon is now negatively charged. The negative charges on the wall are pushed away a little. This lets the balloon be attracted to the positive charges on the wall. The balloon sticks to the wall.

Have you ever walked across a carpet and then touched a metal doorknob? You might have seen a spark and felt a *shock.* What caused that?

When your shoes moved on the carpet, they caused the charges on the carpet to separate. Negative charges moved from the carpet to your body. Your body became negatively charged.

Touching the metal doorknob gave the charges a place to go. They "jumped" to the doorknob in a spark, and you felt the shock. Then the charges became balanced again. Similar electric sparks in giant form are lightning bolts.

What causes a negatively charged balloon to stick to a neutral wall? This happens because there is another way to separate charges.

The negative charges on the balloon repel negative charges in the wall. The wall's negative charges move away a little. They are separated from the wall's positive charges. This allows the balloon's negative charges to be attracted to the wall's positive charges.

After a while, the balloon falls. This is because the extra charges on the balloon move to the air.

CAUSE AND EFFECT What are two ways you can cause charges to separate?

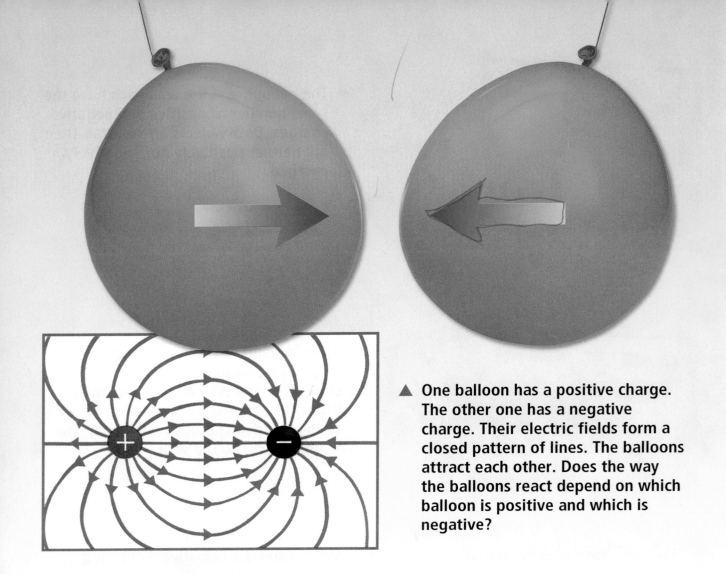

▲ One balloon has a positive charge. The other one has a negative charge. Their electric fields form a closed pattern of lines. The balloons attract each other. Does the way the balloons react depend on which balloon is positive and which is negative?

Electric Forces

In the Investigate, you saw how a charged balloon pushed or pulled another charged balloon. The push or pull between objects that have different charges is an *electric force.*

Both positive and negative electric charges have electric fields around them. An **electric field** is the space in which an electric force acts. The force gets weaker as you move farther from a charged object. The field extends in all directions from the charge. The field of a positive charge attracts a nearby negative charge. It also repels a nearby positive charge.

The diagram on this page shows an electric field. The arrows show how a force would act on a positive charge. A positive charge would be pushed away from the positive charge and pulled toward the negative charge. The arrows form a pattern of closed loops.

The diagram on the next page shows the electric fields around two negatively charged balloons. Suppose a positive

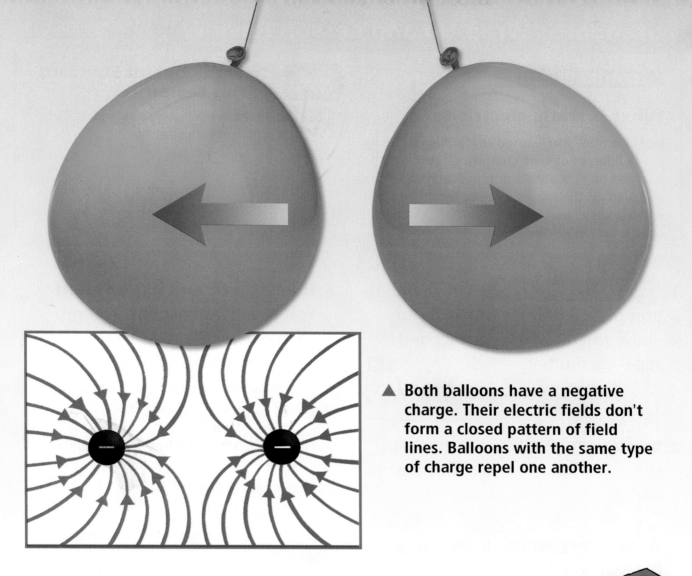

▲ Both balloons have a negative charge. Their electric fields don't form a closed pattern of field lines. Balloons with the same type of charge repel one another.

charge entered the electric field around either balloon. The electric force would cause the positive charge to be attracted toward the negative charges.

What would the field look like if both balloons had a positive charge? This time, the electric force would push a positive charge away. The arrows from both balloons would point away from the balloons. Because the arrows on both charges are pointing in the same way, the balloons would still repel.

 **CAUSE AND EFFECT** What causes an electric force?

Static Cereal

Place some puffed rice cereal on a sheet of paper. Hold a plastic comb above the cereal. Observe what happens. Rub the comb with a piece of wool cloth. Hold the comb over the cereal again. Now what happens?

Essential Question

What is static electricity?

In this lesson, you learned that static electricity is a buildup of electric charges. Electrically charged objects attract or repel each other. You also learned that objects get an electric charge when charges are separated and that an electric charge has an electric field.

Science Content Standard in This Lesson

1.e *Students know* electrically charged particles attract or repel each other.

1. **Focus Skill** **CAUSE AND EFFECT** Draw and complete a graphic organizer to show when particles attract and repel each other. **1.e**

2. **SUMMARIZE** Write two sentences that tell what the lesson was mainly about. **1.e**

3. **DRAW CONCLUSIONS** If you rub a balloon on a wool sweater, the balloon will stick to the wool. What causes this to happen? **1.e**

4. **VOCABULARY** Write a sentence that explains how charges cause *static electricity*. **1.e**

5. **Critical Thinking** What causes plastic wrap to stick to your hands when you pull it off the roll on a dry day? **1.e**

6. **Investigate and Experiment** You have two balloons. You rub each one with a different type of material. When you bring the materials near one another, they repel each other. What can you infer happened? **6.a**

7. How can a plastic ruler get a positive charge?
   A by gaining negative charges
   B by losing negative charges
   C by gaining positive charges
   D by losing positive charges **1.e**

8. Two charged objects attract each other. Which statement is true?
   A neither is positive
   B neither is negative
   C they have the same charge
   D they have opposite charges **1.e**

The Big Idea

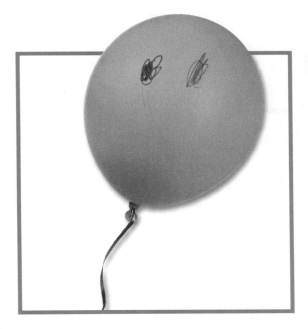

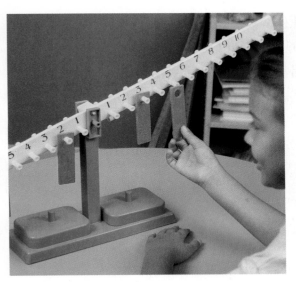

 Writing ELA—W 2.1.b

Write a Description

Suppose you're a balloon. Describe what happens to you as you gain a negative charge from a piece of wool. Write a narrative about this for a classmate.

9÷3 **Math** NS 1.8

Use Math Symbols

The balloon and wool at the bottom of page 60 show charges. How many single negative charges must each object gain or lose to become neutral? Use numbers and math symbols to show how you found your answer.

 Health

Lightning Safety

Lightning is a big movement of charged particles. It can hurt or kill people and animals, and it can start fires. Find out the safety rules you should follow during a thunderstorm. Make a poster illustrating the rules.

 For more links and activities, go to **www.hspscience.com**

Benjamin Franklin

► **BENJAMIN FRANKLIN**

► **Born 1706—Died 1790**

► **Scientist and inventor**

► Co-author of the Declaration of Independence

Curious is the word that best describes Benjamin Franklin! He was fascinated by storms and suspected that lightning was an electrical current. His famous experiment with a kite and a key helped him prove it.

Franklin explained electricity in words we still use today: *charge, discharge, positive, negative, conductor,* and *electric shock.* He experienced electric shock firsthand, describing it as "a universal blow through my whole body."

In his 40s, Franklin figured out how to make a battery, but he saw no use for it. He also invented the lightning rod. A metal spike on top of a building is connected by wire to the ground. During a storm, electric charges collect on its point. They then flow along the wire to the ground instead of destroying the building.

Think and Write

❶ What did Franklin's experiments show people about lightning? **1.e**

❷ How do you think his discoveries have helped later scientists who have studied electricity? **1.e**

Ben Franklin designed the lightning rod that protects the Maryland State House. This lightning rod is 8.5 m (28 feet) tall.

Modern lightning rod

John Brooks Slaughter

As a young boy, John Brooks Slaughter loved to read popular science magazines. He enjoyed building the projects they described. His father began buying old radios for him to repair. His father then sold the radios and bought John more equipment. The money from radio repairs helped John pay for college. He was the only African American student in his engineering class.

After college, Slaughter developed computer programs to analyze electrical signals. He worked at General Dynamics in San Diego and in the Navy Electronics Lab. His knowledge of electricity helped solve problems involving the ocean and the environment. He has won many awards related to his job. However, his real interest is in education.

Today, Slaughter works to encourage young people to study science and math. He is excited about what is happening in engineering. He hopes more boys and girls will develop the interest in science that he had as a young boy. It has taken him a long way!

▶ **JOHN BROOKS SLAUGHTER**

▶ **Winner of the first U.S. Black Engineer of the Year award, in 1987**

▶ Used computers to solve problems in the ocean and the environment

Radio

✐ Think and Write

❶ How did Slaughter begin his study of electrical energy? **1.d**

❷ What is he most interested in now? **1.d**

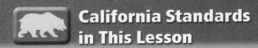

Science Content

1.a *Students know* how to design and build simple series and parallel circuits by using components such as wires, batteries, and bulbs.

Investigation and Experimentation

6.c Formulate and justify predictions based on cause-and-effect relationships.

6.d Conduct multiple trials to test a prediction and draw conclusions about the relationships between predictions and results.

LESSON 2

Essential Question

What Makes a Circuit?

California Fast Fact

Light It Up!

At Disneyland in Anaheim, California, the Electrical Parade uses more than half a million light bulbs. Each parade float has circuits that control thousands of bulbs.

This parade float uses thousands of electric bulbs.

Vocabulary Preview

electric current [ee•LEK•trik KER•uhnt] A flow of electric charges (p. 72)

electric circuit [ee•LEK•trik SER•kit] A  continuous pathway that can carry an electric current (p. 72)

series circuit [SEER•eez SER•kit] An electric circuit with only one path for current (p. 74)

parallel circuit [PAIR•uh•lel SER•kit] An electric circuit with two or more paths for current (p. 76)

resistance [ree•ZIS• tuhns] How much a material  opposes, or resists, the flow of electric current (p. 78)

short circuit [SHORT SER•kit] A flaw in a circuit that allows a large current to flow through where it isn't wanted (p. 79)

Make a Light Bulb Light Up

Directed Inquiry

Start with Questions

Light bulbs come in many different shapes and colors.

- What parts can you use to make a light bulb light up?

- How does a light bulb need to be connected to other materials?

Investigate to find out. Then read to find out more.

Prepare to Investigate

Investigation Skill Tip

Making predictions involves figuring out what will happen in the future. Use what you have observed or what you have experienced to help you predict.

Materials

- D-cell battery
- insulated electrical wire with ends stripped
- flashlight bulb (1.5 V)
- masking tape

Make an Observation Chart

Arrangement of Wire, Battery, and Bulb	Drawing	Observations

Follow This Procedure

1 **Predict** a way to arrange the materials you have been given so that the bulb lights up. Make a drawing to **record** your prediction.

2 Test your prediction. **Record** whether the bulb lights up.

3 Repeat Steps 1 and 2 several times. Try different arrangements to get the bulb to light up. For each try, **record** the **prediction** and the results.

Draw Conclusions

1. What did you observe about the arrangement of materials when the bulb lit up?

2. **Standards Link** How should you connect the parts to make the bulb light up? `1.a`

3. **Investigation Skill** What conclusions can you draw after testing your **predictions**? How will these results help you make predictions in the future? `6.c`

Step 1

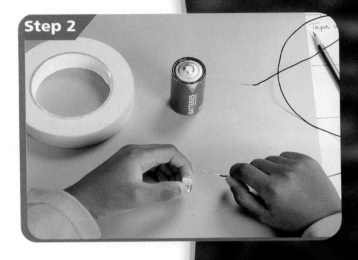

Step 2

Independent Inquiry — **Make Predictions**

Think about your observations. If you had two light bulbs, how would you predict that you could make them both light up at the same time?

Write a plan for an investigation to test your prediction. Be sure to include the materials, the steps of the procedure, and the data you will collect. `6.d`

VOCABULARY
electric current p. 72
electric circuit p. 72
series circuit p. 74
parallel circuit p. 76
resistance p. 78
short circuit p. 79

SCIENCE CONCEPTS

▶ what causes an electric current

▶ how to make series circuits and parallel circuits

Focus Skill **CAUSE AND EFFECT**

Look for the cause of a short circuit.

| cause | → | effect |

Moving Charges

In static electricity, an object becomes charged when it gains or loses negative charges. Once the charge forms, it stays put. It jumps only if it has a path, such as from your finger to a metal doorknob.

Another kind of electricity is current electricity. When electric charges have a path to follow, they flow, or move. A flow of electric charges is called an **electric current.** It's like a moving

▼ An electric current in a circuit moves like a bike wheel. The energy of motion moves through the whole wheel at once. When you connect a circuit, a battery moves energy to all parts of the circuit at the same time.

stream. Current electricity is a steady flow of moving charges.

In the Investigate, you arranged a wire, a bulb, and a battery to make a closed path. An **electric circuit** is a closed path that electric current follows. The battery you used was an important part of the circuit. It provided the energy to move the electric charges through the circuit. That energy was changed to light and heat by the bulb.

Current electricity is more useful to people than static electricity. That's because it can be controlled more easily.

Focus Skill **CAUSE AND EFFECT** What causes electric charges to flow?

▲ Use your finger to trace the path of the current through each part of the circuit. What do you notice?

Controlling Current

The water in this fountain follows an unbroken path, or a circuit. The pump lifts the water, which then falls down through the fountain. The water returns to the pump through the pipe. You can shut the fountain off by turning off the pump. ▶

pump

Just as water flows in a fountain, an electric current follows a circuit. Like the pump, the battery provides energy for the circuit. Current flows through bulbs in the circuit just as it flows through the trays of the fountain. You can control the current in an electric circuit by opening the switch. This breaks the path. ▶

For more links and animations, go to **www.hspscience.com**

Series Circuits

There are different kinds of electric circuits. One kind is the wiring in a flashlight. It's simple, like the circuit you made in the Investigate. It has two or three batteries. There is only one bulb to turn on and off. What if you wanted more than one bulb?

The kind of circuit you built in the Investigate is called a series circuit. A **series circuit** has only one path for its current to follow. It's like a Ferris wheel. Once you're on it, you have to go all the way around to get back to the start.

A series circuit can have more than one bulb. It also can have a buzzer or other devices. The order of the devices doesn't matter. The electric current moves from the battery, which is the power supply, through the wire. Next, it passes through each device. Then it returns to the battery.

In a series circuit, the same amount of current flows through each device. Removing any device breaks the circuit. All of the devices stop working. A circuit with a break in its conducting pathway is called an *open circuit*.

Series Circuit

In this diagram, the thin line stands for a wire. The long and short lines stand for a battery. The circles stand for light bulbs. More than one item can run in a series circuit. ▶

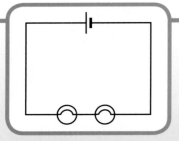

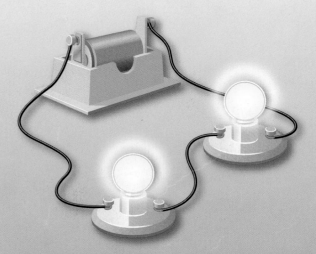

▲ A *closed* series circuit can light up two or more bulbs.

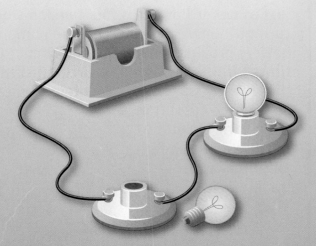

▲ If the circuit is open at any point, neither bulb will light up. How could you open the circuit if both bulbs are in place?

Series circuits work well for simple devices such as flashlights. Series circuits were once used in lighted signs that had only a few lights. They were also used in scoreboards that had just a few lights. There may be a series circuit running the lights on your bicycle. However, these circuits aren't used for most wiring in buildings. Can you guess why?

Current can flow in a series circuit only when everything is connected at the same time. Would it make sense to use only series circuits in a house? All the electric devices would have to be turned on all the time. If you unplugged a radio, it would cause all the lights in the house to go out!

You have probably seen trees decorated with strings of tiny lights. These strings of lights used to be wired in a series circuit. If one light burned out, all the lights went out! People didn't know which bulb had burned out, so they had to check them all. That took a lot of time. The next section will give you information about circuits in which the rest of the string stays lit when one light burns out.

(Focus Skill) **CAUSE AND EFFECT** **What causes the devices in a series circuit to turn off?**

▼ **In a series circuit, the same current goes through all the bulbs. Adding bulbs to a series circuit causes each bulb to be less bright. Do you think there's a limit to how many bulbs you can add to a series circuit?**

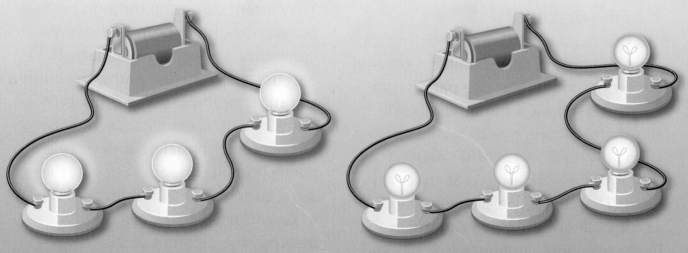

▲ These bulbs are dimmer than those in the two-bulb circuit.

▲ These bulbs are dimmer than the bulbs in the three-bulb circuit.

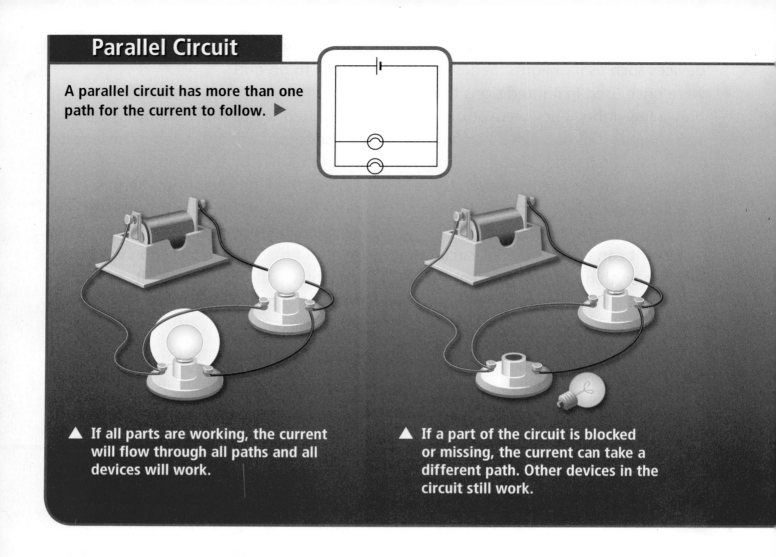

Parallel Circuit

A parallel circuit has more than one path for the current to follow. ▶

▲ If all parts are working, the current will flow through all paths and all devices will work.

▲ If a part of the circuit is blocked or missing, the current can take a different path. Other devices in the circuit still work.

Parallel Circuits

A practical way to wire buildings involves using parallel circuits. A **parallel circuit** has more than one path for the current to follow. If something blocks the charges along one path, the charges keep flowing along another path.

Think of electric circuits as streets in a city. Then think of a parallel circuit as the different ways you can get from home to school. If one street is blocked off or if the traffic is backed up, you can go on another street.

Look at the first picture of a parallel circuit. You can see two complete paths.

The current can travel through both bulbs and light up both of them. What if one bulb is missing or damaged? Because there are two paths, the current can still flow through the other bulb.

Just as with series circuits, you can put a number of different devices in parallel circuits. In series circuits, the same current flows through each device. In parallel circuits, the current is split between the different paths.

Schools and homes have lots of lights. Devices such as lights and computers can be plugged into sockets in the wall. That way, people can turn the devices

▼ In a parallel circuit, the current splits between the different paths. Adding bulbs to a parallel circuit doesn't change the brightness of each bulb.

▼ The bulbs in the two-, three-, and four-bulb circuits are the same brightness.

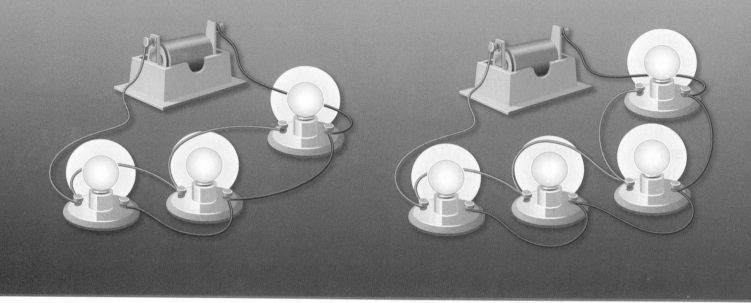

on or off at different times. They don't want one device to cause a change in another device. Parallel circuits let people use each device separately.

Parallel circuits have another advantage over series circuits. Each time you add a light bulb to a series circuit, it causes all the bulbs to become dimmer. In parallel circuits, adding more bulbs doesn't cause a change in how bright the bulbs are.

Focus Skill **CAUSE AND EFFECT** In a parallel circuit, what effect does removing one device have on the other devices?

Insta-Lab

Lights Out!
Use a line of several students to represent a wire. Use a two or three balls to represent current. Arrange the "wire" to represent a series circuit. Move "current" through the circuit. What happens if the wire "breaks?" Repeat to model a parallel circuit. Compare and contrast the two models.

Resistance

The flow of electric current in a circuit is like traffic on a road. If the road has a lot of lanes, a lot of cars can move easily. What happens to the flow of cars if the road narrows to one lane? The traffic slows down and backs up.

The same thing happens when electric current moves through a circuit. The amount of current that can flow through a circuit depends on resistance. **Resistance** is how much a material opposes the flow of current.

The greater the resistance, the less current can pass through a circuit. Thin wire has greater resistance than thick wire. Light bulbs and other devices have higher resistance than copper wire. They produce a "traffic backup" in electric current.

For example, a light bulb glows because the *filament*—or thin wire— inside the bulb has high resistance. As the current passes through the filament, it resists the flow. First, the filament gets hot. Then, it glows. High resistance is used to produce heat and light. Toasters and space heaters have high resistance.

To find out the total resistance for a series circuit, you add up the resistances of all the devices. For a parallel circuit, you need to find out the resistance of the devices in each path.

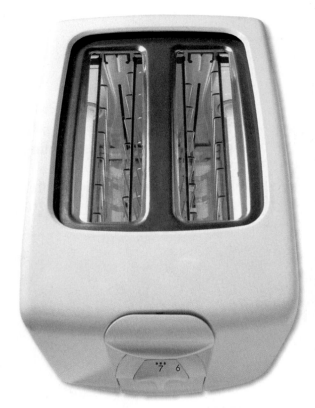

▲ **The wires in a toaster have high resistance compared to the copper wires in the circuits that you built. The high resistance causes the wires to get hot enough to toast bread.**

Some outlets have a built-in circuit breaker. If there is a short circuit or if the wires overheat, the red button pops out, breaking the circuit. ▶

This table compares the resistance of metal wires. All the wires are the same thickness and length. Use the information in the table to answer the questions.

Resistance of Some Metals	
Material	Resistance (Ohms)
Aluminum	2.65
Lead	22
Silver	1.59
Iron	9.71
Copper (alloy)	1.68
Nichrome	100

Which metal shown has the least resistance? Why do you think it isn't used in common circuits? Which material shown would most likely be used in a toaster or a space heater? Why?

Most wires have low resistance. When resistance gets *too* low, though, too much current passes through a wire. Suppose one path in a parallel circuit is a wire that runs directly between the two ends of a battery. The current takes a shortcut, or a short circuit. In a **short circuit**, current flows where it isn't wanted. Short circuits prevent the rest of the circuit from working properly. They have low resistance and high current, so they also produce a lot of heat.

The wires in a lamp cord run side by side. They are covered in plastic so they don't touch. What happens if the plastic wears away and the wires touch? If that happens, the current takes a shortcut. The current cannot light the lamp, and the wire heats up.

Many circuits have safety devices such as fuses. A fuse contains a substance that melts if it gets hot. If a short circuit happens, the heat causes the fuse to melt. The circuit is broken. Because the current stops, no damage is done.

Focus Skill CAUSE AND EFFECT What effect does adding devices have on the resistance of a series circuit?

Essential Question

What makes a circuit?

In this lesson, you learned how to use wires, batteries, and bulbs to design and build simple series circuits and parallel circuits. You also learned how resistance affects electric circuits and how damage due to short circuits is prevented.

Science Content Standard in This Lesson

1.a *Students know* how to design and build simple series and parallel circuits by using components such as wires, batteries, and bulbs.

1. **Focus Skill** **CAUSE AND EFFECT** Copy and complete a graphic organizer to explain how electric circuits work. **1.a**

2. **SUMMARIZE** Use at least four of the lesson vocabulary words to write a summary of the lesson. **1.a**

3. **DRAW CONCLUSIONS** Why are the metal prongs of a plug sealed in plastic or rubber? **1.a**

4. **VOCABULARY** Compare and contrast *series circuits* and *parallel circuits.* **1.a**

5. **Critical Thinking** If you want a switch to turn off all the lights in a room, should you use a series circuit or a parallel circuit? **1.a**

6. **Investigate and Experiment** Predict what would happen if you connected the ends of a battery in a series circuit with wire. **6.c**

7. What two things are needed to make current flow in a circuit?
   A wires and a light bulb
   B a current source and a closed path
   C a current source and a light bulb
   D a battery and a bulb **1.a**

8. Why are parallel circuits more useful in more applications than series circuits are?
   A Parallel circuits are cheaper to build.
   B They allow many appliances to be used at one time.
   C Parallel circuits take up less room.
   D Series circuits produce short circuits, but parallel circuits do not. **1.a**

The **Big Idea**

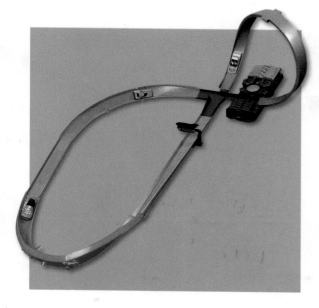

Writing

 ELA—W 2.1

Write a Narrative

Write a story that tells about the journey of an electric charge as it flows through the circuit you built in the Investigate. For example, you might compare the circuit to a race track. Make sure your story includes facts you learned in this lesson.

9÷3 Math

 MG 2.0

Make a Bar Graph

Keep a record of the ways you use electricity at home. For example, keep track for one day of the number of hours the lights are on and the number of hours you use the TV and other devices. Make a bar graph to show your use of each device.

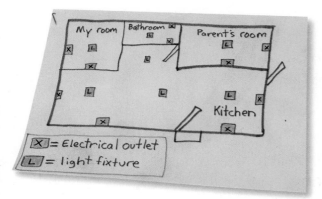

My room   Bathroom   Parent's room

Kitchen

X = Electrical outlet
L = light fixture

Art

VPA—CE 2.8

Wiring Art

Make a home circuit design that shows the difference between series circuits and parallel circuits. Attach magazine pictures to show the devices in the circuits.

 For more links and activities, go to **www.hspscience.com**

Science Content

1.f *Students know* that magnets have two poles (north and south) and that like poles repel each other while unlike poles attract each other.

Investigation and Experimentation

6.f Follow a set of written instructions for a scientific investigation.

LESSON 3

Essential Question

What Are Magnetic Poles?

California Fast Fact

What's Holding Them Up?

Los Angeles sculptor Bruce Gray made this sculpture, which he called *Suspension*. Its cords are suspended, or held in place in midair, by an invisible force. This force is the pull of magnetism between strong magnets on the ends of the cords and on the frame.

magnet [MAG•nit] An object that attracts iron and some other metals (p. 86)

magnetic poles [mag•NET•ik POHLZ] The places on a magnet where the force is the strongest (p. 86)

magnetic field [mag•NET•ik FEELD] The space in which the magnetic force acts around a magnet (p. 88)

The sculpture *Suspension* is on display at a gallery in Los Angeles, California.

Testing Magnets

Start with Questions

Many people hold papers to their refrigerator doors with magnetic letters like those shown below.

- What causes the letters to stick to the door?

- Is there a pattern in the way letters stick to one another?

Investigate to find out. Then read to find out more.

Prepare to Investigate

Investigation Skill Tip
When you predict, you use what you know to tell what you think will happen.

Materials
- 2 bar magnets with poles labeled *N* and *S*
- string
- masking tape
- 2 disk or doughnut magnets

Make an Observation Chart

Arrangement of Magnets	Observations
N pole of hanging magnet and N pole of hand-held magnet	
N pole of hanging magnet and S pole of hand-held magnet	
Stacked disk magnets	

Follow This Procedure

1. Tie one end of an 25- to 30-cm piece of string to the middle of a bar magnet. Use the string to pick up the magnet. Move the string until the magnet balances. Tape the string in place.

2. Use the string and tape to hang the magnet from a desk or table.

3. Hold the other bar magnet by the end marked *S*. Bring the end marked *N* close to the end of the hanging magnet marked *N*. **Record** your **observations**.

4. Turn the magnet in your hand so that you are holding it by the end marked *N*. Then repeat the rest of Step 3.

5. Place one disk magnet on top of another one. **Record** your **observations**. Turn over the top magnet. **Observe** and **record**.

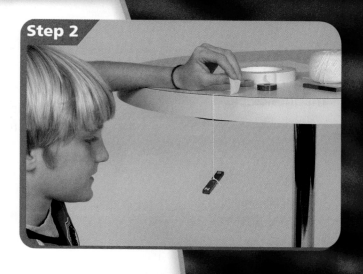
Step 2

Step 3

Draw Conclusions

1. What conclusion can you draw about the way magnets affect one another?

2. **Standards Link** What can you infer about properties of the letters stuck to a refrigerator door and of other magnets? **1.f**

3. **Investigation Skill** What do you **predict** would happen if you put one letter on top of another?

Independent Inquiry | Write and Follow Directions

Think about how you tested the magnets. Write directions for an investigation that tests how a disk magnet or a refrigerator magnet will react to a bar magnet. Make your directions as clear as possible.

Exchange your directions with a partner's. Follow your partner's directions for testing the magnets. Record your observations. **6.f**

VOCABULARY
magnet p. 86
magnetic poles p. 86
magnetic field p. 88

SCIENCE CONCEPTS

▶ what magnetic poles are

▶ how magnetic fields cause magnetic forces

MAIN IDEA AND DETAILS

Look for details about how magnetic fields form around magnets.

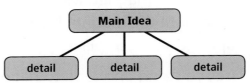

Two Poles

A **magnet** is an object that attracts certain materials. These materials—for example, steel—usually contain iron. A few other metals also have magnetic properties.

In the Investigate, you observed that the two ends of a magnet behave in different ways. The two ends of a magnet are called **magnetic poles**. The magnetic forces of a magnet are strongest around the poles.

If a bar magnet is allowed to swing freely, one end will always point north. This end is called the *north-seeking* pole. It is usually marked with the letter *N*. The other end is the *south-seeking* pole. It is marked with the letter *S*.

In the Investigate, you noticed that one end of the magnet in your hand attracted one end of the hanging magnet. The other end of the magnet in your hand pushed away the same end of the hanging magnet.

◀ **A magnet has a north-seeking pole at one end and a south-seeking pole at the other.**

◀ **If you cut a magnet in half, each half becomes a magnet with an *N* pole and an *S* pole.**

◀ **No matter how many times you cut a magnet, each piece becomes a magnet with an *N* pole and an *S* pole.**

Magnetic Poles

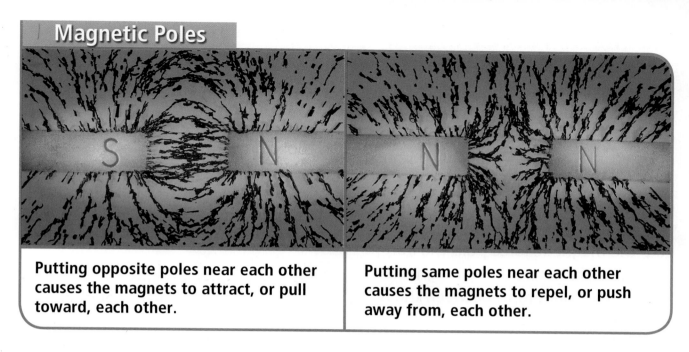

Putting opposite poles near each other causes the magnets to attract, or pull toward, each other.

Putting same poles near each other causes the magnets to repel, or push away from, each other.

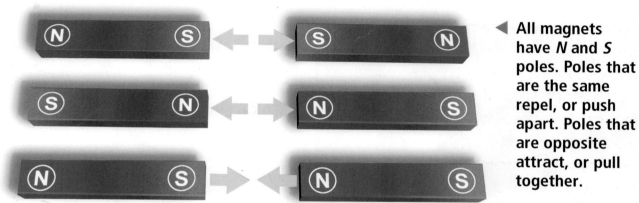

◀ All magnets have *N* and *S* poles. Poles that are the same repel, or push apart. Poles that are opposite attract, or pull together.

Forces between magnetic poles act like forces between electric charges. Opposite poles attract, and poles that are the same repel. When you hold two *S* poles or two *N* poles near each other, you feel them push apart. When you hold an *N* pole and an *S* pole near each other, you feel them pull together.

Magnets keep their poles even if their shapes are changed. If you cut a bar magnet into pieces, each of the pieces becomes a magnet. Each piece has an *N* pole and an *S* pole.

Magnets of different shapes all have *N* and *S* poles. Try holding two disk magnets near each other. When you put them together one way, they attract. When you flip one of them over, they repel.

What do you think would happen if you cut a disk magnet into thin slices? Would each slice have an *N* pole on one side and an *S* pole on the other? Yes, it would!

 **MAIN IDEA AND DETAILS** How are all magnets alike?

Magnetic Forces

A **magnetic field** is the area where the magnetic force around a magnet acts. You can't see the field. What you can see and feel is how it affects other magnets and objects that contain iron.

One way to show a magnetic field is to lay a plastic bag full of iron filings over the magnet. When you tap the bag, the magnetic force pulls the iron filings into the shape of the magnetic field. Curved lines form between the N and S poles of the magnet.

The lines are called magnetic field lines, or lines of force. In the picture, you can see that the lines form closed loops. The loops get bigger as you move away from the magnet.

Look at the arrows on the lines in the picture. Which way do they point? Remember that the arrows in an electric field show how the field acts on a positive charge. The lines of force in a magnetic field always run from the N to the S pole.

Magnetic Field

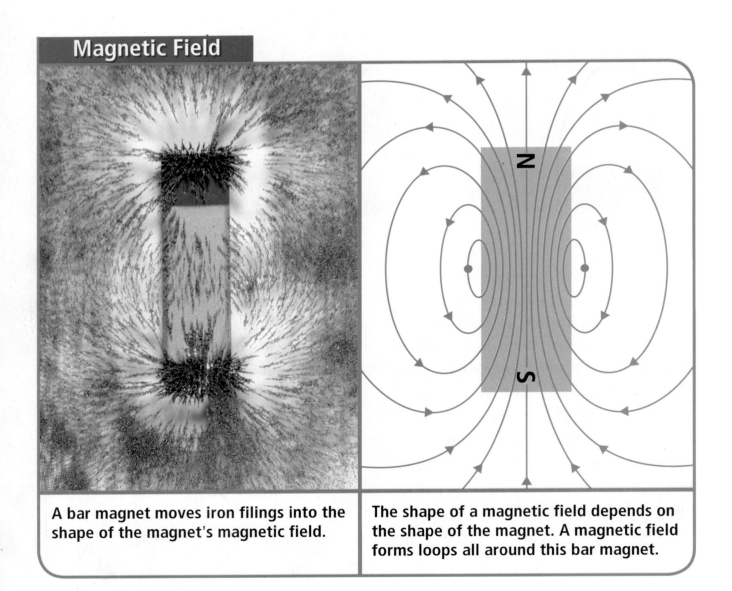

A bar magnet moves iron filings into the shape of the magnet's magnetic field.

The shape of a magnetic field depends on the shape of the magnet. A magnetic field forms loops all around this bar magnet.

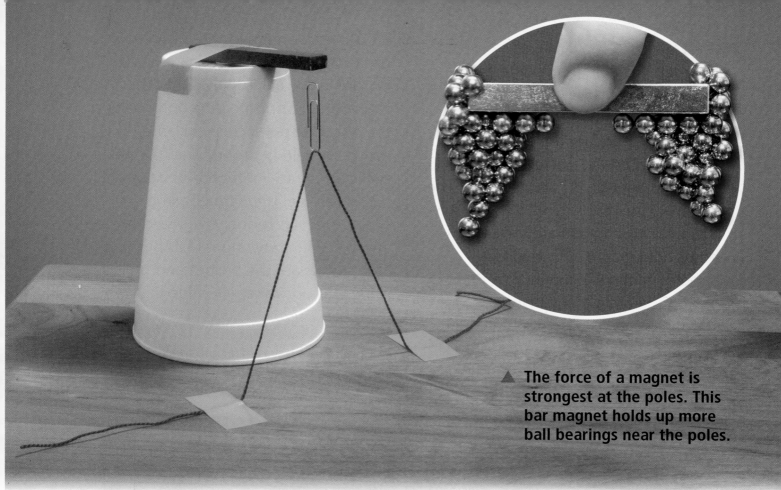

▲ The force of a magnet is strongest at the poles. This bar magnet holds up more ball bearings near the poles.

▲ Magnetic forces can act without touching. The bar magnet is holding up the paperclip.

What happens when you pick up a paper clip with a magnet? You know that the clip jumps to the magnet only when the magnet is close. The force is stronger when the distance between the magnet and the object is smaller.

Not all magnets cause the same force. Some, like the ones in the sculpture on the first page of this lesson, are very strong. Others can pull only small, light objects. Magnets can also become less magnetic if they are heated or dropped.

Focus Skill MAIN IDEA AND DETAILS In what direction do the lines of magnetic force around a magnet run?

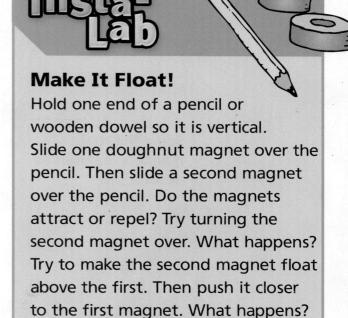

Insta-Lab

Make It Float!
Hold one end of a pencil or wooden dowel so it is vertical. Slide one doughnut magnet over the pencil. Then slide a second magnet over the pencil. Do the magnets attract or repel? Try turning the second magnet over. What happens? Try to make the second magnet float above the first. Then push it closer to the first magnet. What happens? Why do you think this happens?

Magnet Shapes

Magnets come in many different shapes and sizes. They are made for different uses. Some are shaped like a horseshoe. Where are the poles? If you could straighten the horseshoe to look like a bar magnet, you would know. The poles are at the ends.

Square, flat magnets are sometimes used to hold cabinet doors closed. Magnets shaped like a pencil can be used to separate a mix of sawdust, dirt, and old nails. Some companies make magnetic business cards on flat rubber strips. They hope you will stick the cards on your refrigerator so you will remember the companies' names.

Flat rubber magnets are often made up of strips of magnetic material. The picture in the circle shows that the strips run in opposite directions. With the opposite poles close together, the magnetic field is strong. The magnet sticks tightly to a refrigerator door.

You can feel the different strips by sliding one flat rubber magnet over another. The movement feels bumpy! The bumps are the pushes and pulls as same and opposite poles line up.

Focus Skill **MAIN IDEA AND DETAILS** Why do magnets have different shapes?

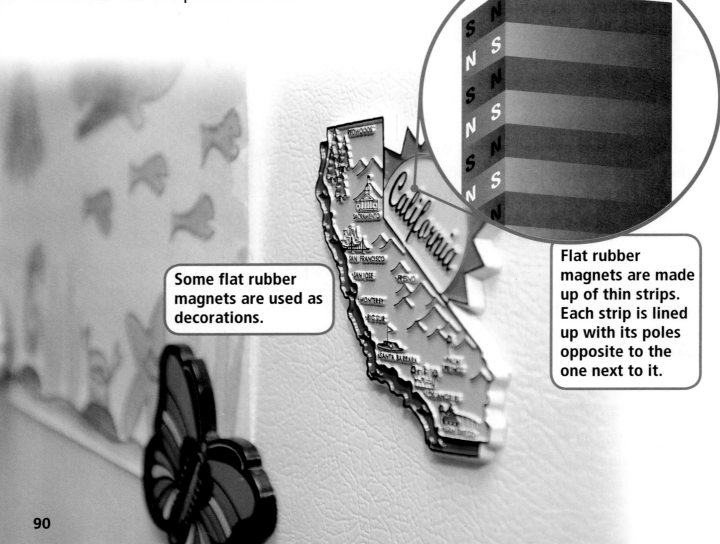

Some flat rubber magnets are used as decorations.

Flat rubber magnets are made up of thin strips. Each strip is lined up with its poles opposite to the one next to it.

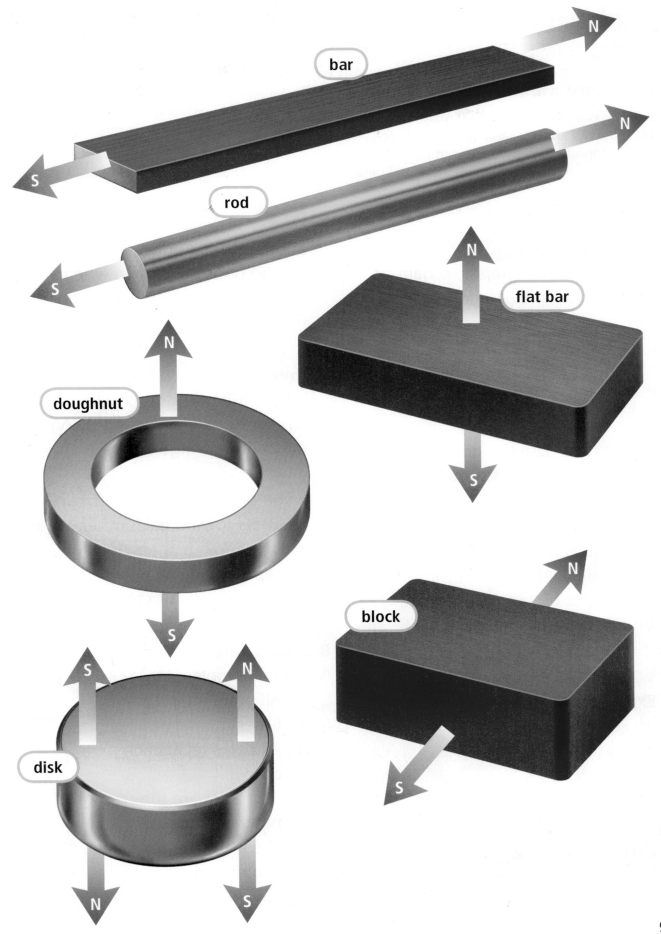

bar

rod

flat bar

doughnut

block

disk

What are magnetic poles?

In this lesson, you learned that magnets have two poles (*N* and *S*). Same poles repel each other. Opposite poles attract each other. You also learned that every magnet has a magnetic field around it.

Science Content Standard in This Lesson

1.f *Students know* that magnets have two poles (north and south) and that like poles repel each other while unlike poles attract each other.

1. 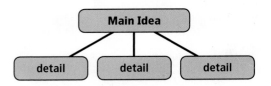 Copy and complete a graphic organizer for the main idea *Magnets affect one another.*   **1.f**

```
        Main Idea
      /    |    \
  detail  detail  detail
```

2. **SUMMARIZE** Use the graphic organizer to write a summary of the lesson.   **1.f**

3. **DRAW CONCLUSIONS** Describe the magnetic field lines that form when the *S* poles of two magnets are brought close together.   **1.f**

4. **VOCABULARY** Explain how you can use iron filings to show a *magnetic field*.   **1.f**

5. **Critical Thinking** You glue a small magnet to a box lid and another to the edge of the box. The lid pops back open when you close it. What can you infer about the two magnets?   **1.f**

6. **Investigate and Experiment** Why is it important to follow directions carefully when doing a scientific investigation?   **6.f**

7. If you bring the *N* poles of two magnets toward each other, what will they do?
   A repel   **C** spin
   B attract   **D** create sparks   **1.f**

8. Which statement about magnetic poles is true?
   A All poles attract each other.
   B All poles repel each other.
   C The poles are the strongest parts of a magnet.
   D The poles are the weakest parts of a magnet.   **1.f**

The Big Idea

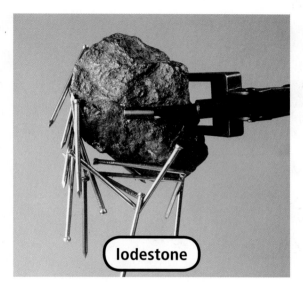

lodestone

Writing

ELA—W 2.3

Write a Report

Research magnets. Then write a report about how people first used magnets. Tell how magnetic materials were discovered and what people thought was the cause of magnetism.

9÷3 Math

SDAP 1.2

Use Data

Test the strength of a bar magnet by measuring how many paper clips it can pick up. Repeat the test 12 or more times. What are two different statistics that you could use to describe the strength of the magnet? Calculate them.

Literature

ELA—R 3.5

Figurative Language

Some concepts from this lesson are used as metaphors. Survey five adults. Ask for one or two examples of magnet concepts used figuratively. Record the answers. Tell whether or not the figurative use matches the science fact.

 For more links and activities, go to **www.hspscience.com**

LESSON

4

Science Content

1.b *Students know* how to build a simple compass and use it to detect magnetic effects, including Earth's magnetic field.

Investigation and Experimentation

6.c Formulate and justify predictions based on cause-and-effect relationships.

6.d Conduct multiple trials to test a prediction and draw conclusions about the relationships between predictions and results.

Essential Question

How Can You Detect a Magnetic Field?

California Fast Fact

Where's North?

Northern lights are caused by particles from the sun interacting with Earth's magnetic field. The shimmering ribbons of light are rarely visible as far south as California.

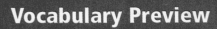
compass
[KUM•puhs] A
tool used to
determine
direction
(p. 100)

Northern lights photographed
over north California foothills
in 2003

Make a Compass

Start with Questions

People in a boat use a compass to find out which way to sail.

- How does a compass help them find a direction?

- Does a compass always work?

Investigate to find out. Then read to find out more.

Prepare to Investigate

Investigation Skill Tip
When you make predictions, you often use information from experiences you have had in the past. Think about your experiences as you predict in this Investigate.

Materials

- safety goggles
- cork square
- bar magnet
- bowl of water
- paper clips
- large craft needle (4–5 cm long)
- tape

Make an Observation Chart

Step Number	Observations
1	
3	
5	
6	

Follow This Procedure

CAUTION: Put on the safety goggles. Be careful with sharp objects.

1. Hold the magnet near a paper clip. Then hold the needle near a paper clip. **Record** your observations.

2. Hold the needle by its eye. Drag it slowly over the magnet 20 times, always in the same direction.

3. Repeat Step 1.

4. Tape the needle onto the cork. Move the magnet at least 1 m away from the bowl.

5. Float the cork in the bowl. Record your **observations**.

6. Carefully and slowly turn the bowl. Record your **observations**.

Step 2

Step 5

Draw Conclusions

1. What happened to the needle as you stroked it on the magnet?

2. **Standards Link** How does a compass show direction? `1.b`

3. **Investigation Skill** Suppose you didn't move the bar magnet away from the bowl and cork. **Predict** what would happen when you turned the bowl. `6.c`

Independent Inquiry — **Test a Prediction**

Test the prediction you made in question 3. How many different ways can you test it? How do your different tests affect the correctness of your prediction? `6.d`

VOCABULARY
compass p. 100

SCIENCE CONCEPTS
▶ how a compass works
▶ how magnets affect one another

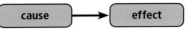
CAUSE AND EFFECT
Look for the effects magnets can have on one another.

| cause | → | effect |

Finding the North Pole

How would you describe Earth's North and South Poles? You might think about the top and bottom of a globe. Or you might picture Earth as a tennis ball with a pencil stuck through it. The pencil stands for the imaginary line around which Earth rotates.

Earth really has two sets of north and south poles. One set is the true, or geographic, North and South Poles. These are where the pencil comes out of the ball.

Earth also has magnetic poles because its core is a huge magnet. Like every magnet, Earth has an *N* and an *S* pole. These are located about 2100 kilometers (1300 mi) away from the true poles. Also like every magnet, Earth has a magnetic field.

The picture shows a bar magnet hanging from a string. When the magnet swings freely, it lines up along Earth's magnetic field lines. If you use a ring-shaped magnet and look through the hole, you'll look north or south.

If allowed to swing freely, the north-seeking end of a magnet will point toward Earth's north magnetic pole. ▶

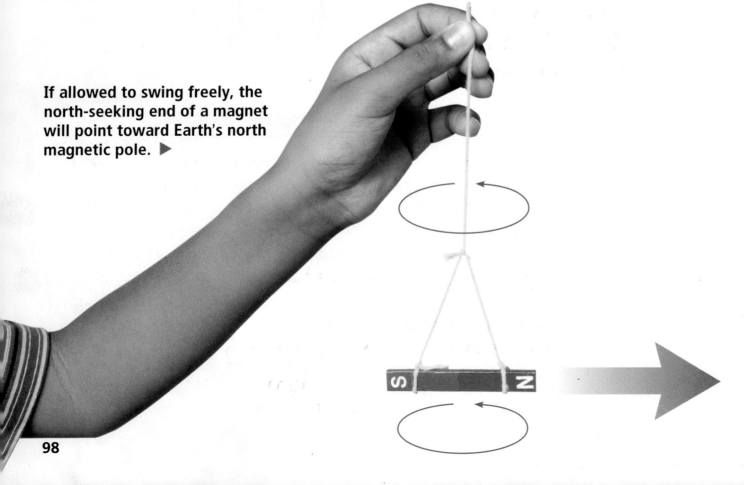

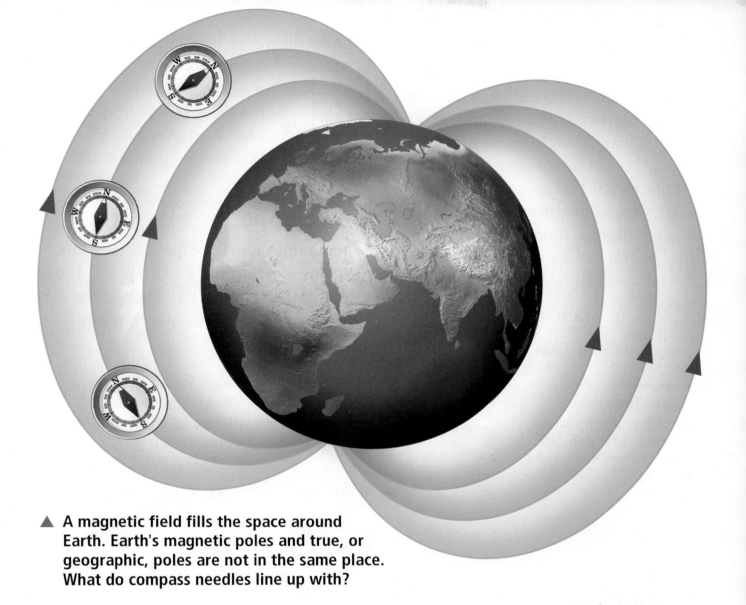

▲ A magnetic field fills the space around Earth. Earth's magnetic poles and true, or geographic, poles are not in the same place. What do compass needles line up with?

What causes the *N* pole of a magnet to point to the north magnetic pole? Remember that a magnet's end that is marked *N* is the *north-seeking* pole. The north-seeking poles of magnets repel one another, but they all point to Earth's north magnetic pole. That means that the magnetic pole near Earth's North Pole is an *S* pole.

Think about the iron filings that show the magnetic field around a bar magnet. The lines of iron filings are close together around the poles of the magnet. That

is also true of Earth's magnetic field. If you hang a magnet near the poles, the magnet will point toward the ground!

Are there any places on Earth where you can't use a magnet to find north? Magnets attract the iron in steel. Some buildings have a lot of steel parts. Inside these buildings, a compass may point to the steel instead of the north magnetic pole.

Focus Skill CAUSE AND EFFECT What causes a hanging magnet to line up in a certain direction?

Compasses

Early sailors used the positions of the sun, moon, and stars to figure out where they were. What did they do when it was cloudy? Few were brave enough to sail out of sight of land.

In time, a naturally magnetic type of rock called *lodestone* (LOHD•stohn) was discovered. Today we know it as a type of iron ore. By the 1100s, people in China and Europe were using it to make a floating magnetic compass. A **compass** is a tool used to determine direction. Compasses helped sailors find their way in bad weather, which happened often in some areas.

In the Investigate, you caused a needle to become magnetic by stroking it along a magnet. A needle makes a much better direction pointer than a chunk of rock does!

The first compasses were quite large and heavy. Compasses today can be made small and light for easy carrying. The needle turns on a sharp point. The face of the compass has labels at the four major directions—north, south, east, and west.

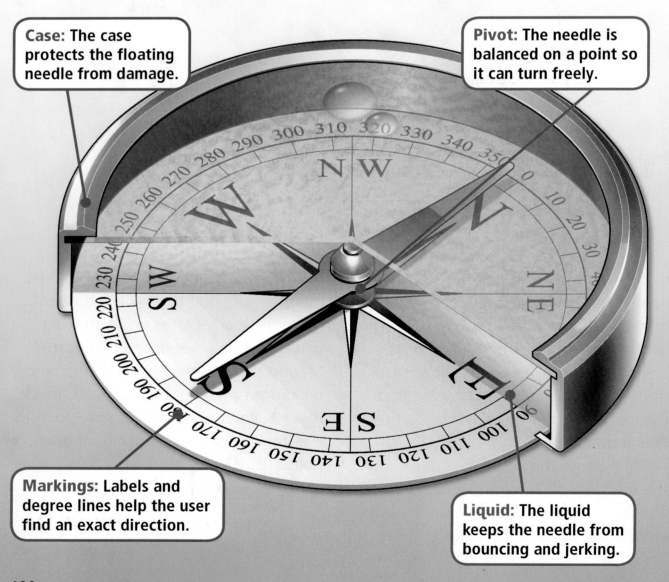

Case: The case protects the floating needle from damage.

Pivot: The needle is balanced on a point so it can turn freely.

Markings: Labels and degree lines help the user find an exact direction.

Liquid: The liquid keeps the needle from bouncing and jerking.

Because the compass background is a circle, it has 360 degrees. North is at zero degrees (or 360 degrees). East is at 90 degrees. South is at 180 degrees, and west is at 270 degrees. There are degree markings between the four directions, also. The markings help people find the exact direction in which they want to travel.

Ships today are mostly made of steel, which can affect the way a compass works. They still carry magnetic compasses, but they also use other ways of finding direction. These new kinds of technology don't need to use Earth's magnetic field.

Focus Skill **CAUSE AND EFFECT** **What effect did the invention of the compass have on ocean travel?**

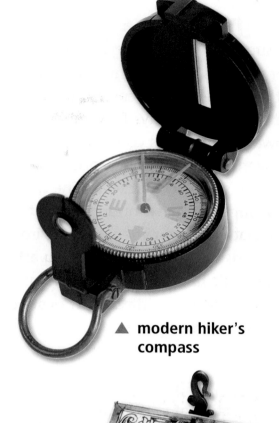

▲ **modern hiker's compass**

▲ **brass compass case with gold trim from the 1600s**

▲ **This miner's compass from the 1600s was hooked on a rope and used to map ore deposits.**

Compasses have been built for many people over the years.

Magnetic Interference

Suppose you're using a compass for an investigation. The needles on other students' compasses are pointing toward the windows. Yours is pointing toward the wall! Is your compass broken? Maybe it's fine.

What's behind that wall? The beams that support many modern buildings are made of steel. There may be iron pipes inside the wall. Concrete walls and floors may have steel rods in them. The compass may be sitting right over an iron nail in your desk!

Any of these things may cause your compass needle to point the wrong way. It points toward the metal materials instead of toward Earth's north magnetic pole. You might try carrying a compass around your classroom to find all the trouble spots!

Many objects around your home contain magnetic materials. Television sets contain powerful magnets. Radios, stereos, and appliances can all cause a compass needle to point to them instead of to the north.

The red arrow shows the true direction of north. Why is the compass on the stereo speaker pointing the wrong way? ▶

▲ A compass works correctly when it's kept away from all metal objects that might attract or repel its magnetic needle. The red arrow shows the direction of true north.

The best place to use a compass is outdoors. Stay away from buildings, power lines, cars, and magnets.

Magnets can also interfere with the way other devices operate. Playing with magnets near a television can cause wavy patterns on the screen. Magnets can damage a computer hard drive because computers store information as patterns of magnetic fields.

Focus Skill CAUSE AND EFFECT How can metal objects and magnets cause problems with compasses and with electronic items that use magnets?

Needle Dance

Place a compass near one pole of a magnet. Then move the compass all around the magnet. Where does the needle point in each position? What causes the needle to move? What can you infer about the strength of the magnetic fields of the magnet and of Earth?

Standards Wrap-Up and Lesson Review

Essential Question

How can you detect a magnetic field?

In this lesson, you learned that Earth has a magnetic field. You also learned how to make a simple compass and use it to observe magnetic effects, including Earth's magnetic field.

 Science Content Standard in This Lesson

1.b *Students know* how to build a simple compass and use it to detect magnetic effects, including Earth's magnetic field.

1.  (Focus Skill) **CAUSE AND EFFECT** Copy and complete a graphic organizer to show how a magnetic field affects objects. **1.b**

```
cause ➔ effect
```

2. **SUMMARIZE** Write a sentence that tells the most important information in this lesson. **1.b**

3. **DRAW CONCLUSIONS** Which type of magnet has a field that is about the same shape as Earth's magnetic field? **1.b**

4. **VOCABULARY** Explain how a *compass* works. **1.b**

5. **Critical Thinking** You have a bar magnet on which the poles are not labeled. How can you use a compass to identify the poles? **1.b**

6. **Investigate and Experiment** Make a **prediction** about how you can make a needle a stronger magnet than the one in the Investigate. **6.c**

7. Could you use a compass if you were south of the equator?
   A No. The compass couldn't point to the north magnetic pole.
   B No. There is no pole to point to.
   C Yes. However, directions would be opposite to directions here.
   D Yes. A compass lines up with a magnetic field anywhere. **1.b**

8. Which statement best explains why a compass needle points to Earth's north magnetic pole?  **The Big Idea**
   A Earth is like a huge magnet.
   B Earth's core is lodestone.
   C Compasses are lodestone.
   D The land near the North Pole has large deposits of iron. **1.b**

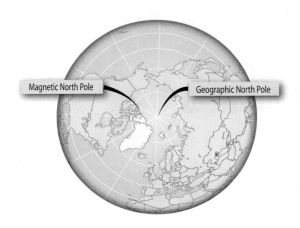

Magnetic North Pole   Geographic North Pole

 Writing ELA—W 2.4

Write a Report

Write a report that includes the most important information about Earth's magnetic field and the use of compasses. Include several main ideas and supporting details.

9÷3 **Math** MG 1.1

Measure an Area

Use a small compass to test the magnetic field of a magnet. Move the compass away from the magnet until the needle no longer points to the magnet. Make a mark at this point. Keep moving the compass around until your marks outline a rectangle. Then calculate the area where the field can be detected.

 Social Studies HSS 4.4.7

Mapping the Pole

Find the current longitude and latitude of the north magnetic pole. If you traveled there, how many degrees of longitude would you cross? Of latitude?

 For more links and activities, go to **www.hspscience.com**

Science Content

1.c *Students know* electric currents produce magnetic fields and know how to build a simple electromagnet.

Investigation and Experimentation

6.e Construct and interpret graphs from measurements.

6.d Conduct multiple trials to test a prediction and draw conclusions about the relationships between predictions and results.

Essential Question

What Makes an Electromagnet?

California Fast Fact

BIG Magnets!

The synchrotron (SINK•ruh•trahn) at Stanford uses 294 magnets. The magnets control the path of electrically charged particles. The particles zoom around an 80-meter diameter circular track. Scientists use this device to study properties of matter.

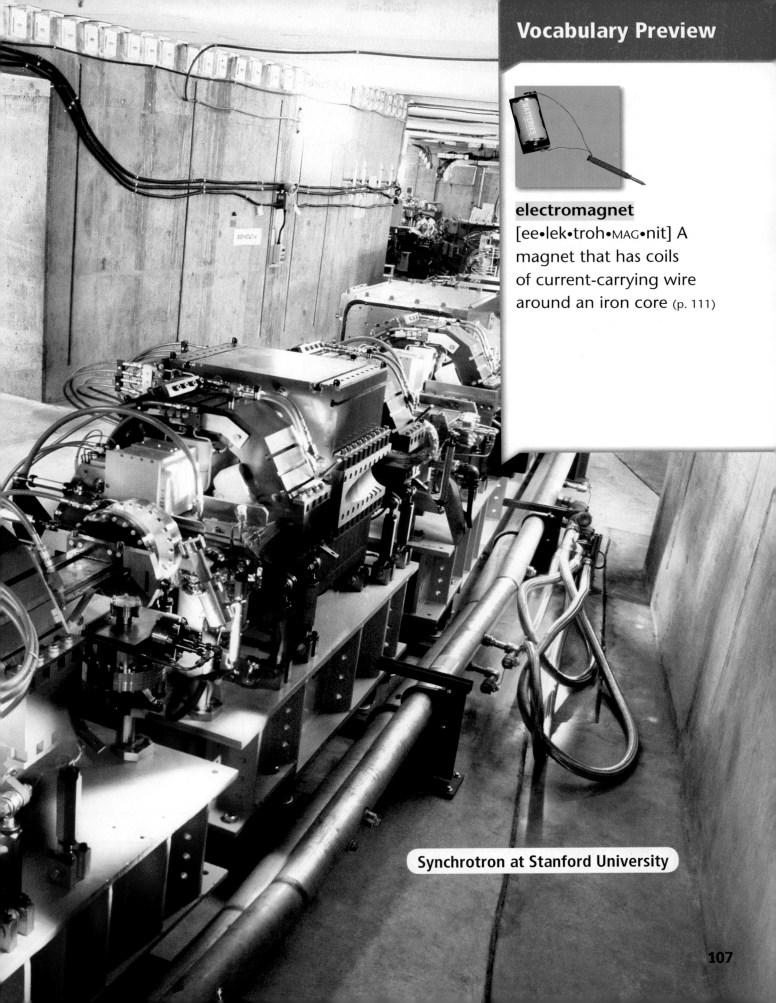

electromagnet
[ee•lek•troh•MAG•nit] A
magnet that has coils
of current-carrying wire
around an iron core (p. 111)

Synchrotron at Stanford University

Make an Electromagnet

Start with Questions

What makes headphones work? Each headphone speaker has an electromagnet inside it that changes electrical energy into sound energy.

- What is an electromagnet, and how does it work?

- How is an electromagnet like a bar magnet?

Investigate to find out. Then read to find out more.

Prepare to Investigate

Investigation Skill Tip

Making and interpreting graphs helps scientists see patterns in data. Think about the kind of graph that will best show the data you collect in this Investigate.

Materials

- insulated copper wire in lengths of 100 cm, 150 cm, and 200 cm
- iron nail, 9 cm long
- D-cell battery in holder
- paper clips
- bar magnet

Make a Data Table

Length of Wire	Number of Coils	Number of Paper Clips Lifted
1 m		
1.5 m		
2 m		

Follow This Procedure

1. Wrap the 1-m length of wire tightly around the nail. Leave 20 cm of wire loose at each end. Record the number of coils.

2. Connect one end of the wire to the battery holder. Touch the other end to the holder, lower the nail toward a pile of paper clips, and lift. **Record** the number of clips lifted. Disconnect the wire.

3. Repeat Steps 1 and 2 with the 1.5-m and 2-m lengths of wire.

4. Hold the point of the nail near the poles of the bar magnet. **Observe** which pole the nail attracts.

5. Turn the battery the other way in the holder. Repeat Step 4.

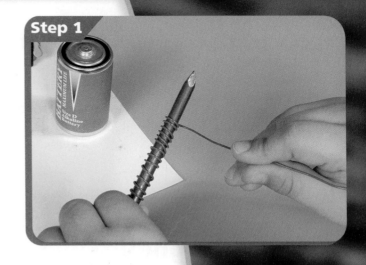

Step 1

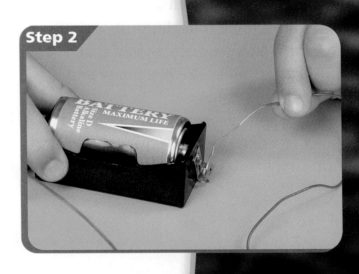

Step 2

Draw Conclusions

1. How does the number of coils relate to the electromagnet's strength? How do you know?

2. **Standards Link** How do you know that an electromagnet has magnetic properties? `1.c`

3. **Investigation Skill** Graph the data in your table. Put the length of the wire on the *x*-axis and the number of lifted paper clips on the *y*-axis. How could you use the graph to make predictions? `6.e`

Independent Inquiry → Make a Prediction

Predict what would happen if you added another battery to your electromagnet. Plan an investigation to test your prediction. If your teacher approves, conduct your investigation. Is your prediction correct? `6.d`

VOCABULARY
electromagnet p. 111

SCIENCE CONCEPTS
▶ what an electromagnet is
▶ how to control an electromagnet

MAIN IDEA AND DETAILS
Look for the main idea about how electricity and magnetism are related.

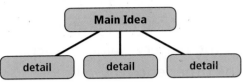

Making a Magnetic Field

You know that electric charges produce a force that can push or pull. Magnets also produce a force that pushes and pulls. Are electricity and magnetism related?

If you sprinkle iron filings around a piece of copper wire, no magnetic field appears. If you run a current in the wire, a magnetic field forms around the wire. The field around one wire is weak. The field gets much stronger if you wrap the wire into a tight coil. Iron filings inside or around the coil show the field.

The magnetic field around a wire that carries current looks different from the field around a bar magnet. The lines of the field circle around the wire instead

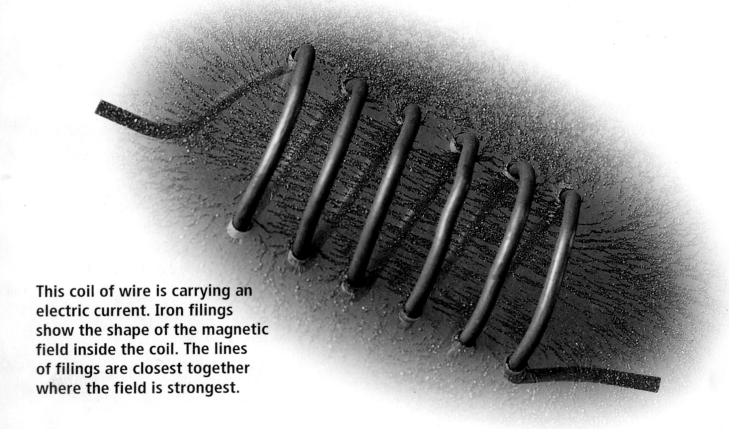

This coil of wire is carrying an electric current. Iron filings show the shape of the magnetic field inside the coil. The lines of filings are closest together where the field is strongest.

An iron nail is not normally a magnet. It becomes one when an electric current runs around it. How can you tell that this nail is now a magnet? What would happen if you took one end of the wire off the battery?

of looping out from the end. A compass needle placed near the wire points straight out, away from the wire.

The magnetic field around a current-carrying wire can move a compass needle but not heavier objects. One way to make the field stronger is to wrap the wire around a magnetic material, such as an iron nail. The material inside the coil of wire is called a core.

In the Investigate, you wrapped a coil of wire around an iron nail. When you attached the battery, an electric current ran through the wire. The nail became

a magnet and attracted paper clips. A magnet that has coils of current-carrying wire around an iron core is called an **electromagnet**.

An electromagnet is a temporary magnet. It has a magnetic force only when an electric current passes through the wire coil. If you turn the electricity off, the electromagnet no longer works. How might you use this property to make a useful tool?

 **MAIN IDEA AND DETAILS** How can electricity be used to make a magnet?

Controlling Electromagnets

An electromagnet is a temporary magnet. One way to control it is to turn it on and off. For example, a very powerful magnet can be used to pick up tons of iron and steel scrap in a junkyard. By turning the electromagnet on and off, a worker can pick up the metal in one place and drop it in another.

There are two ways to make an electromagnet stronger. In the Investigate, you observed one way. The more coils you use, the stronger the magnet becomes. The wire can be coiled in several layers.

The second way to increase the strength of an electromagnet is to increase the electric current. For example, you could add one, two, or three batteries in a series.

In the Investigate, you saw another way to control an electromagnet. Switching the connections to the battery switches the direction of the magnetic

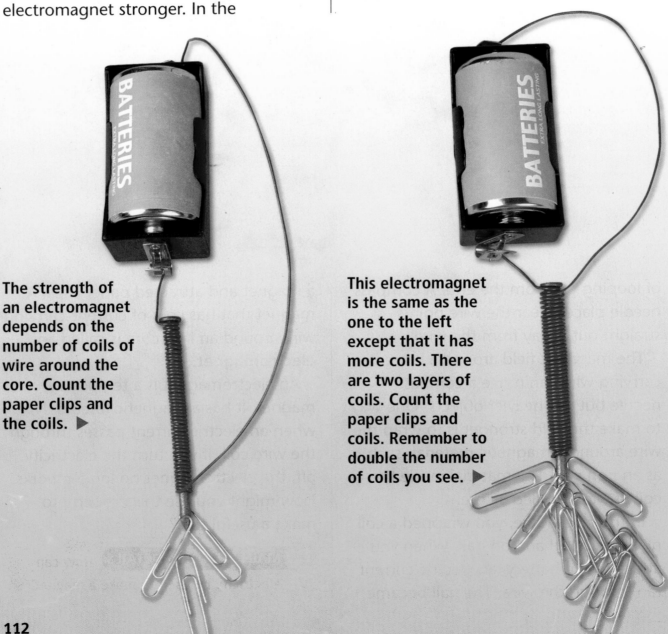

The strength of an electromagnet depends on the number of coils of wire around the core. Count the paper clips and the coils. ▶

This electromagnet is the same as the one to the left except that it has more coils. There are two layers of coils. Count the paper clips and coils. Remember to double the number of coils you see. ▶

field. The *N* pole of the electromagnet becomes the *S* pole.

Electromagnets are an important part of many kinds of technology, from telephones to construction equipment. People use many electromagnets every day, often without knowing it!

Focus Skill **MAIN IDEA AND DETAILS** What are four ways to control electromagnets?

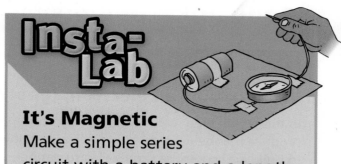

Insta-Lab

It's Magnetic
Make a simple series circuit with a battery and a length of wire. Attach one end of the wire to one end of the battery. Place a small compass near the wire. Then briefly touch the other free end of the wire to the other end of the battery. What happens to the compass needle? What can you conclude?

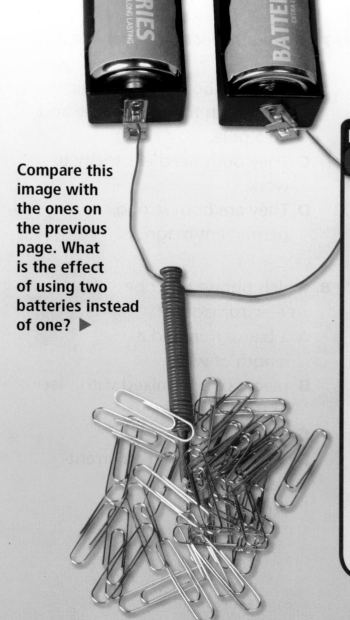

Compare this image with the ones on the previous page. What is the effect of using two batteries instead of one? ▶

Math in Science
Interpret Data

A student built and tested an electromagnet. This graph shows the results. What was the student testing? What conclusion can you draw from the graph? How many paper clips would an electromagnet with 15 coils of wire pick up?

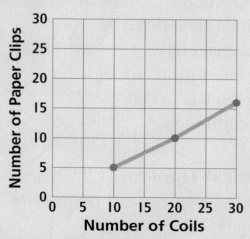

What makes an electromagnet?

In this lesson, you learned that electric currents produce magnetic fields. You also learned how to build and control a simple electromagnet.

Science Content Standard in This Lesson

1.c *Students know* electric currents produce magnetic fields and know how to build a simple electromagnet.

1. ⭐ **MAIN IDEA AND DETAILS** Copy and complete a graphic organizer to show the details about electromagnets.

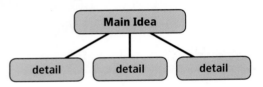

Main Idea

detail   detail   detail

2. **SUMMARIZE** Write a summary of this lesson. Begin with the sentence *Electricity and magnetism are related.*   **1.c**

3. **DRAW CONCLUSIONS** Why is it useful to have a magnet that can be turned on and off?   **1.c**

4. **VOCABULARY** Write a sentence to explain how the strength of an *electromagnet* can be controlled.   **1.c**

5. **Critical Thinking** Why is an electromagnet not a permanent magnet?   **1.c**

6. **Investigation Skill** How would you change the graph in the Interpret Data to show the effect of changing the number of batteries?   **6.e**

7. How is an electromagnet like a bar magnet?
   A They are both made of wire.
   B They both have an *N* pole and an *S* pole.
   C They both need electricity to work.
   D They are both strong, permanent magnets.   **1.c**

8. Which phrase describes an electromagnet?
   A a bar of iron and a length of wire
   B pieces of iron mixed with pieces of wire
   C a coil of wire
   D an iron core with a current-carrying wire coiled around it   **1.c**

The **Big** Idea

Hans Oersted

 Writing ELA—W 2.2

Write a Report

Use several sources to find out how the connection between electricity and magnetism was discovered. Write a report that includes details about the discovery.

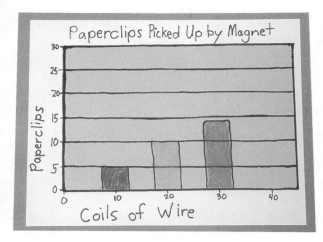

 Math MR 3.1

Extend a Pattern

A student found that an electromagnet with 10 coils of wire could pick up 5 paper clips. With 20 coils of wire, it could pick up 10 paper clips. The student predicted that with 40 coils of wire, the electromagnet could pick up 25 paper clips. How would you evaluate the student's prediction? Explain.

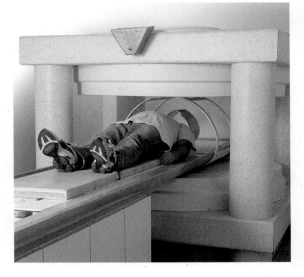

 Health

Electromagnets and Health

Find out how electromagnets are used in tools, such as MRIs, that doctors use for checkups on patients. Make a poster to communicate how one tool is used to get information about the body.

 For more links and activities, go to **www.hspscience.com**

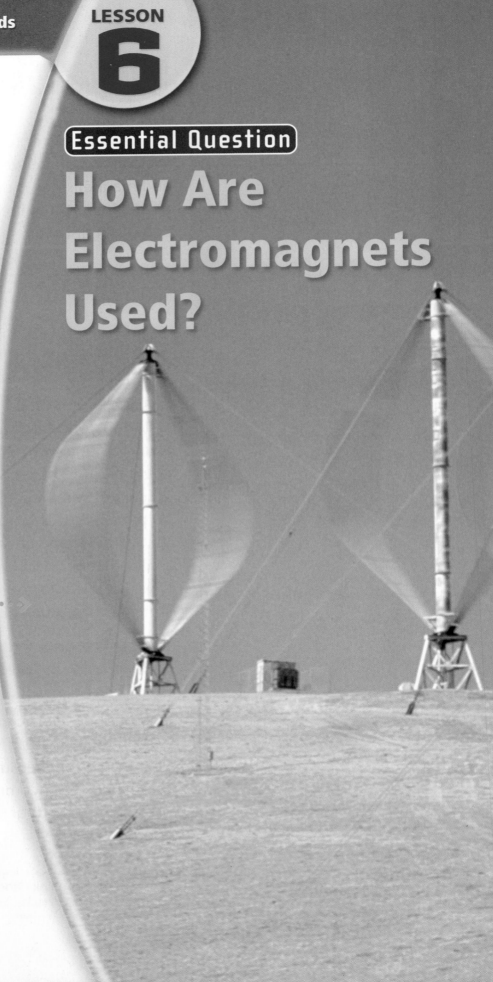

Science Content

1.d *Students know* the role of electromagnets in the construction of electric motors, electric generators, and simple devices, such as doorbells and earphones.

Investigation and Experimentation

6.d Conduct multiple trials to test a prediction and draw conclusions about the relationships between predictions and results.

6.f Follow a set of written instructions for a scientific investigation.

California Fast Fact

Farming the Wind

Does a wind farm grow wind? No, but on a wind farm, the wind spins turbines that use magnets and wires to produce electricity. Wind blows steadily through California mountain passes. The three largest wind farms in the world are in California. In 2004, wind energy produced about 1.5% of the state's electricity.

LESSON 6

Essential Question

How Are Electromagnets Used?

Darius wind turbines near Altamont Pass in California

kinetic energy [kih•NET•ik EN•er•jee] The energy of motion (p. 120)

electric motor [ee•LEK•trik MOH•ter] A device that changes electrical energy into kinetic energy (p. 124)

generator [JEN•uh•ray•ter] A device that changes other forms of energy into electrical energy (p. 126)

117

Build a Motor

Directed Inquiry ## Start with Questions

Motors contain electromagnets. The motor in this toy car makes the wheels turn.

- How can an electromagnet make something move?

- What parts does a motor have?

Investigate to find out. Then read to find out more.

Prepare to Investigate

Investigation Skill Tip
When you compare, you tell how two things are alike and how they are different.

Materials

- insulated copper wire, 50 cm
- ruler
- paper towel tube
- fine sandpaper
- 2 large paper clips
- thick rubber band
- D-cell battery
- tape
- ceramic magnet (3 cm × 1 cm × 1 cm)

Make an Observation Chart

	Observations
While building	
Step 6, coil in cradle after a push	
Step 6, after a push	

Follow This Procedure

1. Wrap the wire around the tube. Leave a 7-cm "tail" on each end.

2. Take the coil off the tube. Wrap each tail around one side of the coil to hold the coil together.

3. Use the sandpaper to rub away all insulation from about 2 cm of one end of the wire. On the other end, rub away 2 cm of insulation from *only* one side of the wire.

4. Bend the two paper clips into the shape shown. Use the rubber band to hold them against the battery.

5. Tape the magnet to the battery.

6. Place the coil in the cradle. What happens? Give it a gentle push. What happens?

Step 1

Step 5

Draw Conclusions

1. How would you rewrite the activity steps to help a younger student read and follow the directions? `6.f`

2. **Standards Link** Can an electromagnet move by itself? What is needed to move it? `1.d`

3. **Investigation Skill** How does this wire coil compare with the one you made in Lesson 5?

Independent Inquiry

Make Predictions

What prediction can you make about how the motor would behave if you added more coils to the wire? What do you predict would happen if you added more batteries? Plan a simple investigation to test one of these predictions. `6.d`

VOCABULARY
kinetic energy p. 120
electric motor p. 124
generator p. 126

SCIENCE CONCEPTS

▶ how electromagnets produce motion

▶ how motors and generators work

COMPARE AND CONTRAST

Look for ways in which devices that use electromagnets are alike and different.

alike ———— different

Electromagnetism and Motion

In the Investigate, you saw that a magnetic coil with a permanent magnet can produce a turning motion. A coil can also produce a straight motion.

Suppose you have a plastic drinking straw. You wrap many coils of wire around the straw, leaving the ends free. You lay the straw on the table and place a thin iron nail inside it. You strip the ends of the wire and attach them to a battery. The nail moves! The magnetic field inside the coil produces a force that moves the nail.

This is like the electromagnet you built in Lesson 5. This time, however, the wire isn't touching the iron nail, so the nail is free to move.

This device converts, or changes, the energy stored in the battery into electricity, another type of energy. Then the electrical energy is converted to the energy of motion. Energy of motion is called **kinetic energy**.

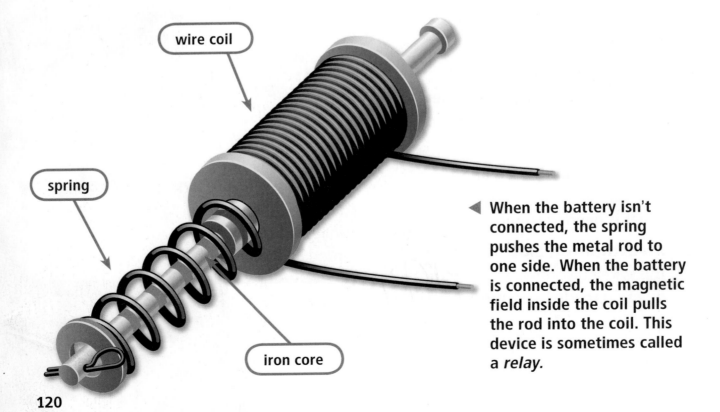

wire coil

spring

iron core

◀ When the battery isn't connected, the spring pushes the metal rod to one side. When the battery is connected, the magnetic field inside the coil pulls the rod into the coil. This device is sometimes called a *relay*.

The diagrams on these two pages show a device that works the same way. Turning the current on and off produces motion, or kinetic energy.

People use this kinetic energy in many ways. One example is in a relay. A relay can use electricity in one circuit to close a switch in a different circuit. Here's how it works in a car.

A driver turns the key in the car. This closes a switch, letting a tiny current flow through a relay. The relay's coil becomes an electromagnet and pulls a rod inside it. The rod touches another piece of metal, closing a circuit. Electricity then can flow from the battery to the starter motor. The car starts.

You may wonder why the key switch can't just connect the battery directly to the starter. Starting a car takes a lot of electricity. The wires connecting the battery to the starter must be thick. Extending them to the key switch would take up a lot of space under the hood. The relay saves space and energy.

Focus Skill **COMPARE AND CONTRAST** How is the electromagnet in a relay different from the electromagnet you built in Lesson 5?

The switch turns the current on and off. When it is on, the electromagnet moves the rod.

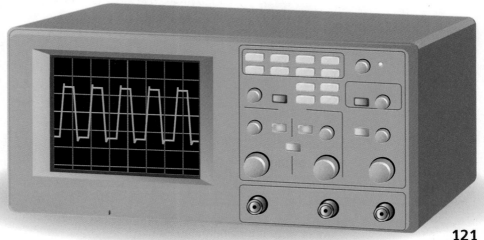

The line on the screen shows when current is on and off. It also shows the rod's position (in, out, or moving). ▶

Doorbells and Speakers

Imagine that you have an electromagnet with a freely moving rod. Pushing and releasing a button turns the current on and off. When the current is on, the rod moves into the coil. When the current is off, a spring pushes the rod out of the coil.

Now put a metal chime at each end of the rod. When you push the button, the rod moves into the coil and strikes one chime. Ding! When you release the button, the rod moves back out. It strikes the second chime. Dong! It's a doorbell.

In another type of doorbell, you don't have to push and release the button. The electricity in your home is called *alternating* current. The current keeps changing direction.

If your doorbell is connected to your home's electrical wiring, what happens when you push the button? The current goes on and stays on. Because it keeps changing direction, the magnetic poles keep reversing. First they push a bar called the clapper, and then they pull it. No spring is needed, because the clapper keeps going back and forth. The doorbell keeps ringing until you take your finger off the button.

Inside a Doorbell

This type of doorbell has a clapper instead of chimes and a rod. When the doorbell button is pushed, current flows through the wire. As the current switches direction, the electromagnet first attracts and then repels the clapper. The clapper vibrates back and forth, ringing the bell.

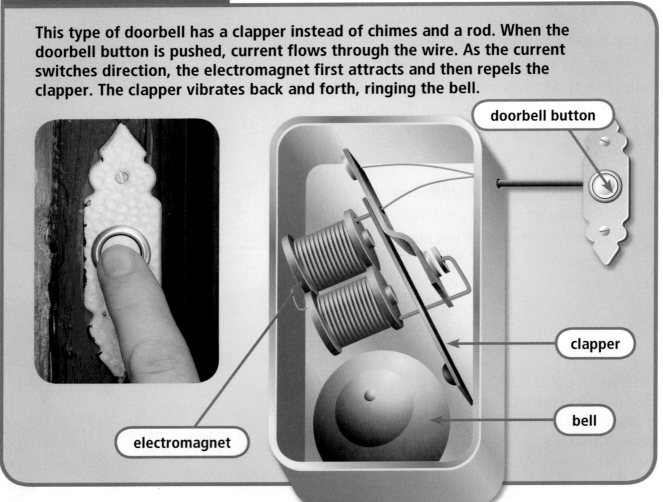

doorbell button

clapper

bell

electromagnet

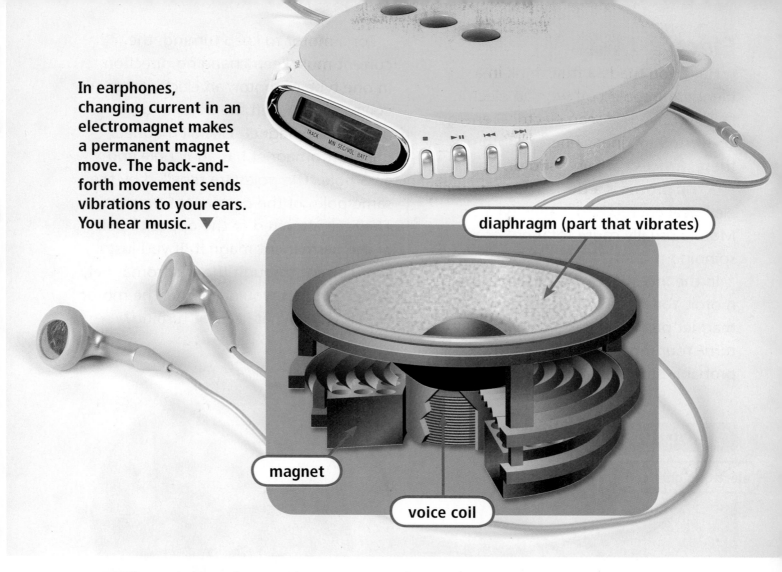

In earphones, changing current in an electromagnet makes a permanent magnet move. The back-and-forth movement sends vibrations to your ears. You hear music. ▼

diaphragm (part that vibrates)

magnet

voice coil

Speakers and earphones also use electromagnets. When you sing into a microphone, you send sound energy through the air. The microphone changes the sound energy to electrical energy that flows through wires as a current. The electrical energy is converted back into sound energy when it reaches the speaker. Here's how that happens.

A speaker diaphragm (DY•uh•fram) is made of flexible, or bendable, material. The diaphragm is attached to a magnet. A wire coil wraps around the magnet.

An electric current passes through the coil. The current direction changes in the same patterns as the sound did. This causes the coil to push and pull on the diaphragm. The diaphragm's movements vibrate the air in front of the speaker, making sound waves. When the waves reach your ear, you hear the sound. Earphones work in the same way, but their speakers are much smaller.

Focus Skill **COMPARE AND CONTRAST** **Compare and contrast a doorbell that runs on a battery and a doorbell connected to a home's electrical wiring. How are they alike? How are they different?**

Electric Motors

Have you made a fruit drink in a blender or cooled off with an electric fan? If so, you've seen electrical energy converted to kinetic energy. Both of these devices contain a motor. An **electric motor** is a device that changes electrical energy into kinetic energy. Motors usually cause rotation, or a spinning motion.

In the Investigate, you built a simple motor. You observed a permanent magnet push and pull a coil, making it turn. Your motor wasn't very strong. It probably stopped turning at times.

For a motor to keep turning, the current must keep changing direction. In one type of motor, an electromagnet coil turns between the poles of a permanent magnet. Like all magnets, the electromagnet has an *N* pole and an *S* pole. The poles are repelled by the same poles of the permanent magnet. They are attracted to the opposite poles of the permanent magnet. If you just sent current through the electromagnet, opposite poles would line up. The motor would stop. What keeps it turning?

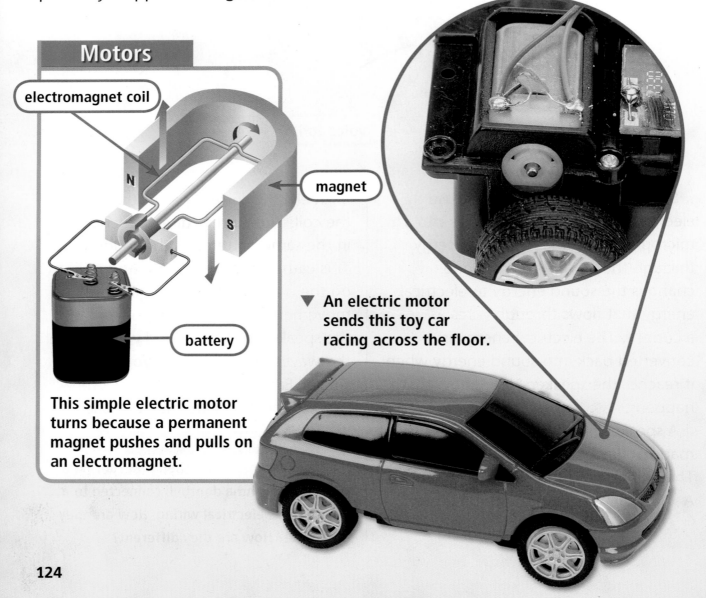

Motors

electromagnet coil

magnet

N

S

battery

This simple electric motor turns because a permanent magnet pushes and pulls on an electromagnet.

▼ An electric motor sends this toy car racing across the floor.

124

How an Electric Motor Works

The electric motor inside a fan contains a coil of wire and a permanent magnet. When the fan is turned on, the coil becomes an electromagnet. The poles of the electromagnet are attracted to the opposite poles of the permanent magnet, so the coil turns. To keep the coil moving, the direction of the electric current keeps changing. This causes the coil and the permanent magnet to keep attracting and then repelling each other.

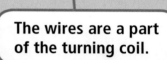

The wires are a part of the turning coil.

For more links and animations, go to www.hspscience.com

The shaft of the motor turns until the poles of the electromagnet are near the opposite poles of the permanent magnet. Then the direction of the current changes. The *N* pole becomes the *S* pole, and the *S* pole becomes the *N* pole. The coil keeps turning. Each time the shaft makes a half turn, the current reverses.

Electric motors that work this way are used to start cars. They also change electrical energy to a turning motion in CD players.

Focus Skill **COMPARE AND CONTRAST** What can a motor do that an electromagnet by itself cannot do?

Insta-Lab

Is It Magnetic?

Hold a compass near some metal objects. Observe the direction in which the needle points. Now hold the compass next to an electric fan. Turn on the fan. What happens to the needle? Why do you think this happens?

Generators

You have seen how an electric current passing through a wire produces a magnetic field. Is the opposite true? Can a magnetic field produce an electric current in a wire?

Suppose you have a coil of wire and a bar magnet. You attach the ends of the wire to a meter. If a current flows through the wire, the meter will show it. Now you move the magnet back and forth through the coil. The meter shows some current. You have produced electricity!

You can also produce an electric current by moving the coil instead of the magnet. If you spin a coil of wire inside a horseshoe magnet, a current will flow through the wire. Moving a wire through a magnetic field produces an electric current in the wire.

A motor converts electrical energy into kinetic and other forms of energy. A **generator** is a machine that converts other forms of energy into electrical energy. Any kind of energy that can move a coil of wire inside a magnetic field can run a generator. For example,

Inside a Generator

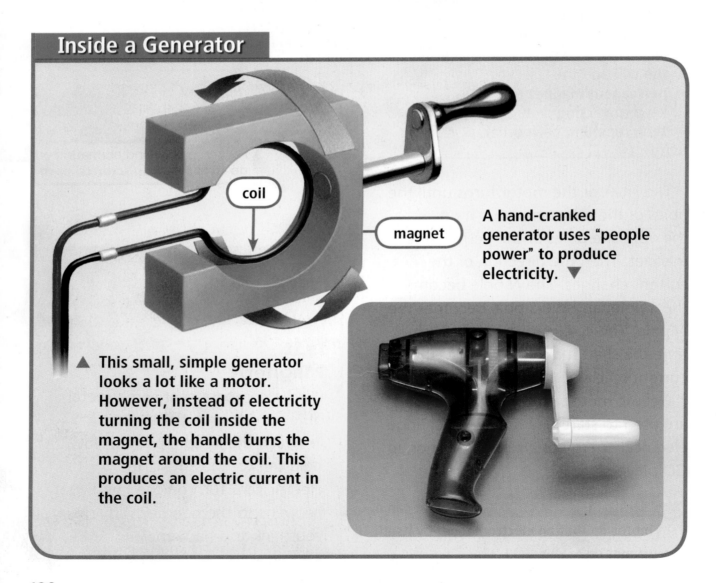

coil

magnet

A hand-cranked generator uses "people power" to produce electricity. ▼

▲ **This small, simple generator looks a lot like a motor. However, instead of electricity turning the coil inside the magnet, the handle turns the magnet around the coil. This produces an electric current in the coil.**

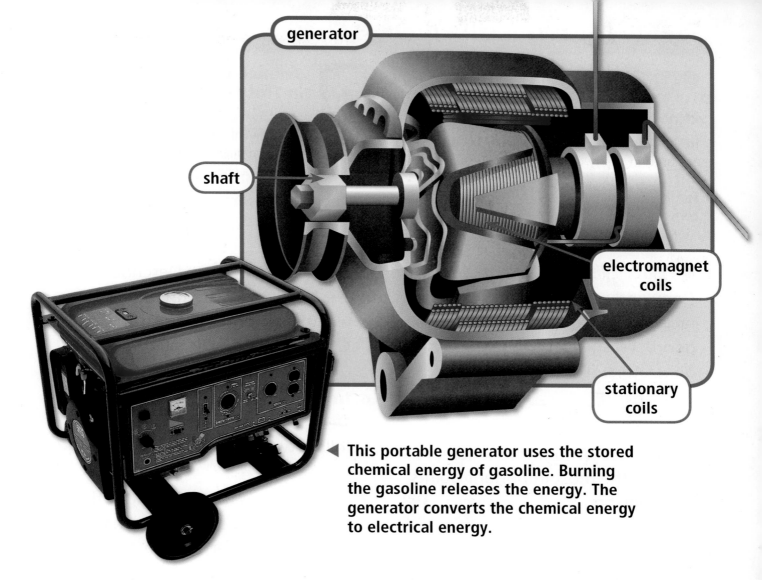

generator

shaft

electromagnet coils

stationary coils

◄ This portable generator uses the stored chemical energy of gasoline. Burning the gasoline releases the energy. The generator converts the chemical energy to electrical energy.

you can use your own kinetic energy to move a wire coil over a bar magnet.

In an emergency, people might use a gasoline-powered generator. It can provide electricity for the lights or a stove in one home. Energy plants use huge generators that have electromagnets.

Most energy plants burn fuel, such as coal, oil, or natural gas. The fuel heats water to change it to steam. The steam pushes against fan blades on a shaft. This makes the shaft turn very fast. At the other end of the shaft are electromagnets. They turn inside

heavy coils of copper wire. The spinning magnets cause charges in the wire to move. This produces electric current.

At the start of this lesson, you saw wind turbines. Instead of steam, wind makes generator shafts turn, converting the wind's kinetic energy to electricity.

Some energy plants are near waterfalls or dams. There, the kinetic energy of falling water spins the shafts of generators to produce electricity.

 COMPARE AND CONTRAST How are generators that run on steam, wind, and water alike?

127

Essential Question

How are electromagnets used?

In this lesson, you learned how electromagnets are used in many devices, such as electric motors, electric generators, doorbells and earphones. You also learned how energy can be converted from one form to another.

Science Content Standard in This Lesson

1.d *Students know* the role of electromagnets in the construction of electric motors, electric generators, and simple devices, such as doorbells and earphones.

1.  **COMPARE AND CONTRAST**
Copy and complete the graphic organizer to compare and contrast doorbells, speakers, motors, and generators. **1.d**

> alike ———— different

2. **SUMMARIZE** Write three sentences that tell the most important points in the lesson. **1.d**

3. **DRAW CONCLUSIONS** Why is it important for a hospital to have a generator? **1.d**

4. **VOCABULARY**
Show how the three vocabulary terms are related by using them together in a sentence. **1.d**

5. **Critical Thinking** Describe how electromagnets are used to get electricity from a wind farm to a CD player and play music. **1.d**

6. **Investigate and Experiment** Describe two things that help you follow written directions. **6.f**

7. A student has a portable light that does not use a battery. She has to turn a handle very fast to make the light come on. What is inside the device? **1.d**
   A a fuel   **C** a generator
   B a motor   **D** a wind turbine

8. Which of the following does not work by using an electromagnet?
   A blender
   B electric racing toy
   C compass
   D CD player   **1.d**

The **Big** Idea

Writing

ELA—W 2.3

Write a Report

You want to help a friend fix the motor in a toy. Write a report that tells about the parts of a motor. Suggest some things that might have caused the motor to fail. Read more about motors if you need ideas for your report.

Math

NS 3.3

Solve a Problem

A student wants to build a motor like the one in the Investigate but with a bigger coil. The motor will use 12 centimeters of wire for one loop. How many centimeters of wire will the student need if he wants to have 15 loops of wire in the coil? What is the answer in meters?

Social Studies

HSS 4.4.7

Hydroelectric Power

Locate a hydroelectric plant near you. Make an information sheet that shows the location, the name of the lake, when the dam was built, and how much electricity the plant generates.

For more links and activities, go to **www.hspscience.com**

California Wind Farms

On some "farms" in California, hundreds of giant turbines use wind to produce electricity. Wind farms are located in areas where there are steady winds above 19 km per hour (12 mi/hr). Most wind farms are built by private companies. Some are on land that's rented from ranchers. The land between the turbines can still be used to grow crops or graze cattle. The wind farms sell electricity to utility companies or to the government. Wind is free! Is electricity produced on wind farms also free?

The energy from California's wind farms could light a city the size of San Francisco.

How Wind Turbines Work

Although wind is free, it costs a lot to build and run a wind farm. A wind turbine changes the energy of the wind into electricity. The electricity flows through underground wires to a power station. From there it is sent to the grid, the network of wires that carries electricity to homes and businesses. A single wind turbine can produce huge amounts of electricity—enough to light a few thousand 100-watt light bulbs.

There are more than 13,000 wind turbines at Altamont Pass, Tehachapi, and San Gorgonio. These high-wind areas are near electric power lines and large cities. In 2004, about 1.5 percent of California's electricity came from wind.

generator

gear box

Wind Farm Pros and Cons

Wind is a renewable source of energy that does not cause pollution. Turbines can be quickly built when more electricity is needed. Today, electricity produced from wind farms is more expensive than the electricity from traditional sources. However, the price is dropping. Wind farms also add jobs.

Wind farms are usually built on hills. Some people think this spoils the view. Wildlife habitats are often harmed. More than 40 different bird species fly at or below the level of the spinning blades. At Altamont Pass, several thousand birds are killed by the turbines each year. Scientists are looking for ways to avoid this.

✎ Think and Write

❶ What electrical devices are part of wind farms?   1.d

❷ What problems must be solved before wind farms can provide more of California's electricity?

LESSON
7

Science Content

1.g *Students know* electrical energy can be converted to heat, light, and motion.

Investigation and Experimentation

6.a Differentiate observations from inference (interpretation) and know scientists' explanations come partly from what they observe and partly from how they interpret their observations.

Essential Question

How Is Electrical Energy Used?

California Fast Fact

Neon Art

You've seen neon lights in advertising signs. By bending glass for lights like those, two artists from Wrightwood, California, create fantastic sculptures. When electric current is put through gases inside the glass, bright colors appear. Some of the sculptures are a few inches in size. Others are as big as a room!

insulate [IN•suh•layt] To protect from electricity by covering with a material that does not carry current (p. 140)

Sculpture on exhibit in Oceanside, California

Using Electricity

Start with Questions

Electricity lights up this scene, but electricity has other uses, too.

- To what other kinds of energy can electricity be converted?

- How do you use electricity in your everyday life?

Investigate to find out. Then read to find out more.

Prepare to Investigate

Investigation Skill Tip
An inference is a conclusion you draw based on observations and what you already know. To make an inference, connect what you observe to what you know.

Materials
- large sheet of poster board
- colored markers
- magazines
- scissors
- glue or tape

Make an Observation Chart

Example	How We Classified It	Explanation

Follow This Procedure

CAUTION: Be careful when using sharp objects such as scissors.

1. On the large sheet of poster board, draw a grid like the one shown in the picture.

2. Find magazine pictures of things that convert electricity to heat, light, sound, and motion. Cut out several examples for each use of electricity.

3. Discuss with a partner how to **classify** each picture. **Record** your classification and explanation on the observation chart.

4. Arrange the pictures in the grid as you agreed. Glue or tape the pictures in place. Display your finished poster.

Draw Conclusions

1. How did you classify the pictures? Name some devices that could go in more than one square. Tell why.

2. **Standards Link** Do you use any electrical devices that don't produce heat, light, sound, or motion? Explain. **1.g**

3. **Investigation Skill** Explain how you **inferred** the type of energy produced by each device. **6.a**

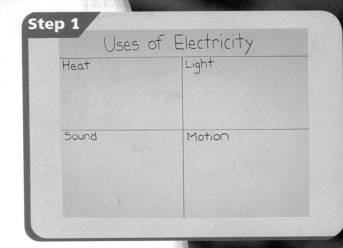

Step 1

Uses of Electricity

| Heat | Light |
| Sound | Motion |

Step 4

Independent Inquiry > **Observing and Inferring**

What might you observe as you look at an automobile? What could you infer about uses of electricity from those observations? Classify the inferred uses as you did in the activity. **6.a**

VOCABULARY
insulate p. 140

SCIENCE CONCEPTS
▶ ways people use electricity
▶ how to use electricity safely

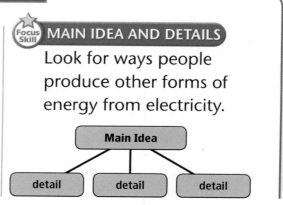

Focus Skill **MAIN IDEA AND DETAILS**
Look for ways people produce other forms of energy from electricity.

Main Idea
detail   detail   detail

Converting to Heat and Light

Can you picture a world without electricity? Strange as it may seem, people have been using electricity for only a short time. Thomas Edison made his first successful light bulb in 1879. The first energy plant to produce electricity opened in the same year. However, even by the 1920s, only about 60 percent of homes were wired for electricity.

Today we take electricity for granted. We never realize how much we use electricity until the power fails. If you live in a hot climate, you may use electricity to cool your home. If it's cold outside, you may use electricity to keep warm. Electricity heats water for showers. It keeps food cold so that it doesn't spoil. It provides heat for cooking and light to read by.

▼ The stove burner on high produces heat and red light. It can also be hot without making light that you can see.

▲ This arc welder can fix cracks in metal under water. Electricity changes to heat that melts the metal pieces together. Light is also produced.

▲ These holiday lights change electricity to light and heat.

Electricity often produces light and heat at the same time. You have seen what happens when you turn the burner of an electric stove on high. As it gets hot, it begins to glow red.

The filament in a light bulb also produces light and heat. If you need to change a light bulb that has been on, you must wait for it to cool. Heat from the filament has made it too hot to touch.

Focus Skill MAIN IDEA AND DETAILS What are three ways in which heat produced from electricity is used?

Insta-Lab

Hot Field

Make an electromagnet with a 9-volt battery, an iron nail, and wire. Connect the battery. After a few seconds, carefully touch the wire coils around the nail. Leave the battery connected only until you feel something. What happens?

Decorative lights come in all shapes and colors.

In how many ways is electricity used in the pictures on these two pages?

Converting to Motion

Think about the electrical devices you use during your day. How many of them change electricity to motion? Perhaps you use an electric alarm clock to get you up in the morning. An electromagnet makes part of the buzzer vibrate. A hair dryer moves air. An electric toothbrush replaces the movement of your hand and arm.

A parent may use a blender to make a fruit smoothie for breakfast. You open the refrigerator. A fan inside moves the cold air.

Perhaps you ride a train to school. Bay Area Rapid Transit (BART) trains run on electricity. If your school has more than one floor, some students may take an elevator between floors.

After school, you may go with a parent to a grocery store. An electric motor opens the door for you. Air conditioners move cool air around the store. A butcher slices meat with an electric slicer. A moving belt carries your groceries from one end of the checkout counter to the other.

When you arrive home, maybe you vacuum your room. Electricity runs the motor that spins the brushes. You might

Each car on a Bay Area Rapid Transit (BART) train has four electric motors. Electricity is supplied through a rail next to the tracks. Part of the braking system also runs on electricity. ▼

A bumper car gets electricity through a pole. The top of the pole connects to a grid in the ceiling.

◄ A knob lets you change a fan's speed by controlling the amount of electricity that goes to the motor.

watch an adult trim the bushes with an electric hedge trimmer.

Some electrical devices that produce motion run on batteries. To save fuel and make less pollution, some cars now run on batteries. Instead of buying more gas after driving for a while, the owner plugs the batteries into a charger.

In factories, many machines contain electric motors. For example, objects such as cars and appliances are made on a factory assembly line. An object travels from one worker to another on a moving belt. Each worker has a tool, such as an electric screwdriver or an electric paint sprayer. The worker does a single job on the object. Then the object travels to the next person. What would happen in such a factory if the electricity failed?

Focus Skill **MAIN IDEA AND DETAILS** What are three ways in which you use motion produced by electricity?

▲ A grass trimmer converts electricity to motion.

▲ An electric motor turns the blades of this blender so fast that they chop the food into tiny pieces.

Electrical Safety

As useful as electricity is, it can also be dangerous. Touching wires that carry electric current can cause injury or even death. For this reason, the makers of electrical devices insulate cords, knobs, and handles. To **insulate** means to protect from electricity with a material that does not conduct current.

Plastic is often used for covers and knobs. Cords and plugs may be insulated with rubber or plastic. These materials will not conduct an electric current. Never use an appliance if the insulation is broken. You could touch the bare wire and get a bad shock.

When you plug an appliance into an outlet, you should hold only the insulated part of the plug. The same is true when you remove a plug. Never pull on the cord. This can cause the wire to break and start a fire.

Devices such as space heaters or microwave ovens need a lot of current. When a lot of current flows through wires, they can become very hot. The wires and plugs for these devices are thicker than those for lamps. An extension cord should always be at least as thick as the appliance cord that plugs into it.

▲ **Always remove a cord by holding onto the plug as you pull it out.**

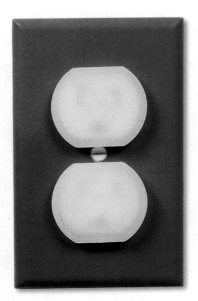

▲ **Plastic plates can be used to cover unused outlets. Then no one can reach the metal parts that carry current.**

▲ **Pulling on the cord can break the insulation. The bare wire could shock you. If it touches something that will burn, a fire could result.**

Each part of a home's wiring can carry only a certain amount of current. Using an expander to plug three or four devices into a single socket is a bad idea. If you turn on all the devices at once, too much current flows. The wires can overheat and cause a fire inside the walls of the home.

A home is wired with several separate circuits. Every circuit should be protected with a fuse or a circuit breaker. These shut down the current in a circuit if too much flows at once.

▲ **Most newer homes have a circuit breaker for each circuit in the home. The breaker shuts the circuit down if there is a short circuit or too high a current.**

Focus Skill **MAIN IDEA AND DETAILS** What does an insulator do?

Before plugging in an appliance, check the cord for breaks or worn places. Broken wires can cause a shock or a fire from a short circuit. ▶

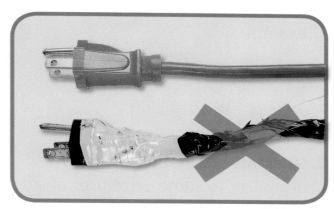

◀ **Plugging too many devices into one outlet can cause the wires in the wall to overheat. This could start a fire.**

If you use a power strip, be sure it has a built-in circuit breaker. ▼

Standards Wrap-Up and Lesson Review

How is electrical energy used?

In this lesson, you learned that electrical energy can be converted to heat, light, and motion. You also learned that electrical devices can be dangerous and must be handled safely.

Science Content Standard in This Lesson

1.g *Students know* electrical energy can be converted to heat, light, and motion.

1. **Focus Skill** **MAIN IDEA AND DETAILS** Copy and complete the graphic organizer to show ways electricity can be converted. Include examples. **1.g**

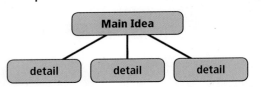

Main Idea

detail   detail   detail

2. **SUMMARIZE** Use the graphic organizer to summarize uses of electricity. **1.g**

3. **DRAW CONCLUSIONS** What would be a benefit of a light bulb that gave off only light and no heat? **1.g**

4. **VOCABULARY**
Write a sentence that explains how to *insulate* a wire. **1.g**

5. **Critical Thinking** You are watching television in one room when someone plugs in a space heater in another room. The television goes off. What conclusion can you draw? **1.g**

6. **Investigate and Experiment** What observation would make you **infer** that electrical power has failed in a whole neighborhood? **6.a**

7. What happens as the burner of an electric stove gets hot?
   A Electrical energy changes to heat.
   B Heat changes to electrical energy.
   C Light changes to heat.
   D Heat changes to light. **1.g**

8. Which appliance is **not** used to convert electricity to motion?
   A electric toothbrush
   B hair dryer
   C digital clock
   D CD player **1.g**

The **Big** Idea

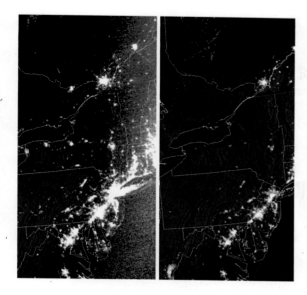

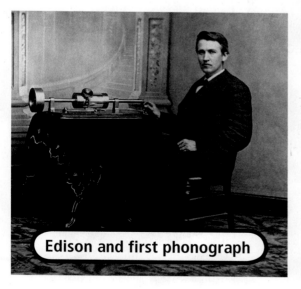

Edison and first phonograph

Write a Description

Suppose you wake up one morning and one use of electricity from this lesson has disappeared. Write a description telling how your life would change and how your community would change.

Solve a Problem

Electric power is measured in kilowatt-hours (kWh). *Kilo-* means "one thousand," so 1 kWh equals 1000 watts used for 1 hour. How long would five 100-watt bulbs need to burn to use 1 kWh?

Music Players

The first phonograph was spring-powered. Modern music players use electricity. Make a time line that shows the year each type of player was first made. Include a major historical event from the same year.

For more links and activities, go to **www.hspscience.com**

These Boots were made for Walking

In the future, recharging the battery in your MP3 player may be as simple as taking a walk. Why? A California company has developed a material that can be placed in a pair of boots. It changes the mechanical energy of walking into electrical energy that can charge batteries and other devices.

Charge It!

The material is a thin, rubbery sheet called artificial muscle. It bends when an electric current flows through it. It moves when it gets an electric signal just as your muscles do. This is why it is called *artificial muscle.*

The material can work in reverse, too. When a person walks, the material in the boots' soles compresses and releases. This makes a weak electric current. A wire connected to the sheet can then send the energy to recharge a battery or to power a device, such as a cell phone.

Used in the Field

A team of scientists worked for 15 years to develop the artificial muscle. Some of the first people to make use of the material might be U.S. soldiers in the field. By going on a march, soldiers could power up hand-held gear such as computers.

Scientists working on the project believe that the artificial muscle material could also be used by recreational hikers and walkers to power such things as a radio or a CD player.

Think and Write

1. What other inventions can you think of that might help U.S. soldiers in the field? **1.g**

2. How might artificial muscles in your shoes help you?

Find out more. Log on to www.hspscience.com

Wrap-Up

▶ Visual Summary

Tell how each picture helps explain the **Big Idea**.

The Big Idea Electricity and magnetism are related. They are part of things you use every day.

1.a, 1.e

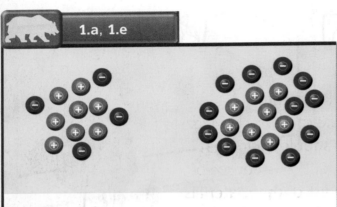

Electricity
Same electric charges repel each other. Opposite charges attract each other. An electric circuit is a closed path for flowing electric charges.

1.b, 1.f

Magnets
All magnets have north and south poles. Same poles repel. Opposite poles attract. The magnet in a compass shows Earth's magnetic field.

1.c, 1.d, 1.g

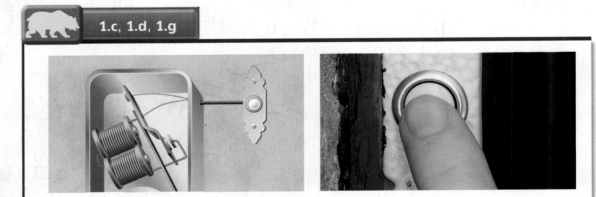

Electrical Energy and Electromagnets
Electric currents produce magnetic fields. Doorbells and motors use this to change electric energy to sound and motion.

Show What You Know

Unit Writing Activity

Magazine Article

Write a magazine article that other fourth-grade students will read. In the article, summarize what you have learned in this unit. Include details that make the article interesting. Explain how electricity and magnetism work together. Illustrate your article with photos, drawings, or diagrams.

Unit Project

Model for a Home

Plan and build a model for a home that uses electricity in several ways. You might use boxes to make rooms and pieces of cardboard to make a roof. Your model should include at least two lights, one switch, one magnet, and one source of sound. After you finish your plan, make a list of the materials you will need. Show your plan and materials list to your teacher before you begin building.

Vocabulary Review

Use the terms below to complete the sentences. The page numbers tell you where to look in the unit if you need help.

static electricity p. 59

series circuit p. 74

parallel circuit p. 76

magnetic field p. 88

compass p. 100

electromagnet p. 111

generator p. 126

insulate p. 140

1. A circuit that has two or more paths that electricity can follow is a _____. **1.a**

2. You _____ electrical wires to avoid dangerous short circuits. **1.g**

3. A temporary magnet made up of a wire wrapped around a core is an _____. **1.c**

4. A _____ converts other forms of energy into electricity. **1.d**

5. You find direction with a _____. **1.b**

6. The buildup of charges on an object is _____. **1.e**

7. The space around a magnet in which a force acts is a _____. **1.f**

8. A circuit that has only one path that electricity can follow is a _____. **1.a**

Check Understanding

Choose the best answer.

9. **CAUSE AND EFFECT** Why do the balloons react as shown? **1.e**

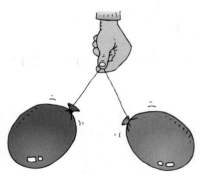

A Neither balloon has a charge.
B Both balloons have the same charge.
C The blue balloon is positive and the red balloon is negative.
D The red balloon is positive and the blue balloon is negative.

10. **MAIN IDEA AND DETAILS** What is true of all magnets? **1.f**
A They are made of iron.
B They stick to all surfaces.
C They have north and south poles.
D To work, they need a current.

11. Which device produces motion when a coil of wire carrying a current produces a magnetic field? `1.d`
 A electric motor **C** generator
 B magnet **D** electromagnet

12. What increases when you add a second bulb to a series circuit? `1.a`
 A current **C** electrons
 B magnetic field **D** resistance

13. What can an electromagnet do that a permanent magnet can't do? `1.c`
 A pick up paper clips
 B produce a magnetic field
 C turn on and off
 D make electricity

14. What will happen to the bulbs in this circuit? `1.a`

 A Both A and B will light.
 B Neither A nor B will light.
 C B will light and A will not.
 D A will light and B will not.

Use the table to answer questions 15 and 16.

Appliance	Electrical units/hr	Appliance	Electrical units/hr
Refrigerator	500	Microwave	800
Stove burner	1500	TV	300
Oven	3410	Water heater	4450
Washing machine	1150	Clothes dryer	5400

15. Which would use the least electricity? `1.g`
 A using the stove burner for two hours
 B using the oven for one hour
 C washing clothes for two hours
 D drying clothes for one hour

16. How much electricity will you use if you watch TV for 4 hours? `1.g`
 A 120 units **C** 1500 units
 B 1200 units **D** 3000 units

Investigation Skills

Give your answers in complete sentences.

17. As you walk toward a building, your compass's needle turns to point toward the building. What can you **infer** from this observation? `6.c`

18. Electromagnet A has 20 coils of wire. Electromagnet B has 40 coils of wire. Everything else is the same. Electromagnet A picks up 13 paper clips. How many do you **infer** Electromagnet B will pick up? `6.c`

Critical Thinking

19. The lights of a bicycle are on whenever the wheels turn. There is no battery on the bicycle. What can you infer about the source of electricity for the lights? `1.d`

20. Describe a practical use for an electromagnet.

The **Big Idea**

149

UNIT 2 LIFE SCIENCE

Energy for Life and Growth

California Standards in This Unit

2 All organisms need energy and matter to live and grow. As a basis for understanding this concept:

2.a *Students know* plants are the primary source of matter and energy entering most food chains.

2.b *Students know* producers and consumers (herbivores, carnivores, omnivores, and decomposers) are related in food chains and food webs and may compete with each other for resources in an ecosystem.

2.c *Students know* decomposers, including many fungi, insects, and microorganisms, recycle matter from dead plants and animals.

This unit also includes these Investigation and Experimentation Standards: **6.a** **6.d** **6.f**

What's the Big Idea?

All living things need energy and matter to live and grow.

Essential Questions

San Rafael Wilderness

Dear Kelly,

You would NOT believe what I saw while hiking in the San Rafael Wilderness with my family. There were beautiful plants everywhere! The sun was shining through the leaves. Plus, there were lots of different animals. I took some pictures with my camera. They turned out really well. I can't wait to show them to you!

Your friend,
Sue

How might the sunshine and plants that Sue saw while hiking be important? How do you think they relate to the

Big Idea?

Unit Inquiry

Back to the Soil

Some soils have more nutrients for plants than others. The decomposers in different soils can affect this. How could you determine which soils had the most efficient decomposers? Plan and conduct an experiment to find out.

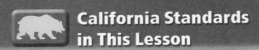
Science Content

2.a *Students know* plants are the primary source of matter and energy entering most food chains.

2.b *Students know* producers and consumers (herbivores, carnivores, omnivores, and decomposers) are related in food chains and food webs and may compete with each other for resources in an ecosystem.

Investigation and Experimentation

6.f Follow a set of written instructions for a scientific investigation.

California Fast Fact

Nothing Fishy About Eating

This archerfish is leaping for its prey. It eats insects to get energy for living. Archerfish also hunt by spitting at insects to knock them into the water. Some archerfish are eaten by other animals or die and then decay in the water.

LESSON

1

Essential Question

What Are Producers and Consumers?

Archerfish in an estuary

producer [pruh•DOOS•er] A living thing, such as a plant, that can make its own food (p. 158)

---

consumer [kuhn•SOOM•er] A living thing that can't make its own food and must eat other living things (p. 158)

---

herbivore [HER•buh•vawr] An animal that eats only plants or producers (p. 160)

---

carnivore [KAR•nuh•vawr] An animal that eats only other animals (p. 160)

---

omnivore [AHM•nih•vawr] An animal that eats both plants and other animals (p. 160)

What Eats What?

Start with Questions

Like the goldfish in the picture, all organisms need energy to live.

- How do organisms get energy?

- Does energy get passed from one organism to another?

Investigate to find out. Then read to find out more.

Prepare to Investigate

Investigation Skill Tip
When you classify things, you can better see relationships among them.

Materials

- encyclopedia
- markers
- index card
- bulletin board
- pushpins
- yarn

Make an Observation Chart

Animal	Plant	Animal That Eats Plants	Animal That Eats Meat	Animal That Eats Dead Organisms

Follow This Procedure

1. Choose an organism. Use a reference book to find out what it eats. **Classify** your organism into one of these groups: plants, plant-eating animals, meat-eating animals, animals that eat both plants and meat, animals that eat dead organisms. Use markers to draw your organism or write its name on an index card.

2. Work in a team. Work together to order your team's cards to show what eats what. Draw or write more cards if you need them.

3. Display the cards on the bulletin board, and connect them with yarn to show what eats what.

Draw Conclusions

1. When your team put its cards in order, which group of organism was eaten first and did not eat other organisms?

2. **Standards Link** How do organisms get energy? How does energy get passed along by eating? **2.b**

3. **Investigation Skill** How did **classifying** and **ordering** the living things help you understand how they are related?

Step 1

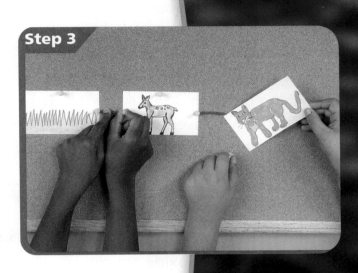

Step 3

Independent Inquiry | **Follow Written Instructions**

Look again at your team's cards on the bulletin board. Could you classify or order them in any other way to show what eats what? Make a set of written instructions that someone else could follow to rearrange your cards. **6.f**

VOCABULARY
producer p. 158
consumer p. 158
herbivore p. 160
carnivore p. 160
omnivore p. 160

SCIENCE CONCEPTS
▶ how living things use the energy from sunlight
▶ how living things get energy from other living things

MAIN IDEA AND DETAILS
Look for details about the movement of energy among living things.

```
        Main Idea
    ┌──────┼──────┐
  detail  detail  detail
```

Food from the Sun

Think about what you feel when you raise your face to the sun. The warmth that you feel is part of the sun's energy. The sun is important to almost everything on Earth. Most living things get the energy to live from sunlight.

Green plants and algae (AL•jee) use solar energy, the energy of sunlight, and change it to chemical energy through a process called photosynthesis (foh•toh•SIN•thuh•sis). In this process, water and carbon dioxide are combined in the presence of sunlight to form sugars and oxygen.

The sun provides energy for this producer.

The green leaves of this bush use photosynthesis to make food for the bush. The berries are a source of food for other living things.

Plants use the sugars for food. The sugars provide the energy the plants need for growth and good health. They use some of this energy right away. The rest is stored. The plants may use the stored energy later. Other organisms may use it by eating the plants.

MAIN IDEA AND DETAILS What process do plants use to make food with energy from the sun?

Solar energy is used to make food almost everywhere on Earth!

The berries on this plant provide food for other organisms.

The bush's roots absorb nutrients from the soil.

Producers and Consumers

Any living thing that can make its own food is called a **producer**. Plants are producers. They can be as small as tiny moss plants or as large as redwood trees. Whatever their size, plants are important to life on Earth.

Some animals, such as deer and cattle, get the energy they need to live by eating plants. When these animals eat, the energy stored in the plants moves into the animals' bodies. The animals can then use this energy for their own growth and health.

Not all animals eat plants. Lions and hawks, for example, get the energy they need by eating other animals.

An animal that eats plants or other animals is called a **consumer**. Consumers can't make their own food, so they must eat other living things.

Some consumers eat the same kind of food all year. Horses, for example, eat grass during warm weather. During the winter, they eat hay, a kind of dried grass.

Other consumers eat different things in different seasons. For example, black bears eat grass in the spring. Later on,

Plants are called producers because they make their own food.

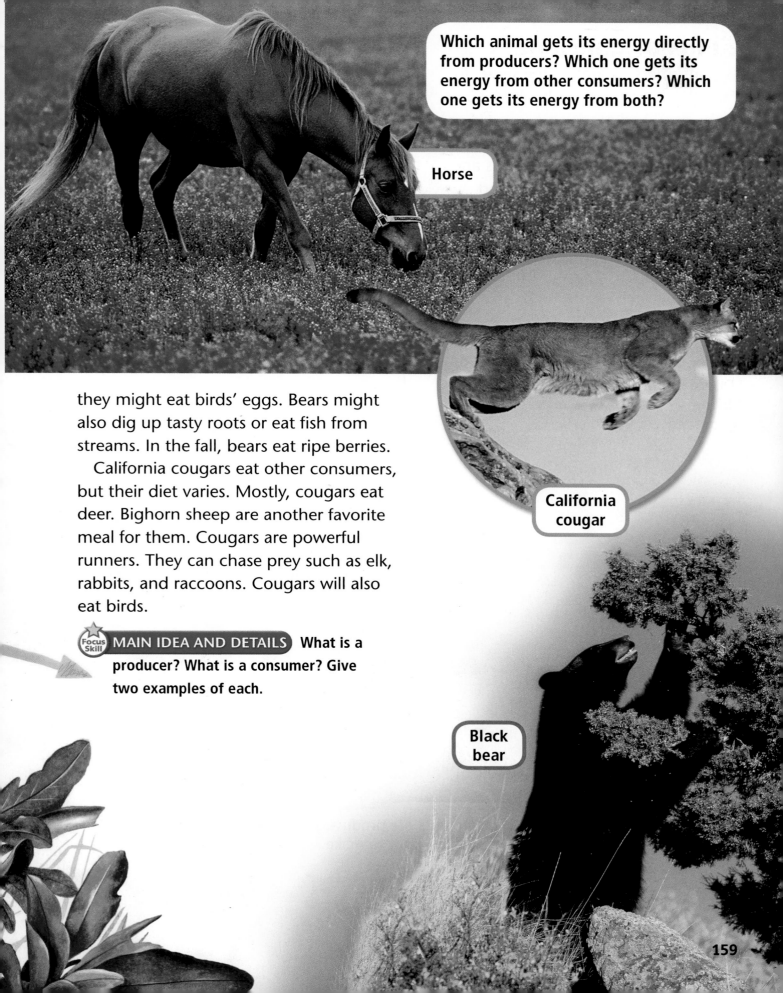

Which animal gets its energy directly from producers? Which one gets its energy from other consumers? Which one gets its energy from both?

Horse

they might eat birds' eggs. Bears might also dig up tasty roots or eat fish from streams. In the fall, bears eat ripe berries.

California cougars eat other consumers, but their diet varies. Mostly, cougars eat deer. Bighorn sheep are another favorite meal for them. Cougars are powerful runners. They can chase prey such as elk, rabbits, and raccoons. Cougars will also eat birds.

Focus Skill **MAIN IDEA AND DETAILS** What is a producer? What is a consumer? Give two examples of each.

California cougar

Black bear

Kinds of Consumers

Consumers are not all the same. In fact, there are three kinds—herbivores, carnivores, and omnivores.

A **herbivore** is an animal that eats only plants, or producers. Horses are herbivores. Giraffes, squirrels, and rabbits are also herbivores.

A **carnivore** is an animal that eats only other animals. The California cougar and the lion are carnivores. A carnivore can be as large as a whale or as small as a spider.

An **omnivore** is an animal that eats both plants and animals. That is, omnivores eat both producers and other consumers. Bears and hyenas are omnivores. Do any omnivores live in your home?

Producers and all three kinds of consumers can be found living in water. For example, algae are producers that live in water. They use sunlight to make

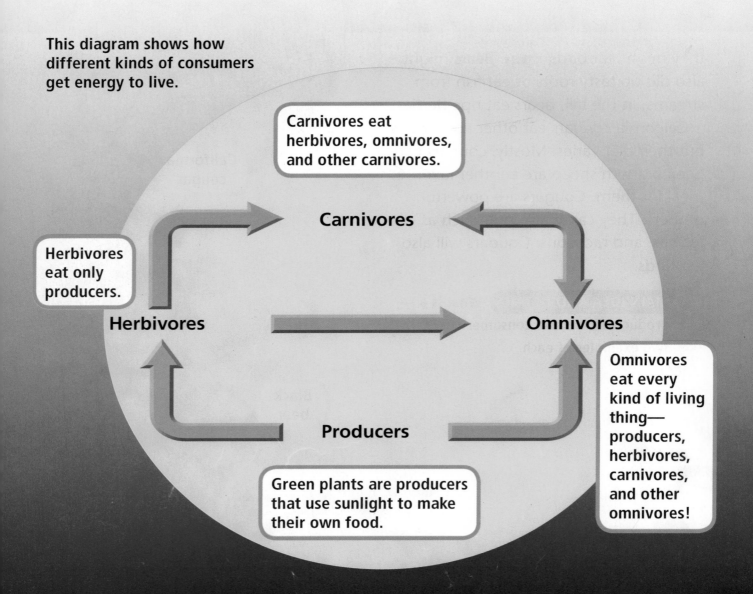

This diagram shows how different kinds of consumers get energy to live.

Carnivores eat herbivores, omnivores, and other carnivores.

Carnivores

Herbivores eat only producers.

Herbivores

Omnivores

Omnivores eat every kind of living thing—producers, herbivores, carnivores, and other omnivores!

Producers

Green plants are producers that use sunlight to make their own food.

their own food. Tadpoles, small fish, and other small herbivores eat algae. Larger fish that are carnivores eat the tadpoles. Some animals, including green sea turtles, are omnivores. Green sea turtles eat seaweed, algae, and fish. Algae are what make the flesh of the green sea turtle green.

 MAIN IDEA AND DETAILS Name the three kinds of consumers. Give two examples of each.

Insta-Lab

Who's an Omnivore?

Read the nutrition labels on several food containers. Think about the source of each kind of food. What does the food's source tell about consumers who eat it?

The sea otter, a carnivore, eats crabs, sea urchins, and other consumers.

Crabs are omnivores. They eat both producers and consumers.

Sea urchins are mainly herbivores. They get energy from eating plants such as kelp.

This plant is a producer. It makes its own food and provides stored energy for consumers.

Standards Wrap-Up and Lesson Review

Essential Question

What are producers and consumers?

In this lesson, you learned that plants produce food for themselves from the energy of the sun. Other organisms consume the plants or organisms that have eaten the plants to get energy for themselves.

Science Content Standards in This Lesson

2.a *Students know* plants are the primary source of matter and energy entering most food chains.

2.b *Students know* producers and consumers (herbivores, carnivores, omnivores, and decomposers) are related in food chains and food webs and may compete with each other for resources in an ecosystem.

1. (Focus Skill) **MAIN IDEA AND DETAILS** Draw and complete a graphic organizer to show the supporting details of this main idea: Living things get energy from other living things. **2.b**

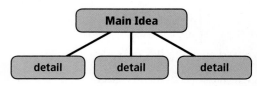

Main Idea

detail · detail · detail

2. **SUMMARIZE** Write two sentences that tell what this lesson is mainly about. **2.b**

3. **DRAW CONCLUSIONS** Why are omnivores consumers? **2.b**

4. **VOCABULARY** Which is **not** a consumer?
   A carnivore
   B herbivore
   C omnivore
   D producer **2.b**

5. **Critical Thinking** How do hawks depend on sunlight for their energy? **2.b**

6. **Investigate and Experiment** In an investigation, why is it important to follow written instructions exactly? **6.f**

7. Which term describes a hyena?
   A carnivore
   B herbivore
   C omnivore
   D producer **2.b**

8. What are the two things that all living things need? **2.a**

The **Big** Idea

 Writing ELA—W.2.1

Write a Narrative

Write a science fiction story. Tell about a time when all the producers on Earth disappear. Describe what happens to the consumers. Be sure to include a main idea and details.

 Math NS 3.0

Solve Problems

A shrew eats about $\frac{2}{3}$ of its body weight daily. Suppose a child who weighed 30 kilograms (66 lb) could eat $\frac{2}{3}$ of his or her body weight every day. How many kilograms of food would that be?

Tidal Pool Community

sea urchin

crab

starfish

 Social Studies HSS 4.1

Producers and Consumers

Choose a California community like a tide pool or a forest. Research the types of producers and consumers in that community. Use pictures to make a display of what you learned.

 For more links and activities, go to **www.hspscience.com**

THE MOJAVE NATIONAL PRESERVE'S TOP PREDATOR

California cougars are efficient predators in the Mojave National Preserve.

Mojave

The California cougar preys on deer, elk, wild burros, rabbits—even birds. In the Mojave National Preserve, bighorn sheep are a favorite prey. Some people see that as a problem because the numbers of bighorn sheep are quickly dropping. In a healthy food web, there should be a balance between predator and prey. What's tipping the balance?

Losing Ground

The Mojave National Preserve is located in Southern California. The human population in this part of the state is growing fast. As people move in, wildlife is pushed out. New roads disrupt the habitats of both cougars and sheep.

The loss of habitat is especially dangerous for bighorn sheep. They thrive in rocky areas at high elevations. Those areas provide good protection from predators like the California cougar. As the sheep lose safe places to live, they also lose more population to cougars. Illegal hunting has caused the bighorn sheep population to drop even further. So have off-road vehicles in the desert and the loss of water holes and grazing areas.

Bighorn sheep are sure-footed on the rocks.

Changing Status

California cougars have gone from "outlaw" to protected. For about 150 years, cougars were hunted to the point of extinction. In the late 1960s, their status changed. Laws were put into place to protect cougars. As a result, their numbers grew. Now, there are far more cougars than there are bighorn sheep for them to prey upon. Between a big increase in cougars and a loss of habitat, bighorn sheep are facing extinction. The balance between predator and prey has been affected.

 Think and Write

1. How does this article relate to what you've learned about food chains? 2.b

2. What are two things that have affected the predator-prey balance between cougars and bighorn sheep? 2.b

MOUNTAIN LION

Mountain lions are important members of the natural community and may be found in this area. Although these animals are seldom seen, they are unpredictable and have been known to attack without warning.

If you should encounter a lion:
- Do not approach lion
- Do not crouch down
- Do not run or make sudden moves
- Stand tall, make yourself look as big as possible
- Pick children up so you appear to be one, large person
- If attacked, fight back

Please protect them by protecting yourself!

Science Content

2.c *Students know* decomposers, including many fungi, insects, and microorganisms, recycle matter from dead plants and animals.

Investigation and Experimentation

6.a Differentiate observation from inference (interpretation) and know scientists' explanations come partly from what they observe and partly from how they interpret their observations.

California Fast Fact

Strange Hunters

The California condor is the largest flying land bird in North America. It is also a scavenger. Scavengers find and eat dead animals. At one feeding, a California condor can eat from 1 to 2 kilograms (2 to 4 lb) of dead matter from a large mammal.

LESSON 2

Essential Question

What Are Decomposers?

California condor

decomposer
[dee•kuhm•POH•zer] A living thing that feeds on the wastes and remains of plants and animals (p. 170)

scavenger [SKAV•in•jer] A living thing that feeds on large pieces of dead organisms (p. 171)

fungus [FUHNG•guhs] An organism that can't make food and can't move around (p. 172)

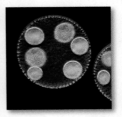

microorganism [my•kroh•AWR•guh•niz•uhm] An organism that is too small to be seen without a microscope (p. 174)

167

Decomposing Bananas

Directed Inquiry **Start with Questions**

You were looking forward to a banana with your lunch, but this one doesn't look good to eat.

- Why is the banana changing?

- Is it becoming food for organisms other than you?

Investigate to find out. Then read to find out more.

Prepare to Investigate

Investigation Skill Tip
Scientists use time relationships to measure change. Think about the amount of time it takes for the change that you observe.

Materials

- 2 slices of banana
- 2 zip-top plastic bags
- marker
- dry yeast
- teaspoon

Make a Data Table

Bag	Day 1	Day 2	Day 3	Day 4	Day 5
P					
D					

Follow This Procedure

❶ Put a banana slice in each bag. Label one bag *P* for *plain.*

❷ Sprinkle $\frac{2}{3}$ teaspoon of dry yeast on the other banana slice. Yeast is a decomposer, so label the bag *D.* Seal both bags. Put them in the same place.

❸ Check both bags every day for a week. Observe and record the changes you see in each bag.

Draw Conclusions

1. Which banana slice shows more change? What is the cause of the change?

2. **Standards Link** Why does the banana change? Is it becoming food for organisms other than you? **2.c**

3. **Investigation Skill** Scientists use time relationships to understand how objects and events change over different amounts of time. How long did it take for each banana slice to start decomposing? How long do you think it would take for each banana slice to decompose completely?

Step 2

Step 3

Independent Inquiry

Observe/Infer

What would happen if you put flour, instead of yeast, on one banana slice? Use the results of the Investigate to infer what would happen. Then carry out the experiment and observe what happens.

2.c

VOCABULARY
decomposer p. 170
scavenger p. 171
fungus p. 172
microorganism p. 174

SCIENCE CONCEPTS
► how decomposers recycle plant and animal matter
► why different types of decomposers are needed

Focus Skill COMPARE AND CONTRAST
Look for ways decomposers are the same and ways they are different from each other.

alike —— different

Decomposers

A **decomposer** is a living thing that feeds on wastes and the remains of dead plants and animals. Decomposers break down wastes and remains into nutrients. Nutrients are substances that living things need to help them grow.

Soil contains many nutrients. Plants take them in through their roots. When animals eat the plants, animals get the nutrients. When plants and animals die, decomposers break down the dead matter into nutrients and return the nutrients to the soil. Then the nutrients can be used again. This cycle keeps repeating. Decomposers *recycle* nutrients.

Decomposers are important consumers. They come in many shapes and sizes. Some are tiny bacteria that you can see only with a microscope. Other decomposers, such as mushrooms, are bigger. Without decomposers, Earth would be covered with dead plants and animals. Instead, decomposers turn waste and dead matter into useful nutrients. They allow living things to use recycled nutrients.

Focus Skill COMPARE AND CONTRAST How is a decomposer also a consumer?

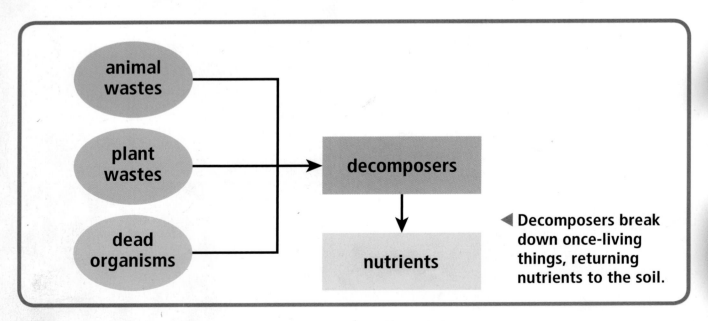

► Decomposers break down once-living things, returning nutrients to the soil.

Scavengers

A **scavenger** is an animal that eats large pieces of plant and animal remains. When scavengers eat these things, they break them down into smaller pieces. Decomposers take over from the scavengers by breaking down dead matter still more.

Like decomposers, scavengers come in all sizes. Some, such as sow bugs and millipedes, usually eat dead plant matter. Other scavengers, such as flies, California condors, and crows, eat dead animal matter.

Scavengers and decomposers work together. Both return the nutrients from animal and plant matter to the soil, where the nutrients can be used again.

Focus Skill COMPARE AND CONTRAST How are scavengers and decomposers alike?

Sow bugs help plant matter decay.

Millipedes chew up dead plant material In the forest. Sow bugs and millipedes are not insects.

Maggots are fly larvae. Flies lay their eggs on dead animal matter. When the eggs hatch, the larvae feed on the animal's flesh.

California condors eat large dead animals. They break down the animal matter into smaller pieces for the decomposers.

171

Fungi

A **fungus** is an organism that absorbs nutrients from living plants and dead plant materials. The plural of fungus is fungi (FUHN•jy). Fungi that break down dead plant materials are decomposers. They break down the materials into nutrients and absorb some of the nutrients into their own cells. The rest of the nutrients return to the soil.

Fungi are divided into several groups. These include molds, mushrooms, and sac fungi. There are thousands of varieties of fungi within the groups.

Some, such as slime mold, look like sticky puddles. Other types of fungi include colorful mushrooms called toadstools.

In many forests, fungi are the main decomposers of wood. These fungi have special ways of digging into wood and releasing a chemical that breaks down the cells of the wood. Other types of fungi feed on plant leaves and plant matter in soil. Fungi are found in both fresh water and seawater. They are

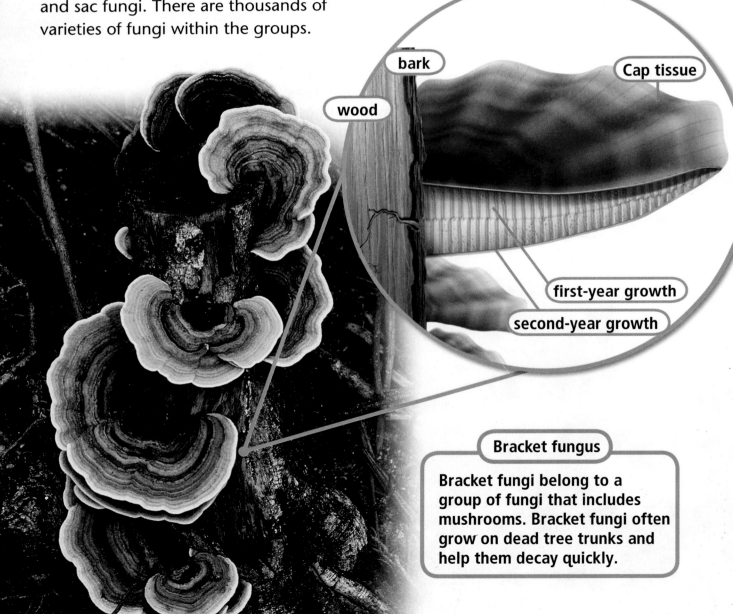

bark

wood

Cap tissue

first-year growth

second-year growth

Bracket fungus

Bracket fungi belong to a group of fungi that includes mushrooms. Bracket fungi often grow on dead tree trunks and help them decay quickly.

important decomposers in whatever environment they live in.

Even though fungi are decomposers, they are also a food source for other living things. Certain beetles and ants eat fungi as part of their regular diet. Have you eaten mushrooms lately? If so, you have eaten fungi. Certain mushrooms are a favorite food for people around the world. Not all mushrooms are safe to eat, though. Some are deadly.

 **COMPARE AND CONTRAST** How are molds, mushrooms, and other types of fungi alike?

Puffball fungi are usually found on decaying wood. Some puffballs crack open to send spores into the wind.

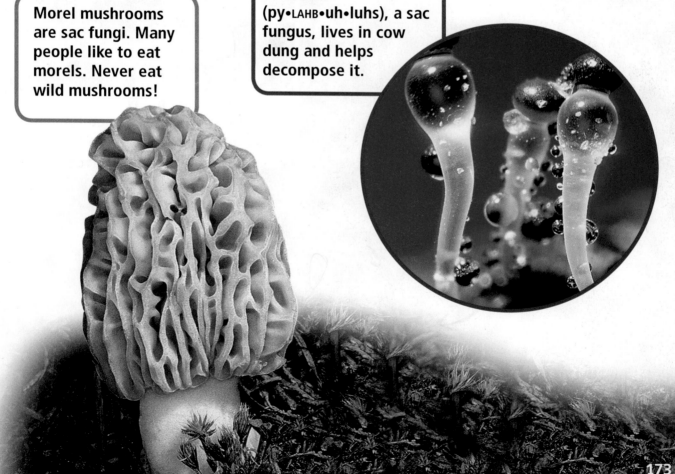

Morel mushrooms are sac fungi. Many people like to eat morels. Never eat wild mushrooms!

Pilobolus (py•LAHB•uh•luhs), a sac fungus, lives in cow dung and helps decompose it.

Microorganisms

Some living things are so small that they cannot be seen without a microscope. Such a tiny living thing is called a **microorganism**.

Bacteria are the most common type of microorganism. Decomposer bacteria are found in soil and in water. Like fungi, the bacteria in soil break down tiny pieces of animal and plant matter. By doing this, they fill the soil with the nutrients that plants need to grow.

Decomposer bacteria found in water are similar to soil bacteria. They break down tiny pieces of plant and animal matter and return nutrients to the water. Other microorganisms use these nutrients for food. Then other living things eat those microorganisms.

Bacteria actually provide food in two ways. They release nutrients by decomposing matter. They are also a source of food themselves for other living things.

Molds can also be microorganisms, although they are a type of fungus.

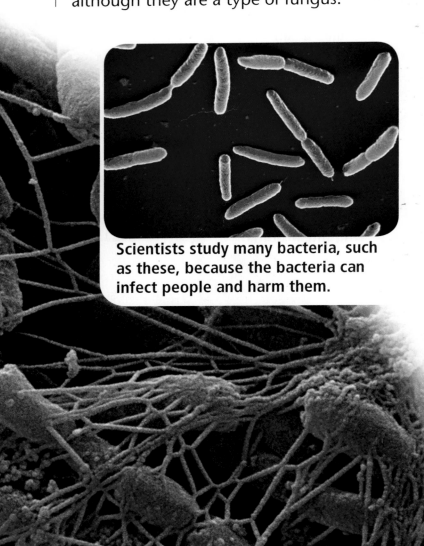

Scientists study many bacteria, such as these, because the bacteria can infect people and harm them.

These bacteria are found in the ground.

Penicillin, a helpful microorganism used in medicine, is growing on this orange.

Yeast is a decomposer microorganism. It lives in soil, on flowers, and on plant leaves. It provides food for living things. It is also used to make bread.

If you look at the penicillin on the orange under a microscope, you will see the individual microorganisms.

When you see mold growing on a piece of fruit or a slice of bread, you are seeing millions of organisms at once. Each organism is too small to see with just your eyes.

Like bacteria, molds are also food for other living things. Many types of cheese are made by molds. Some molds even produce medicine!

 COMPARE AND CONTRAST How are decomposer bacteria in soil similar to decomposer bacteria in water?

Insta-Lab

Take a Close Look!

Use a hand lens to take a close look at the mold colonies on a slice of bread. What color is the mold? What does the mold look like close up?

What are decomposers?

In this lesson, you learned that there are many kinds of decomposers, including fungi and microorganisms. Decomposers recycle matter from dead plants and animals.

 Science Content Standard in This Lesson

2.c *Students know* decomposers, including many fungi, insects, and microorganisms, recycle matter from dead plants and animals.

---

1. 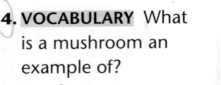 Draw and complete a graphic organizer to compare and contrast a scavenger with a decomposer. **2.c**

alike — different

2. **SUMMARIZE** Write a summary of this lesson by using the lesson vocabulary terms in a paragraph. **2.c**

3. **DRAW CONCLUSIONS** Describe one way that decomposers provide you with the energy you need to live. **2.c**

4. **VOCABULARY** What is a mushroom an example of?
   A a fungus
   B a microorganism
   C a scavenger
   D a producer   **2.c**

5. **Critical Thinking** Suppose you're taking a walk in the forest. You see a dead tree lying on the ground. It is covered with what look like giant mushrooms. Describe what you think is happening to the tree. **2.c**

6. **Investigate and Experiment** Describe how what you inferred about the Investigate differed from what you observed. **6.a**

7. What is the California condor an example of?
   A a decomposer
   B a microorganism
   C a scavenger
   D a fungus   **2.c**

8. How are decomposers part of a cycle? **2.c**

 The Big Idea

 Writing ELA—W 2.3

Write a Report

Some types of bacteria have been used to help clean up oil spills in oceans or in lakes. Gather information about how the bacteria were used, and prepare a report. Share your findings with the other students in your class.

 Math SDAP 1.1

Make a Graph

Healthy soil has large numbers of decomposers living in it. One gram of soil (much less than an ounce) can contain 100,000 algae, 1,000,000 fungi, and 100,000,000 bacteria. Make a bar graph comparing the numbers of these types of decomposers in the soil.

 Health

Eating Decomposers

Find out what vitamins and other nutrients are in mushrooms. Find healthful recipes that have mushrooms as one of the ingredients. Share your findings by making a poster.

 For more links and activities, go to **www.hspscience.com**

Creepy Crawly Surgeons

There you are, taking a walk through the park. You look down. You see the remains of a mouse. You look closer and see other things—tiny, white crawling things. The sight of them may make your stomach flip, but those crawly organisms have a place in modern medicine. Welcome to the world of maggot therapy.

Maggots are helping thousands of people each year.

Eating Machines

Blowflies lay their eggs in rotting animal matter. When the eggs hatch, they become maggots. Maggots are "eating machines." They make quick work of decaying animal matter—including human flesh!

Soldier's Friends

Long ago, army doctors noticed that wounds with maggots were cleaner. Those wounds were less likely to get infected than untreated wounds were. During the Civil War and World War I, maggots were commonly used to treat wounds.

After World War II, antibiotics became popular. Now some bacteria are resistant to antibiotics. Some doctors are looking to the past for proven treatments.

Nature's Surgeons

Dr. Ronald A. Sherman works at the University of California, Irvine. He has researched the use of maggots for decades. Sherman has found that maggots break down infected tissue. When they eat the infected tissue, they also kill bacteria. As the maggots chomp away, the patient feels no pain. The patient doesn't need pain-killing drugs. Recovery time is also faster. The maggots' removal of diseased tissue helps healthy tissue grow.

Many people are uncomfortable with the idea of maggots. Sherman knows that. He approaches maggot therapy with a sense of humor. He wants people to see the benefits of using nature's surgeons.

Think and Write

1 How does the maggot's role as a decomposer enable it to help people? `2.c`

2 How might using maggots in medicine help people conserve resources? `2.c`

Find out more. Log on to
www.hspscience.com

179

Science Content

2.b *Students know* producers and consumers (herbivores, carnivores, omnivores, and decomposers) are related in food chains and food webs and may compete with each other for resources in ecosystems.

Investigation and Experimentation

6.a Differentiate observation from inference (interpretation) and know scientists' explanations come partly from what they observe and partly from how they interpret those observations.

LESSON 3

Essential Question

What Are Food Chains and Food Webs?

California Fast Fact

Ouch!

More than 50 species of mosquitoes live in California. They're found everywhere from the high mountains to the deserts. Only female mosquitoes bite people and other animals. They need the blood to produce eggs. You may think mosquitoes are nothing but pests, but they're an important food source for many animals.

Mosquitoes can be found in almost every place in California.

food chain [FOOD CHAYN] A series of organisms that depend on one another for food (p. 184)

prey [PRAY] Consumers that are eaten by predators (p. 184)

predator [PRED•uh•ter] A consumer that eats prey (p. 184)

food web [FOOD WEB] A group of food chains that overlap (p. 186)

Make a Food Chain

Directed Inquiry > Start with Questions

You watch as a frog uses its tongue to snatch a fly out of the air.

- Why do frogs eat flies? What do flies eat?

- What do snakes eat?

Investigate to find out. Then read to find out more.

Prepare to Investigate

> **Investigation Skill Tip**
> Scientists communicate their ideas in many ways. Before you communicate, think about ways to present the ideas, such as the order in which to put things.

Materials

- 8 to 10 blank index cards
- colored pencils or markers
- reference books about animals

Make a Data Table

Kind of Organism	What It Eats

Follow This Procedure

❶ Choose a place where animals live. Some examples are pine forests, rain forests, deserts, wetlands, and oceans.

❷ On an index card, draw a living thing that lives in the place you have chosen. Repeat with the other cards. Use reference books to help you.

❸ Put your cards in an **order** that shows what eats what. If one of your animals is not a link in the order, you can trade that card for one that shows a different animal. You can also draw another animal on an extra card to link two of your cards.

Draw Conclusions

1. Can the same animal belong to more than one set of cards? Explain your answer.

2. **Standards Link** Why do frogs eat flies? What do flies eat? What kind of animal eats other animals? `2.b`

3. **Investigation Skill** Scientists **communicate** by using spoken words, pictures, and written words. What do your cards communicate about how the living things depend on one another?

Step 2

Step 3

Independent Inquiry **Compare**

Draw a picture of yourself on an index card. What can you infer about your place in the food chain? Make a food chain with yourself at one end. What do you observe? What is the difference between your observation and your inference? `6.a`

VOCABULARY
food chain p. 184
prey p. 184
predator p. 184
food web p. 186

SCIENCE CONCEPTS
▶ how consumers depend on other living things
▶ how energy moves through food chains and food webs

Focus Skill **SEQUENCE**

Look for the order in which things happen.

☐ → ☐ → ☐

Food Chains

Living things depend on one another to live. A **food chain** is the movement of food energy through a sequence, or order, of living things. Every food chain starts with producers. Remember that producers use sunlight to make their food. Some consumers, such as deer, eat these producers. Deer are eaten by other consumers, such as California cougars. Consumers that are eaten are called **prey**. A consumer that eats prey is a **predator**. Prey are what is hunted. Predators are the hunters.

Wherever animals live, some animals are prey and others are predators.

Predators limit the numbers of prey. For example, in grasslands, wolves are predators of antelope. The wolves keep the number of antelope from increasing too much. That keeps the antelope from eating all the producers.

Acorns provide energy for the chipmunk, which then provides energy for the hawk.

184

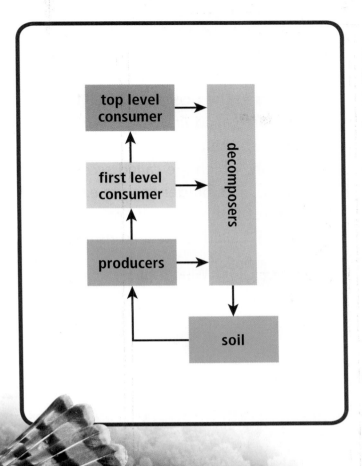

Prey can also limit the numbers of predators. Predators often compete for the same prey. The number of prey limits the number of predators that have enough food to live.

Energy is transferred at each level of a food chain. For example, deer get energy from the grass they eat. California cougars get energy when they eat deer. The energy is cycled from one organism to another throughout the food chain.

Decomposers are important parts of all food chains. Decomposers help return nutrients to the soil in which producers grow. Decomposers break down dead plant matter. They break down wastes from consumers that eat producers. Decomposers also break down dead animal matter and the wastes from consumers that eat other consumers.

Focus Skill SEQUENCE **What would happen next if the number of predators in a place increased too much?**

Without hawks, the chipmunk population would get very large. The chipmunks would eat all the acorns. Once the acorns were gone, the chipmunks would starve.

Insta-Lab

Chain of Life

Cut white paper into strips that are about 3 cm by 14 cm. On each strip, write the name of a producer or a consumer. Then use glue or tape to join the strips into paper food chains. Which food chains are you in?

Food Webs

A food chain shows how an animal gets energy from just one food source. However, food chains can overlap. Some consumers eat several kinds of food, not just one. For example, hawks eat sparrows, mice, and snakes. Also, one kind of producer may be food for different kinds of consumers.

Food chains that overlap form a **food web**. There are food webs in water habitats, as well as on land. For example, herons eat snails and fish.

On the next page, you can see an ocean food web. It shows that energy moves from plankton, which are small producers in the ocean, to small fish. The fish are called *first-level consumers.*

These fish then become prey for bigger fish, which are called *second-level consumers.* The bigger fish are eaten by the biggest fish and by the mammals in the ocean, called *top-level consumers.*

Focus Skill **SEQUENCE** What happens after a first-level consumer eats a producer?

Follow several paths in this food web. Begin at the bottom, with a producer, and trace the movement of energy through the web.

Antarctic Ocean Food Web

The food web begins with energy from the sun. The producers are tiny plants called phytoplankton (fyt•oh•PLANGK•tuhn). They float near the water's surface. Where would decomposers fit in this food web?

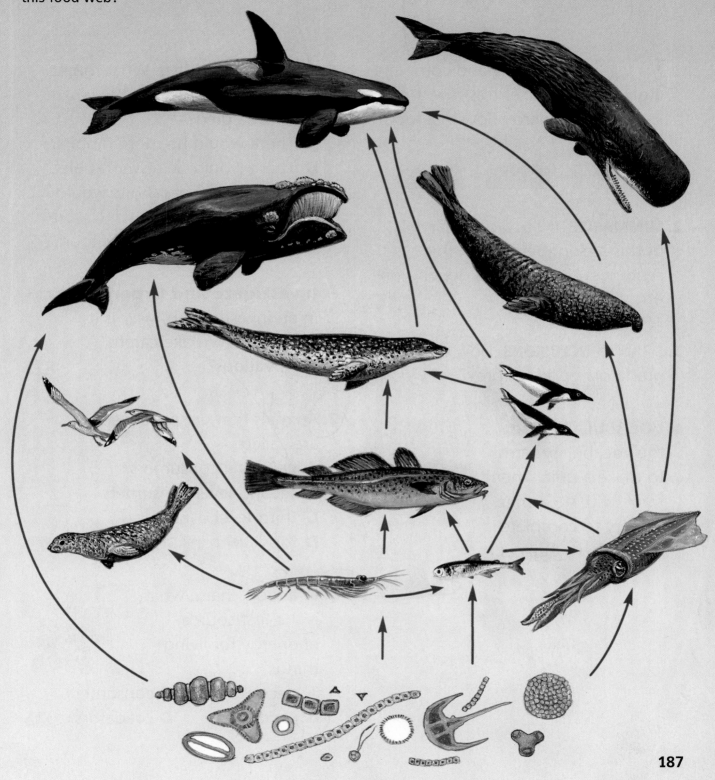

Essential Question

What are food chains and food webs?

In this lesson, you learned that producers and consumers are all connected in food chains and food webs.

Science Content Standard in This Lesson

2.b *Students know* producers and consumers (herbivores, carnivores, omnivores, and decomposers) are related in food chains and food webs and may compete with each other for resources in ecosystems

1. **(Focus Skill) SEQUENCE** Draw and complete a graphic organizer to show the sequence of energy flow in a food chain. **2.b**

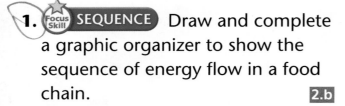

2. **SUMMARIZE** Write a summary of this lesson. Begin with this sentence: Living things depend on one another. **2.b**

3. **DRAW CONCLUSIONS** How are predators good for prey? **2.b**

4. **VOCABULARY** Use the vocabulary terms to make a quiz. Then trade with a partner and try to complete each other's quizzes. **2.b**

5. **Critical Thinking** What might happen to rabbits if all the wolves in an area died?
   A There would be more rabbits.
   B There would be fewer rabbits.
   C The number of rabbits would stay the same.
   D Rabbits would have less food. **2.b**

6. **Investigate and Experiment** In an investigation, why is it important to make careful observations? **6.a**

7. Animals that eat producers are called
   A first-level consumers
   B second-level consumers
   C third-level consumers
   D top-level consumers **2.b**

8. In a food chain, what is the first source of energy for living things?
   A decomposers   C consumers
   B producers   D predators **2.b**

The **Big** Idea

  Writing ELA—W 1.3

Write a Composition

Write about ways that people might affect a food web. For example, people might cut down trees to have a place for building houses or for feeding deer. Tell what might then change. Think about the sequences of organisms in the food web.

  Math NS 3.0

Solve Problems

Producers in a field have stored 20,000 Calories. The first-level consumers that eat all the producers store 2000 Calories. If the pattern continues, how much energy could the next level of consumers store?

  Art VPA—VA 2.0

Food Webs

Choose any form of art, such as watercolor, charcoal, or collage. Use it to show living things in a particular ecosystem. (You don't have to show them eating one another!)

 For more links and activities, go to **www.hspscience.com**

Jargal Jamsranjav

► **JARGAL JAMSRANJAV**

► **Conservationist**

► Chevening Scholar and Whitney Award recipient, training nomadic herders to monitor wildlife in the Gobi Desert.

The Gobi, a desert area in Asia, gets less rainfall than it used to. This means there is less natural vegetation for camels, goats, and horses. These are the animals on which Mongolian herders depend for survival. Jargal Jamsranjav grew up in Mongolia and has witnessed the shrinking of the Gobi's natural resources. Jamsranjav is the grandchild of nomadic herders. She understands the relationship between the nomads' lifestyle and the environment. She recognizes that the resources must support the nomads and wildlife at the same time.

Jamsranjav works with the Mongolian herders of the desert steppe, which is like a plain. They have planted trees to help keep water and soil from washing away. Wells that had been abandoned are being repaired for the herders to use as a water source. The wells allow natural stream and river water to be conserved for wild mammals like gazelle and wild donkeys. This helps prevent overgrazing. Jamsranjav is also teaching the herders to record the numbers and types of wild animals they see. Monitoring wildlife will help ensure that the Gobi has the resources to support herders and animals alike.

✎ Think and Write

❶ What is Jargal Jamsranjav trying to accomplish in her work with the Mongolian herders?

❷ How has Jamsranjav helped the nomadic people of the Gobi?

2.b

Enric Sala

Splashing in the ocean surf is fun. When Enric Sala was a boy in Spain, he spent hours swimming in the Mediterranean Sea. Over time, he saw how some human activities harmed the sea environment. As an adult, he decided to learn more about this problem. Dr. Enric Sala is now the deputy director of the Scripps Center for Marine Biodiversity and Conservation in San Diego, California. He studies how pollution, development, and fishing affect the food webs in ocean environments.

▶ **DR. ENRIC SALA**

▶ **Marine ecologist**

▶ Developed a model to track biodiversity in marine ecosystems

Sala believes that it is important to protect the variety of life, called biodiversity, in the world's oceans. His research on fishing in the Gulf of California has shown that overfishing has caused the numbers of some fish species to become dangerously low. Sala developed a model that showed how all the species in the Gulf of California interact with each other. A drop in the numbers of one species affects all the other organisms in the food web. Other scientists use his model to try to figure out a way to protect the biodiversity in the Gulf of California and in other seas around the world.

✍ Think and Write

❶ What is the focus of Enric Sala's work?

❷ How does a change in one part of a food web affect the food web as a whole?

2.b

Science Content

2.b *Students know* producers and consumers (herbivores, carnivores, omnivores, and decomposers) are related in food chains and food webs and may compete with each other for resources in ecosystems.

Investigation and Experimentation

6.d Conduct multiple trials to test a prediction and draw conclusions about the relationships between predictions and results.

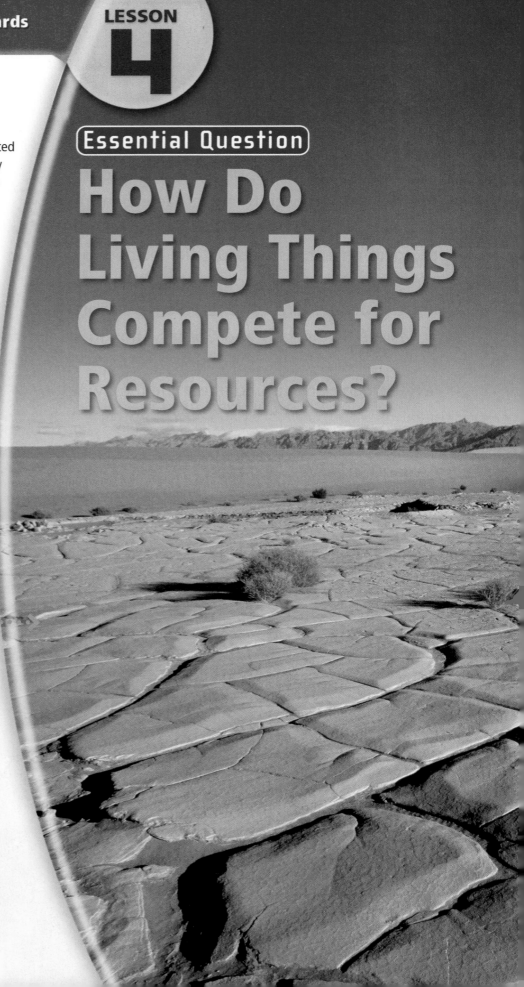

Essential Question

How Do Living Things Compete for Resources?

California Fast Fact

Competing for Water

California's Death Valley desert averages less than 5 centimeters (2 in.) of rainfall per year. With so little water, the plants and animals must compete for it. Some plants start to grow from seeds only when their seed casings are scratched. This may happen in a rare flash flood.

Death Valley, California

habitat [HAB•ih•tat] An environment that meets the needs of an organism (p. 196)

resources [REE•sawr•suhz] Useful things in the environment, such as air, food, water, and shelter, which animals need to survive (p. 197)

competition [kahm•puh•TISH•uhn] A situation in which organisms must work to win limited resources (p. 198)

Using Color to Hide

Start with Questions

Some living things, such as this giraffe, are food for other living things.

● How do organisms that are food for other living things survive?

Investigate to find out. Then read to find out more.

Prepare to Investigate

Investigation Skill Tip
A prediction is what you expect to happen. Think about what you expect the results of this investigation will be.

Materials

● hole punch
● red, blue, green, and yellow sheets of acetate
● large green cloth
● clock or watch with a second hand

Make a Data Table

Number of Insects Collected				
	Red	Blue	Green	Yellow
Hunt 1				
Hunt 2				
Hunt 3				
Hunt 4				
Total				

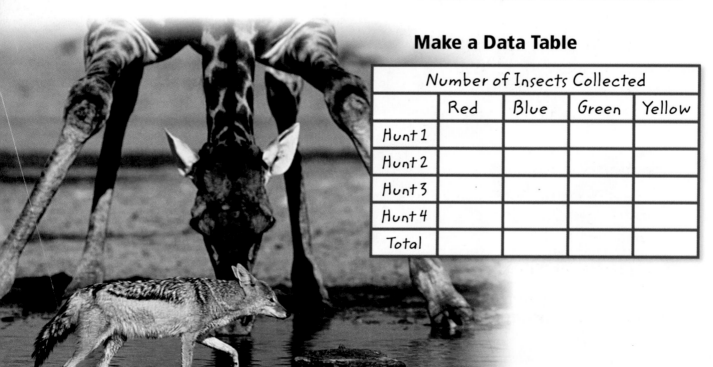

Follow This Procedure

1. Make a table like the one shown. Using the hole punch, make 50 small "insects" from each color of acetate. **Predict** which color would be the easiest and the hardest for a bird to find in grass. **Record** your predictions.

2. Spread the green cloth on the floor, and scatter the insects over the cloth. One group member should time the other group members. They should pick up as many insects, one at a time, as they can in one minute.

3. Count the number of each color of insect your group collected. **Record** the data in the table. Repeat so that you have four "hunts" in all.

Step 1

Step 2

Draw Conclusions

1. Which color did you predict would be easiest for a bird to find? Which color did your group collect the most of? The least of? Why?

2. **Standards Link** What do you think helps living things survive when they are food for some other living thing? `2.b`

3. **Investigation Skill** **Predict** what may happen to green insects if the grass they live in turns brown. `6.d`

Independent Inquiry → **Predict**

Predict how the body shapes of different insects might help them hide in the grass. Justify, or explain, your prediction. Then plan an investigation to test your prediction. `6.d`

VOCABULARY
habitat p. 196
resources p. 197
competition p. 198

SCIENCE CONCEPTS
▶ how habitats contain the resources living things need
▶ how living things compete for resources

CAUSE AND EFFECT
Focus Skill

Look for ways that resources are affected in habitats.

cause ⟶ effect

Habitats

You probably wouldn't see a water bird in a desert or a penguin in a swamp. Animals must live in places that meet their needs. A **habitat** is an environment that meets the needs of a living thing. An insect is small. As a result, its habitat can be as small as the space under a rock. A migrating bird's habitat can cross a continent.

Many habitats overlap. For example, the three living things pictured on this page all live in a desert habitat. This habitat meets all their needs. Sidewinders and tarantulas find many small consumers to eat. Sagebrush grows well in the desert.

The venomous ("poisonous") sidewinder eats mice, rats, lizards, and birds. ▶

Sidewinder

◀ Tarantulas are venomous, too. They eat insects, other spiders, lizards, snakes, frogs, and birds.

Tarantula

Sagebrush can grow where other plants can't. Sheep and cattle often eat sagebrush in the winter. ▶

Sagebrush

Even though this desert habitat is hot and has little water, some living things can thrive there.

Each living thing in a habitat has a *niche*. A niche is a living thing's special role in its habitat. It includes all the things the organism does to live in that habitat. All habitats have the resources that living things need in their niches. **Resources** are useful things in the environment, such as air, food, water, and shelter. Part of a living thing's niche is how it gets and uses its habitat's resources.

Part of a sidewinder's niche is eating the mice, birds, and lizards of its habitat. The small animals are the sidewinder's food resources. If all the sidewinders died, there would be too many of those small animals in the desert. The small animals would soon eat all their food resources and would then starve.

The sidewinder's niche helps keep the number of small desert animals in balance with the habitat's resources.

CAUSE AND EFFECT What would happen if all the sagebrush disappeared from a desert?

Water, food, and shelter are plentiful in a rain forest. With these resources, the rain forest can support many different types of living things. ▶

Competing for Resources

In any habitat, there is only a certain amount of food, water, and shelter. These resources and others are limited. For example, even a rain forest has a limited amount of water that the animals and plants there can use. Because resources are limited, the living things in a habitat must compete to win them.

Competition is a kind of contest among living things to win resources. Groups of living things often compete for the same kinds of food. For example, raccoons and turtles both eat fish. They are competing with each other for the fish resources.

If the number of fish goes down, there will be less food for both raccoons and turtles. The number of fish limits the numbers of raccoons and turtles that can survive. Since it's likely that other animals eat the raccoons and turtles,

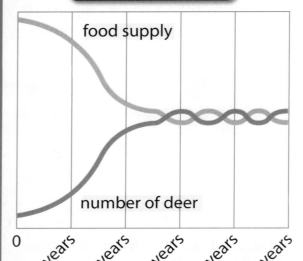

Math in Science
Interpret Data

food supply

number of deer

0 5 years 10 years 15 years 20 years 25 years

What happened to the population of deer as the food supply went down?

Tree leaves are a main source of food for deer. It takes 0.6 to 1.2 square kilometers (15 to 30 acres) of land to provide enough food for one deer.

Plants compete for light under the canopy. When there is a break, called a deadfall, plants quickly grow into the new space.

those other animals are also limited by the number of fish.

Living things also compete for shelter and for other spaces. For example, suppose there are more squirrels than there are trees for nests. Then the squirrels are less likely to survive. Plants may compete for locations that have sunlight. In a rain forest, the leaves at the tops of the trees form a covering. The plants that grow on the rain-forest floor compete for the small amount of sunlight that gets through the covering.

 Focus Skill **CAUSE AND EFFECT** How might a change in the amount of water affect the living things in a habitat?

Insta-Lab

Who Wins?
Gather 20 pencils. Some should be yellow. The rest can be any color. The yellow pencils are worth 50 points each. All the others are worth 5 points. Have a contest with three partners. Try to get the most points by picking up pencils during a limited time. Does the fastest person win? What about the person who spots the yellow pencils first?

Essential Question

How do living things compete for resources?

In this lesson, you learned that living things compete with each other for the resources in a habitat in a sort of contest.

Science Content Standard in This Lesson

2.b *Students know* producers and consumers (herbivores, carnivores, omnivores, and decomposers) are related in food chains and food webs and may compete with each other for resources in ecosystems.

1. **Focus Skill** **CAUSE AND EFFECT** Draw and complete a graphic organizer to show the effects of a drought in a habitat. **2.b**

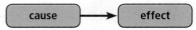

cause → effect

2. **SUMMARIZE** Use your completed graphic organizer to write a lesson summary. **2.b**

3. **DRAW CONCLUSIONS** Which types of resources can living things do without? **2.b**

4. **VOCABULARY** Which term describes the contest among living things to get resources?
A prey
B predator
C competition
D habitat **2.b**

5. **Critical Thinking** How might flooding affect competition within a habitat? **2.b**

6. **Investigate and Experiment** In the Investigate, why was it helpful to have more than one "hunt" for green "insects"? **6.d**

7. Which of these is a name for the ways a living thing uses the resources in its environment? **2.b**
A competition
B niche
C habitat
D life cycle

8. How does competition for resources affect a living thing's ability to survive? **2.b**

The **Big** Idea

Writing   ELA—W 1.2

Write a Letter

Choose a habitat found in California. Write a letter to the editor of a newspaper about the organisms found in that habitat. Tell why it's important to protect the habitat.

9÷3 Math   MR 2.1

Estimate

A sea otter that weighs 25 kilograms needs to eat at least 6.25 kilograms of food a day. What is the total amount of food the habitat must provide the sea otter during 100 days?

Social Studies   HSS 4.4.7

Water Needs

Research a specific dam or aqueduct in California. Find out what the land was like before and after the amount of available water in the area changed. Share your findings in a written or oral report or by making a poster.

 For more links and activities, go to **www.hspscience.com**

◗ Visual Summary

Tell how each picture helps explain the **Big Idea**.

The Big Idea All living things need energy and matter to live and grow.

2.a

Food Energy

The sun is the source of energy for all living things. Producers use sunlight to make food. Consumers get energy by eating producers.

2.b

Food Chains

Organisms in an ecosystem are connected by food chains and food webs. Energy is passed from organism to organism.

2.c

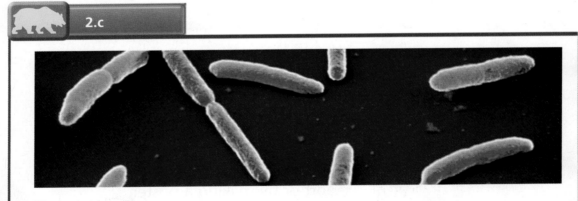

Decomposers

Decomposers break down dead plant and animal matter. This returns nutrients to the soil to be used again by producers.

Show What You Know

Unit Writing Activity

Write an Information Report

Producers, such as plants, are the first source of food in food webs. As cities and towns grow, more and more land is being used. There are fewer resources available for producers. Some cities and towns are trying to use parks to replace some of the resources that producers need. Research how parks are being used. Find out if the parks really help maintain healthy food webs. Explain your idea for the "perfect park."

Unit Project

Food Web Balance

Draw a scene that shows a food web in an ecosystem. Label each member of this food web with its role or roles. Then show the same food web in trouble in some way. Perhaps there are few or none of one kind of producer. Perhaps there are too many of one kind of consumer. Under your drawing, explain what is wrong and predict what is likely to happen.

Vocabulary Review

Use the terms below to complete the sentences. The page numbers tell you where to look in the unit if you need help.

producers p. 158   predators p. 184

consumer p. 158   food chain p. 184

omnivores p. 160   habitat p. 196

decomposers p. 170

microorganisms p. 174

1. An animal that eats other living things is a _____.   `2.b`

2. Nutrients from plant and animal waste would be lost without _____.   `2.c`

3. Animals that eat other consumers are _____.   `2.b`

4. Organisms that are too small to be seen without a microscope are _____.   `2.c`

5. Animals that eat both producers and other consumers are _____.   `2.b`

6. A _____ is a series of organisms that depend on each other for food.   `2.b`

7. _____ can make their own food.   `2.b`

8. The animals and plants on a coral reef share a _____.   `2.b`

Check Understanding

Choose the best answer for each question.

9. **MAIN IDEA AND DETAILS** Which term includes herbivores and carnivores?   `2.b`
   A consumers   C plants
   B predators   D producers

10. **SEQUENCE** Which is the first organism in a food chain?   `2.b`
    A a consumer
    B a decomposer
    C a producer
    D a predator

11. What must every habitat have to support the organisms living within it?   `2.a`
    A resources   C herbivores
    B predators   D consumers

Use the image below to answer Questions 12 and 13.

12. What is shown in the picture? **2.b**
  A niche **C** habitat
  B food chain **D** food web

13. What is the chipmunk? **2.b**
  A carnivore **C** prey
  B predator **D** decomposer

14. Which of the following organisms is an example of a decomposer? **2.c**
  A deer
  B California cougar
  C bracket fungus
  D human being

15. Which of the following do herbivores eat? **2.b**
  A consumers **C** predators
  B omnivores **D** producers

16. Which of these must a coral reef food web have? **2.a**
  A algae **C** tiny fish
  B sunlight **D** whales

Investigation Skills

17. While hiking with your family, you follow a trail that leads past many dead plants. Even the trees seem to be dying. The soil is very dry. What can you infer is happening to the consumers in this area? **6.c**

18. Compare a carnivore and a predator. How are these living things different? **6.a**

Critical Thinking

19. How do California cougars depend on the sun for food? **2.b**

20. Imagine that a new kind of animal has suddenly appeared in a habitat. How might the animal affect the available resources in a habitat? Explain your reasoning.

The **Big** Idea

UNIT 3

LIFE SCIENCE

Ecosystems

California Standards in This Unit

3 Living organisms depend on one another and on their environment for survival.

3.a *Students know* ecosystems can be characterized by their living and nonliving components.

3.b *Students know* that in any particular environment, some kinds of plants and animals survive well, some survive less well, and some cannot survive at all.

3.c *Students know* many plants depend on animals for pollination and seed dispersal, and animals depend on plants for food and shelter.

3.d *Students know* that most microorganisms do not cause disease and that many are beneficial.

This unit also includes these Investigation and Experimentation Standards: **6.a** **6.c** **6.d** **6.f**

What's the Big Idea?

Living things depend on one another and on their environment for survival.

Essential Questions

Hopper Mountain Wildlife Refuge

Dear Sarah,

You'll never guess what just happened! I saw a California condor fly over my house! It must have come from the Hopper Mountain National Wildlife Refuge, which is near here. Can you ask your parents to bring you over soon? We might be able to spot another one!

Your friend,
Kim

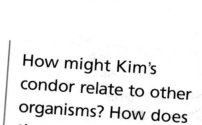

How might Kim's condor relate to other organisms? How does that relate to the **Big Idea?**

Unit Inquiry

Unit Inquiry

Most organisms need water to grow and stay healthy. But does water quality affect living things? Plan and conduct an experiment

Science Content

3.a *Students know* ecosystems can be characterized by their living and nonliving components.

Investigation and Experimentation

6.a Differentiate observation from inference (interpretation) and know scientists' explanations come partly from what they observe and partly from how they interpret their observations.

California Fast Fact

Disappearing Wetlands

Wetlands are one type of ecosystem. California once had about 4 million acres of wetlands. Many of these acres were drained and filled with soil to make land for buildings. Only about 300,000 acres of wetlands remain in California. They provide homes for thousands of kinds of birds, ducks, fish, snakes, frogs, and other animals.

LESSON 1

Essential Question

What Makes Up an Ecosystem?

208

Tioga Pass wetlands, California

ecosystem [EE•koh•sis•tuhm] A community of living things and its physical environment (p. 212)

population [pahp•yuh•LAY•shuhn] All the individuals of one kind living in the same environment (p. 212)

community [kuh•MYOO•nuh•tee] All the populations of organisms living in an environment (p. 214)

biome [BY•ohm] A large area of similar climates and ecosystems (p. 216)

ecology [ee•KAHL•uh•jee] The study of ecosystems (p. 218)

Modeling an Ecosystem

Directed Inquiry ## Start with Questions

Look under a rock. You might find a whole ecosystem there!

- Do you live in an ecosystem?

- Is everything in your ecosystem living?

Investigate to find out. Then read to find out more.

Prepare to Investigate

> **Investigation Skill Tip**
> Using a model can make it easier to understand how things work.

Materials

- gravel
- sand
- soil
- 6 small plants
- clear plastic wrap
- 2 rubber bands
- 2 empty 2-L soda bottles with tops cut off
- water in a spray bottle

Make an Observation Chart

	Day 1	Day 2	Day 3
Sunny Terrarium			
Dark Terrarium			

Follow This Procedure

❶ Put a layer of gravel, a layer of sand, and then a layer of soil into the bottom of each bottle.

❷ Plant three plants in each bottle. Spray the plants and the soil with water. Cover the top of each bottle with plastic wrap. Hold the wrap in place with a rubber band.

❸ Put one of the terrariums you just made in a sunny place. Put the other one in a dark place.

❹ After three days, observe each terrarium and record what you see.

Draw Conclusions

1. What did you observe about each ecosystem after three days? What was missing from one ecosystem?

2. **Standard Link** Which parts of the ecosystems were alive? Do you live in an ecosystem? What can you infer about what every ecosystem needs? `3.a`

3. **Investigation Skill** Scientists learn more about how things affect one another by **using a model**. What did you learn by using a model and observing how its parts interact?

Step 1

Step 2

Independent Inquiry

Tell the Difference Between Observation and Inference
Think about your observations during this investigation. What other inference could you make, based on those observations? `6.a`

Look out a window and make three observations. Then write two inferences you could make, based on those observations. Tell why each is an inference and not an observation.

VOCABULARY
ecosystem p. 212
population p. 212
community p. 214
biome p. 216
ecology p. 218

SCIENCE CONCEPTS
▶ what populations and communities are
▶ how living and nonliving parts of different kinds of ecosystems interact

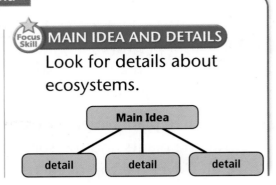

MAIN IDEA AND DETAILS
Look for details about ecosystems.

Individuals and Populations

In the activity, you made two ecosystems. An **ecosystem** is all the living and nonliving things in one area. The living things are plants, animals, and other organisms. The nonliving things are water, sunlight, air, and soil.

Each living thing is an *individual.* You are an individual. So is a clover plant. So is a monkey.

Individuals of the same kind living in an area make up a **population**. You and the other people in your town or city form a population. A lawn might have a population of clover plants. A forest might have a population of monkeys.

Members of a population do not have to live together. They may just live in the same area. All the garter snakes in a meadow are one population. Gopher snakes in the same meadow are a different population. Each kind of grass growing in the meadow is a population, too.

Some plants and animals can live in more than one kind of ecosystem. Red-winged blackbirds live in wetlands, but they can live in other ecosystems, too.

This individual water lily is part of a large population of water lilies.

This individual male red-winged blackbird is part of a large population of blackbirds.

A population of red-winged blackbirds can include several million birds. Some of the birds fly 80 kilometers (50 mi) to find food.

Other plants and animals can live only in certain places. One bird, the willow flycatcher, makes its nest only in willow trees. This means that it can't live in ecosystems without willow trees.

The willow flycatcher used to live all over California. However, many willow trees have been cut down to make room for new buildings. Because the birds now have fewer places to nest, there are fewer willow flycatchers in the state today.

 MAIN IDEA AND DETAILS Name an individual and a population that are not mentioned on these two pages.

Insta-Lab

Eek! Oh System!
Work with a partner to list some populations in the ecosystem around your school. Think about the plants and animals you have seen there. Then compare lists with other students. Did you list the same populations?

213

be able to survive with little water. The populations in a tidal pool must be able to live in water when the tide is in. They must also be able to live in wet sand when the tide is out.

The populations in a forest or taiga community are different, too. However, all of these communities are the same in one way. The plants and animals that make up each community depend on one another. Some animals eat the plants. Other animals eat the plant eaters. The animals help spread the plants' seeds. The plants provide food for the animals. They also provide shelter for the animals.

 MAIN IDEA AND DETAILS Name three populations that might live in a forest community.

215

Communities

A group of individuals is called a population. A group of populations living in the same place is called a **community**. You live in a community with other populations of living things. Your community might include birds, squirrels, insects, trees, and grass.

Death Valley National Park is the hottest, driest place in North America. You might not expect to find many living things forming a community in such a place, yet more than 1,000 plant populations live there. More than 20 of these live *only* in Death Valley.

This desert community includes at least 5 populations of bats. It also has 3 populations of rabbits and 4 populations of squirrels. You might spot mice and rats from as many as 18 populations.

You might also see large animals in Death Valley. They include coyotes, foxes, burros, bighorn sheep, and mountain lions. All of these plant and animal populations are adapted to survive in the hot, dry desert.

As you can see in the photo, the community in a tidal pool looks nothing like the community in Death Valley. The populations in Death Valley must

Nonliving Parts

Plants and animals can't survive without the nonliving parts of their ecosystems. These nonliving parts are water, soil, sunlight, and air.

Climate is a combination of nonliving things. It includes the amounts of rainfall and sunlight that an area receives. It also includes the pattern of air temperatures during the year.

A large area may have similar climates and ecosystems. Such an area is called a **biome**. The taiga, desert, and rain forest are kinds of biomes.

Changes in the nonliving parts of an ecosystem or a biome can affect all the living parts. For example, too little rain causes many plants to wilt and die. Then the animals that eat those plants don't have enough food. Too much rain can cause flooding. This can kill both plants and animals.

An ecosystem with rich soil has many kinds of plants. Where the soil is poor, few kinds of plants grow. An ecosystem with few plants will also have few animals.

The air, the water, and the soil in an biome can contain harmful substances. When gasoline burns, it sends chemicals into the air. Other chemicals run off fields and into rivers and streams. These chemicals can harm both plants and animals.

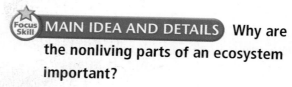 **MAIN IDEA AND DETAILS** Why are the nonliving parts of an ecosystem important?

Science Up Close

Nonliving Parts of an Ecosystem
Without the nonliving parts of an ecosystem, there would be no living parts.

216

Sunlight
Plants need sunlight to produce food. Where trees shade the ground, not many other plants can grow.

Water
Almost all living things need water. Plant roots absorb water, and animals drink it.

Soil
Most plants need soil to grow. The kind of soil in an ecosystem is one of the things that determine what kinds of plants grow there.

For more links and animations, go to **www.hspscience.com**

217

Ecosystems

Each ecosystem has its own set of living and nonliving parts. In a desert ecosystem, you would find cacti, scorpions, plenty of sunlight, and very little rain. In a different ecosystem, such as a forest, you would find different plants and animals and different amounts of sunlight and rain.

An ecosystem can be as huge as a desert or as small as the space under a rock. Like all other ecosystems, the space under a rock has both living and nonliving parts. The living things might include insects and tiny plants. You might need a hand lens to see some of the living things there.

The nonliving parts of this rock ecosystem include the rock itself, pockets of air, and soil. You might find a few drops of water or just dampness in the soil. A little sunlight might reach under the edges of the rock.

The ecosystem under this rock even has a climate. If the rock is in northern California, that climate might be cool and wet. If the rock is in southern California, the climate might be warm and dry.

Ecology is the study of ecosystems. The scientists in this field are called *ecologists.* Ecologists study the ways

▼ **This prairie smoke plant grows well in this hot, dry grassland ecosystem.**

Prairie dogs also live in grasslands.

Moose thrive in a coniferous forest ecosystem.

the living and nonliving parts of an ecosystem affect each other. They look at the ways plants help animals and how animals help plants. They study the ways in which living things depend on the nonliving things in an ecosystem.

Suppose the amount of rainfall in an ecosystem increased. How would the plants there be affected? Then how would the animals be affected? Would the plants and animals be able to adjust to more rainfall? Would the animals try to move to another ecosystem?

Suppose much of the coniferous forest in the photo were cut down for timber. Could the moose survive in the changed ecosystem? What about the other plants and animals there?

 **MAIN IDEA AND DETAILS** Name an ecosystem, and list its living and nonliving parts.

Standards Wrap-Up and Lesson Review

What makes up an ecosystem?

In this lesson, you learned that different types of ecosystems have different living and nonliving parts.

 Science Content Standard in This Lesson

3.a *Students know* ecosystems can be characterized by their living and nonliving components.

1. 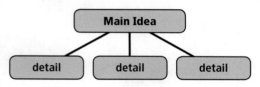 **MAIN IDEA AND DETAILS** Draw and complete a graphic organizer to show the living and nonliving things in an ecosystem. **3.a**

```
          Main Idea
         /    |    \
   detail  detail  detail
```

2. **SUMMARIZE** Write a summary of this lesson by using the vocabulary terms in a paragraph. **3.a**

3. **DRAW CONCLUSIONS** Why do some ecosystems include more living things than others? **3.a**

4. **VOCABULARY** Which statement could **not** be true about a rattlesnake and a cactus?
   A They are members of the same population.
   B They are part of the same ecosystem.
   C They live in the same community.
   D They live in the same biome. **3.a**

5. **Critical Thinking** You are traveling from one ecosystem to another. What can you expect to change? **3.a**

6. **Investigate and Experiment** In an investigation, why is it important to separate observations from inferences? **6.a**

7. Which statement is true?
   A A group of individuals makes up an ecosystem.
   B A community includes living and nonliving things.
   C All the land in a biome has about the same climate.
   D Nonliving things could not exist without living things. **3.a**

8. How do the nonliving parts of an ecosystem affect the survival of the living parts? **3.a**

 The Big Idea

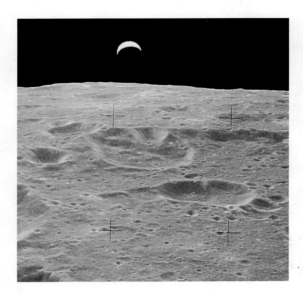

Write a Composition

Imagine that you are a scientist planning an ecosystem for people to set up on the moon. Write several paragraphs explaining what this ecosystem should include.

Find Quotients

A certain community is made up of 650 populations of living things. It has as many plant populations as animal populations. How many plant populations does the community have?

California Ecosystems

On a map of California, identify and label the locations of at least three biomes of different kinds. Describe the ecosystems that the biomes include.

 For more links and activities, go to **www.hspscience.com**

Aquarius:
An Underwater Lab With A View

A buoy marks *Aquarius'* location.

Many kids have to share a bedroom with a brother or a sister. Six scientists know that sharing a room can be a pain! They squeezed into a small underwater laboratory to study a coral reef. They worked and slept in the tiny space for ten days.

A diver checks equipment outside *Aquarius.*

Yellow Submarine

"I've been on missions where people snored," said Celia Smith, who led one of the missions. "You just kind of kick their bunk and try to get to sleep before they do."

The underwater lab is called *Aquarius.* It looks like a little yellow submarine. The *Aquarius* was placed near the Florida Keys National Marine Sanctuary, a protected area of the ocean. Each year, several teams of scientists have lived in *Aquarius* for up to ten days at a time. The scientists who live and work there are called aquanauts [AK•wuh•nawts]. The aquanauts study the nearby coral reef and the creatures that live there.

A Room with a View

A team that recently visited *Aquarius* says the best part of living there is the view. They can see colorful fish swimming in the nearby reef. Smith said it's hard to tell, however, whether the aquanauts are watching the fish or the fish are watching the aquanauts.

Team members spend as much time as they can on the reef studying sea life. They can spend up to nine hours at one time outside the laboratory.

Smith likes to remind people that humans have barely begun to explore the oceans and need to learn more about living underwater. "The really important thing for us to realize is how much we don't know about the oceans," she said.

✍ Think and Write

❶ How might living underwater help scientists learn more about a coral reef ecosystem?　　**3.b**

❷ What might be the best thing about living underwater? What might be the worst thing?

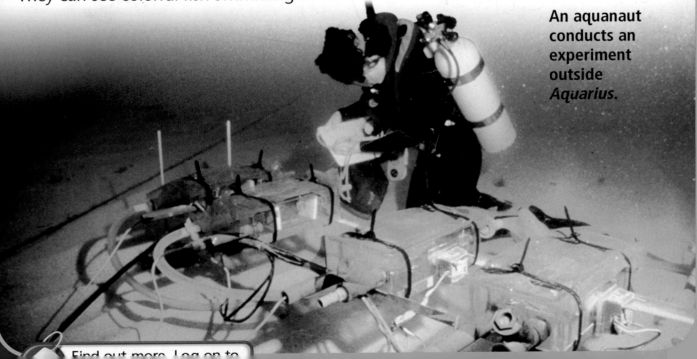

An aquanaut conducts an experiment outside *Aquarius.*

Find out more. Log on to

Science Content

3.b *Students know* that in any particular environment, some kinds of plants and animals survive well, some survive less well, and some cannot survive at all.

Investigation and Experimentation

6.d Conduct multiple trials to test a prediction and draw conclusions about the relationships between predictions and results.

LESSON 2

Essential Question

What Affects Survival?

California Fast Fact

Let's Eat!

The sea otter is one of very few animals that know how to use tools. It cracks open shellfish by hitting them with rocks or other shells. Unlike other sea mammals, the sea otter has no layer of fat to keep it warm. Instead, it has the thickest fur in the animal kingdom. Today, fewer than 3000 sea otters live off California's coast.

adaptation
[ad•uhp•TAY•shuhn] A change in a body part or behavior that helps an organism survive (p. 228)

accommodation
[uh•kahm•uh•DAY•shuhn] A learned behavior that helps the individual members of a species survive (p. 229)

Eating Like a Bird

Start with Questions

The shape and size of your mouth makes it easy to eat foods like watermelon. The shape and size of a bird's beak helps it eat the foods it eats.

- Have you noticed that the beaks of a sparrow, a cardinal, an eagle, and a duck are different?

- Why do you think their beaks are so different?

Investigate to find out. Then read to find out more.

Prepare to Investigate

Investigation Skill Tip
After the investigation, you will draw conclusions about the types of beaks that best handle different bird foods.

Materials

- 2 chopsticks or unsharpened pencils
- pliers
- clothespin
- spoon
- forceps
- plastic worms
- cooked rice
- raisins
- water in a cup
- birdseed
- cooked spaghetti
- peanuts in shells
- small paper plates

Make an Observation Chart

Food	Best Tool (Beak)	Observations

Follow This Procedure

➊ Make a table like the one on the facing page.

➋ Put the first five objects on one side of your desk, and think of them as bird beaks. Put each kind of food on a paper plate.

➌ Place one plate of food in the middle of your desk. Try picking up the food with the "beaks." Try several times with each beak. Decide which kind of beak works best for that kind of food.

➍ Test all the beaks with all the foods and with the water. Use the table to **record** your observations and conclusions.

Draw Conclusions

1. Which kind of beak is best for picking up small seeds? Which kind is best for crushing large seeds?

2. **Standard Link** Why do different kinds of birds have different kinds of beaks? `3.b`

3. **Investigation Skill** After experimenting, what **conclusion** can you **draw** about which beak works best with water?

Step 2

Step 3

Independent Inquiry

Conduct Many Trials and Draw Conclusions

Think about this investigation. How might your conclusions change if you had tried each beak just once with each food? `6.a`

Write a plan for an investigation to find out which kind of food a certain dog likes. Explain why you will conduct many trials with each food before drawing any conclusions. Carry out your plan.

VOCABULARY
adaptation p. 228
accommodation p. 229

SCIENCE CONCEPTS
▶ how living things respond if an environment changes
▶ how living things are adapted to different ecosystems

Focus Skill MAIN IDEA AND DETAILS
Look for details about adaptation and accommodation.

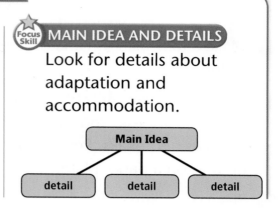

Main Idea

detail   detail   detail

Adaptation and Accommodation

Ecosystems change. They may become drier or wetter, hotter or cooler. When an ecosystem changes, the plants and animals there must change, too. If they cannot change, they must find another ecosystem that meets their needs. If, like most plants, they cannot move, they are likely to die.

However, many plants and animals do change. Over many generations, they develop adaptations. An **adaptation** is a change in a body part or a behavior that helps a living thing survive.

Suppose that an ecosystem begins to have less rainfall every year. The ecosystem includes a population of mice. Some individuals in the population need to drink a lot of water. They die young and have no babies.

Other individuals in that population need less water. These mice live longer and reproduce. Their offspring can survive with less water, too. Those offspring grow up and reproduce.

After several generations, all of the mice in that ecosystem can survive with

▼ A hummingbird's beak helps it survive. This long, slender beak can reach the nectar deep inside a flower.

228

▼ With bears' natural habitats destroyed to build towns, some bears now raid garbage cans to survive. This accommodation allows them to meet their needs. With about 35,000 black bears living in California, this behavior is becoming a problem. Several towns now ask people to use bear-proof trash containers.

less water. This population of mice has adapted to the change in its ecosystem.

Some adaptations are behaviors. When food is hard to find in winter, moose, geese, and some other animals *migrate.* They go to a warmer climate.

Some animals, such as bats, *hibernate.* They go into a state that looks like deep sleep until spring.

No one teaches these animals to migrate or hibernate. However, animals do learn other behaviors that help them survive. The bears in the photo have learned how to find food easily. This change in their behavior is an **accommodation**. These bears raid trash cans to find food to eat.

 **MAIN IDEA AND DETAILS** What kinds of changes can lead to adaptations?

All Thumbs
Use masking tape to tape your partner's thumb to his or her hand. Then ask your partner to write, pick up a pencil, eat, and so on. How is a thumb an adaptation?

The *canopy* is the top layer of the forest. This is where most rain-forest animals live.

The next layer is the cool, dark *understory*. This layer is just right for plants that grow well in shade.

The bottom layer is the dim *forest floor*. Here, decaying matter provides food for plants.

Tropical Rain Forests

You might think that anything could live and grow in a lush tropical rain forest. Why would the plants or animals there need adaptations?

The tall trees that form the rain-forest canopy block sunlight from reaching the understory. Little light reaches the dim forest floor. Many plants growing beneath the canopy have large leaves to catch as much light as possible. Without large leaves, these plants would not grow well here. Some might not survive.

Vines climb up the tree trunks into the canopy to reach the sunlight. In some places, vines make up nearly half of the canopy layer.

Because it rains so often, some plants have leaves with grooves or an oily coating. Both adaptations let the water run off quickly. If the leaves caught and held the rain, the weight might break the branches, harming the plants.

Animals in the rain forest also have adaptations. Adaptations help some animals escape from their predators.

These orchids' roots can take in water and nutrients directly from raindrops. This kind of root allows the orchids to grow on high branches instead of in soil. Up high, they get more sunlight than they would on the dim forest floor. Without these roots, orchids would not be able to live in the rain forest.

▲ The toucan's long beak is an adaptation. It helps the bird reach fruit at the ends of branches. Its beak looks heavy, but because it is hollow, it is actually light.

▲ Many birds do not notice this leaf butterfly because it is camouflaged. The shape and color of its wings hide it from predators.

One adaptation is camouflage. *Camouflage* is a color or shape that helps an animal hide. For example, many rain-forest lizards are green, brown, striped, or dotted. These colors allow them to blend in with the plants in the rain forest. Chameleons can actually change color to match a background.

The sloth is a large, furry animal. It hangs quietly in the rain-forest canopy. Predators often do not notice it. Algae growing in the sloth's fur help it blend in with the green leaves.

Camouflage also helps some rain-forest predators sneak up on their prey. Many large snakes are hard to see among the vines and leaves. Their camouflage helps them get close to their prey without being seen.

MAIN IDEA AND DETAILS How does camouflage help animals?

Coral Reefs

Coral reefs, a living creature made up of many very small organisms, teem with hundreds of populations of living things. These plants and animals have many adaptations that help them survive. Like the animals in a rain forest, many coral reef animals have camouflage. Think about how hard it would be to spot the decorator crab shown on the next page.

Sea horses, too, have special coloring. It helps them hide among the coral formations of the reef.

Many small reef fish swim together in schools, or large groups. Swimming in schools is an adaptation that protects small fish. The large number of fish swirling together confuses many predators. A few fish get eaten, but most survive. If the fish swam alone, very few would survive.

The coral itself is adapted to living in sunlit waters. A coral reef is made up of tiny coral animals. Part of the reef is made of dead coral skeletons. In some reefs, the outer layer is live coral. Coral cannot move around. They eat any plankton that drift past them. However,

Math in Science
Interpret Data

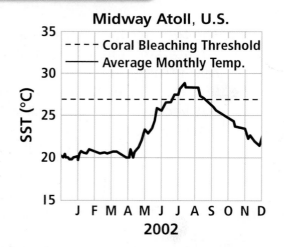

Midway Atoll, U.S.

- - - Coral Bleaching Threshold
— Average Monthly Temp.

SST (°C)

J F M A M J J A S O N D
2002

This graph shows the temperatures at a coral reef near Hawai`i. An increase in temperature killed up to 75 percent of the coral there. When was the water warmest? When was it coolest?

Sponges produce chemicals that taste bad. These chemicals discourage fish from taking a bite. This adaptation helps sponges survive.

the coral could not survive without algae.

Algae living inside the coral help feed it. Like all plants, algae use sunlight to make their own food. They share this food with the coral. In return, the coral provide homes for the algae. The coral also give off carbon dioxide, which the algae need to make food.

Focus Skill **MAIN IDEA AND DETAILS** What do you think happens when the algae living in coral die?

The clownfish has adapted to reef life by living with anemones. The anemone's sting protects the clownfish from predators. In return, the clownfish serves as bait. It lures other fish close to the anemone. Without each other, the clownfish and the anemone might not survive.

This decorator crab hides by attaching seaweed, sponges, and other small animals to its shell. Without this camouflage, the crab would probably not survive.

The colored coral in this reef is alive. Its colors help hide the fish from their predators.

The ocotillo [oh•kuh•TEE•yoh] plant looks dead during dry spells. After a rain, however, it springs to life. In just a few weeks, it grows leaves and flowers and produces seeds.

The mesquite [mes•KEET] bush sends its roots deep underground to reach water. Some roots grow up to 24 meters (78 ft) long.

After a rare rainfall, the stem of the barrel cactus expands. Expanding allows the cactus to store more water.

Deserts

The hot, dry desert challenges both plants and animals. Like animals in other ecosystems, many of the animals here have camouflage. Light brown colors make these animals harder to spot. Light colors also help keep them cool.

Many desert animals avoid the highest temperatures of the day. They sleep under rocks and in burrows until nightfall. Then, when the air is cooler, they come out to hunt. During very hot spells, some desert animals go into a deep sleep that is almost like hibernation.

Some animals, such as jackrabbits and mule deer, have extra-large ears. These ears help them release heat from their bodies into the air.

The bad smell and taste of the creosote bush keep animals away.

Most desert herbivores get the water they need from the plants and seeds they eat. Carnivores get water from the bodies of the animals they eat. Desert animals release very little water when they get rid of wastes.

Desert plants have adaptations that help them survive. Most store water in their stems. A waxy coating on the stems helps to prevent water loss.

Most desert plants have spines, not leaves. A plant with broad, thin leaves, such as an oak tree, could not survive in the desert. The large surface of the leaves would release too much water into the air. Narrow spines help plants save water. They also discourage animals from eating the plants.

The roots of many cacti spread out just below the surface of the desert soil. This adaptation lets the roots quickly absorb any rain that falls, before it dries up.

The cactus wren builds its nests in cholla [CHOHL•yah] cacti. The spines protect the nests from predators. To confuse predators, one pair of wrens might build ten nests. The wrens raise their young in only one of the nests.

MAIN IDEA AND DETAILS How do adaptations help desert animals survive?

◄ **Gila monsters hunt at night to avoid the desert heat. They can store fat in their tails. They can live off the fat for months if food is scarce.**

The kangaroo rat's digestive system can absorb the water in seeds. The rat also has fur-lined pockets in its cheeks. It uses these to carry as many as 900 small seeds back to its burrow.

235

Standards Wrap-Up and Lesson Review

Essential Question

What affects survival?

In this lesson, you learned that in any particular environment, some kinds of plants and animals survive well, some survive less well, and some cannot survive at all.

Science Content Standard in This Lesson

3.b *Students know* that in any particular environment, some kinds of plants and animals survive well, some survive less well, and some cannot survive at all.

---

1. 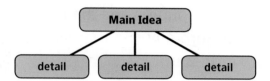 **MAIN IDEA AND DETAILS** Draw and complete a graphic organizer to show details about adaptation and accommodation. **3.b**

Main Idea

detail   detail   detail

2. SUMMARIZE Fill in the blanks. When an environment changes, some living things adapt and _____. Others do not adapt well, but they _____. Some cannot adapt at all, and they _____. **3.b**

3. DRAW CONCLUSIONS In what ways is an animal's body covering important to its survival? **3.b**

4. VOCABULARY Which is an example of accommodation?
A fish swimming in schools
B the spines of a cactus
C mother bear teaching cub to hunt
D chameleons using camouflage to hide **3.b**

5. Critical Thinking An animal is dark brown in color, with a long, shaggy coat. It moves slowly and can't climb trees. How well do you think this animal would survive in a desert ecosystem? A forest? A rainforest? Explain your answer. **3.b**

6. Investigate and Experiment You predict that a plant will survive if it receives twice as much water as usual. To test your prediction, write a plan for an investigation with repeated trials. **6.d**

7. Which adaptation helps a robin catch a worm?
A sharp eyesight
B feather coloring
C perching feet
D nest building **3.b**

8. Describe three accommodations you make to live in your environment. **3.b**

The **Big** Idea

 Writing ELA—W.2.1

Write a Narrative

Explain how a change in your ecosystem would affect your survival. Your narrative can be fiction or nonfiction. Include details that will help readers understand the effects of the change.

 Math NS 3.3

Multiply Whole Number

Clams from the East Coast and green crabs from Asia have nearly wiped out the *Nutricola* clams in San Francisco Bay. The bay once had 10,000 *Nutricola* clams per square yard. Now there are 1000. How many of these clams would you find now in 10 square yards?

 Health

Accommodations and You

Soon your life will change in many ways. For example, you may not grow as tall as your classmates. Think of accommodations you can make to deal with these differences in growth and development. Make a list.

 For more links and activities, go to **www.hspscience.com**

Scripps Institution of Oceanography

Would you like to study the ocean? The Scripps Institution of Oceanography, in La Jolla, is a good place to do it. There, about 1,300 scientists work in 300 programs. Some work to learn more about how the ocean affects Earth's climate. Others study beach erosion or undersea earthquakes.

Many of these scientists are investigating ways in which fish and other living things are adapted to the ocean environment. For example, this anglerfish, like many other deep-sea fish, has huge jaws. They can open wide enough to capture almost any prey that passes.

This anglerfish lives in the deep ocean. The light on its "fishing rod" lures curious prey close enough for it to catch.

This undersea vent produces clouds of chemicals.

Undersea Adaptations

The Ken Smith Laboratory is one part of the Scripps Institution. Scientists who work there focus on the deep ocean, which is dark and cold. The animals that live at this depth have found unusual ways to survive. Some, like the anglerfish, give off light to attract prey. Others catch bits of dead fish that fall from the surface.

Some deep-sea fish have large eyes. This helps them see better in the dark. Many have almost no color. They blend in with the ocean bottom. This helps them hide from predators.

Sea Soup

Scripps scientists have discovered that the deep ocean is far from empty. Many kinds of clams, worms, shrimp, and other animals live there. Deep-sea fish feed on them.

Near the ocean bottom, thousands of microorganisms live near vents, or holes in the ocean floor. They are adapted to be able to use the chemicals coming out of the vents instead of using sunlight to make their own food. Then deep-sea animals feed on them, just as land animals eat plants.

✍ Think and Write

❶ How are some fish and other kinds of ocean animals adapted to life in the deep ocean? **3.b**

❷ How are microorganisms at the bottom of the ocean similar to plants on land? **3.d**

Science Content

3.c *Students know* many plants depend on animals for pollination and seed dispersal, and animals depend on plants for food and shelter.

Investigation and Experimentation

6.c Formulate and justify predictions based on cause-and-effect relationships.

LESSON 3

Essential Question

What Is Interdependence?

California Fast Fact

Going Batty

This Mexican long-tongued bat lives up to its name! This bat, which eats nectar and pollen, has a tongue that can be $\frac{1}{3}$ the length of its body. That helps the bat feed from night-blooming flowers and agaves.

Bat feeds from an agave in southern California.

interdependence
[in•ter•dee•PEN•duhns] The dependence of organisms on one another for survival (p. 244)

relationship
[rih•LAY•shuhn•ship] The connection between organisms (p. 245)

pollinate [PAHL•uh•nayt] To transfer pollen from the male to the female part of a flower (p. 246)

241

Pollination Partners

Directed Inquiry **Start with Questions**

Honeybees, hummingbirds, and butterflies seem to fly to only certain flowers. Is this actually true?

- Can hummingbirds drink nectar from any flower?

- How do honeybees find the flowers they visit?

- What attracts butterflies to certain flowers?

Investigate to find out. Then read to find out more.

Prepare to Investigate

Investigation Skill Tip
A prediction is based on previous observations. Before you predict, think about what you have already observed.

Materials

- drawing materials

Make an Observation Chart

What is your favorite	
Shape?	_____
Color?	_____
Smell?	_____

Barn owl sheltering in tree

Follow This Procedure

① Read the information below.

Honeybees
- cannot see the color red.
- need to land to drink.
- like sweet smells.

Butterflies
- drink through a long, coiled tube.
- are attracted to red and yellow.
- need a wide landing place.

Hummingbirds
- have a long bill and tongue.
- are attracted to the color red.
- do not land to sip nectar.

② Use the information to **predict** the kinds of flowers each animal would land on. Draw the flowers, and label the parts.

③ Make a chart like the one shown. Ask your partner the questions. Draw and label a flower to attract your partner.

Step 2

Step 3

Draw Conclusions

1. **Compare** your first three drawings with those of other students. How are they the same and different?

2. **Standards Link** Why are bees, butterflies, and birds attracted to different flowers? `3.c`

3. **Investigation Skill** How could you test your **predictions** in this Investigate?

Independent Inquiry — **Make and Justify Predictions**

Think about this investigation. What did you use to make your predictions? What causes and effects did you figure out? `6.a`

A honeybee flies near a red rose that has no smell. What do you predict will happen? What is the cause, and what is the effect?

VOCABULARY
interdependence p. 244
relationship p. 245
pollinate p. 246

SCIENCE CONCEPTS
▶ how plants depend on animals
▶ how animals depend on plants

Focus Skill **COMPARE AND CONTRAST**
Compare different examples of interdependence.

alike ──── different

Interdependence

When you depend on people, you trust them and rely on them for support. For example, you depend on your family, teachers, and close friends.

The word **interdependence** means "dependence or reliance on each other." Another term that means the same thing is *mutual dependence*. When two living things are mutually dependent, each depends on the other. They help each other survive.

Groups of living things depend on each other in many ways. For example, elephants live in herds for protection. Lions live in prides for the same reason. Can you name other kinds of animals that live in families or groups?

These ants and aphids are interdependent. The ants bring the aphids into their nests at night. This protects the aphids. The aphids provide a food called honeydew for the ants. In the morning, the ants take the aphids back to the plants they eat.

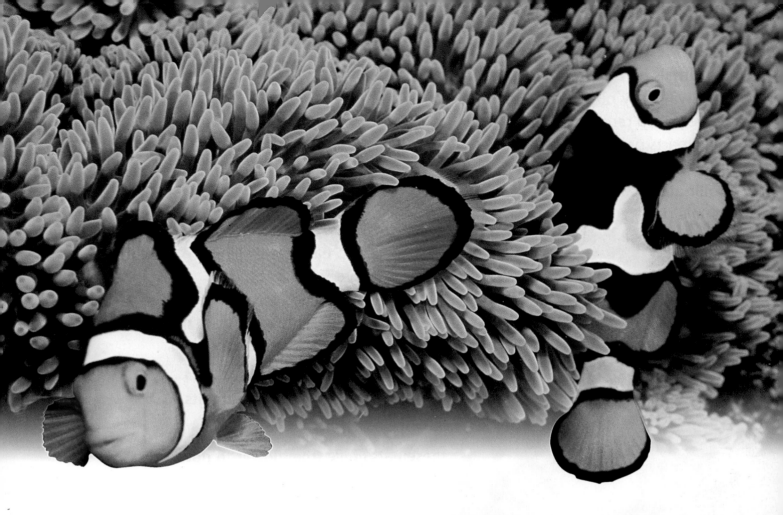

▲ Clownfish and anemones live together in coral reefs. They are mutually dependent.

Sometimes, different kinds of animals help each other. They do not try to eat each other or compete for food. They help each other survive. They have a connection, or **relationship**.

Cleaner shrimp have a relationship with fish. The shrimp depend on the fish for the parasites, harmful organisms that feed on their hosts, that are their food. The fish depend on the shrimp to get rid of parasites.

Red-breasted geese live in the Arctic. They build their nests near the nests of peregrine falcons. As the falcons defend their own nests, they also protect the geese's nests. In return, the geese warn the falcons of predators. In this way, the geese and the falcons are mutually dependent. They help each other survive.

(Focus Skill) **COMPARE AND CONTRAST** How is the relationship between ants and aphids like the one between clownfish and anemones?

Animals Help Plants

Animals help plants in two main ways. One way is by pollinating the plants' flowers. You remember that flowers' male parts produce pollen. Flowers also have a female part called the *pistil*. **Pollinate** means "to carry pollen to the female part of the same kind of flower." When the pollen reaches the pistil, seeds can form.

Bees, other insects, birds, bats, and other small animals help pollinate plants. They do so as they are feeding themselves. When they push deep inside a flower to drink its nectar, some pollen sticks to them. Then they carry that pollen to another flower. The pollinator gets fed, and the flowers get pollinated.

Without animals, fewer seeds would form. Fewer plants would grow. Then herbivores would have less to eat. Soon carnivores and omnivores would have less to eat, too. Pollination is important to every living thing!

After seeds form, animals help plants in a different way. They spread the seeds around in a number of ways.

Fruit bats suck the juices from fruits and flowers. They fly as far as 48 kilometers (30 mi) in search of food. As these bats move from flower to flower, they carry pollen with them.

Honeybees help pollinate many crops. In fact, about 90 different crops—from apples to zucchini—depend on bees to carry pollen from one flower to the next.

Some seeds stick to the coats of dogs, bears, and other furry animals. Birds and other animals eat fruits that are full of seeds. When the seeds come out in the animals' droppings, new plants grow in new places.

Squirrels and other animals carry the seeds they eat to their nests and dens. They may drop some, which then sprout. Some animals bury seeds to eat later. If they forget them, the seeds may grow.

Spreading seeds helps spread plants. This keeps the new plants from crowding the old plants. The new plants do not take space, water, or sunlight that the old plants need.

COMPARE AND CONTRAST How is the way furry animals spread seeds different from the way birds spread seeds?

When birds eat fruit, they often eat the seeds, too. The seeds pass through their digestive systems and come out with their wastes.

These cocklebur seeds stick tight. In the early 1940s, a Swiss inventor noticed how cockleburs stuck to his dog's coat. The hooks on the outside of these seeds gave him an idea. He used it to invent Velcro!

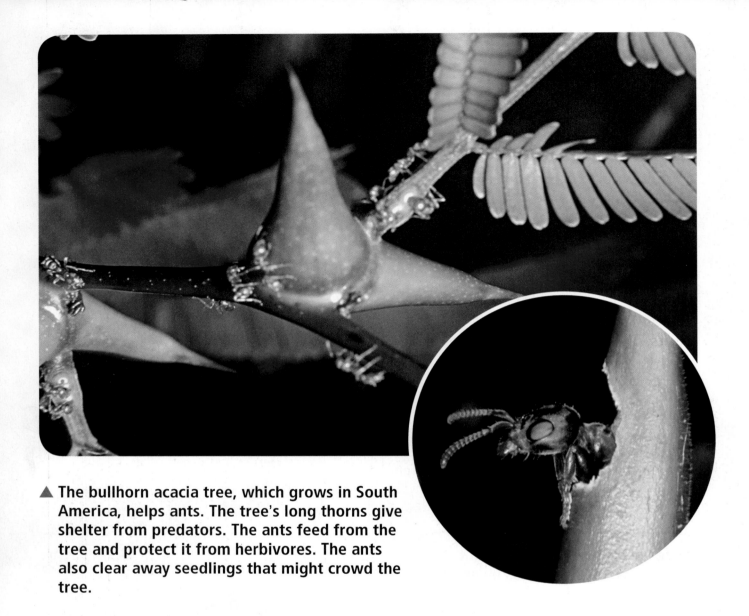

▲ The bullhorn acacia tree, which grows in South America, helps ants. The tree's long thorns give shelter from predators. The ants feed from the tree and protect it from herbivores. The ants also clear away seedlings that might crowd the tree.

Plants Help Animals

You know that herbivores eat plants. Then carnivores and omnivores eat herbivores. Animals, including people, could not survive without plants as food.

However, plants also help animals in other ways. Plants help protect animals from predators. Many kinds of monkeys live high in the canopies of rain forests. Living there prevents leopards and other predators on the ground from reaching them.

Plants help people in many ways. We use wood for lumber, paper, and fuel. Plants that decayed long ago have turned into coal underground. This fuel is used to produce electricity and to make steel.

We use cotton and other plants to make clothing. Many medicines come from plants.

COMPARE AND CONTRAST Do animals help plants more than plants help animals? Explain your answer.

Weaverbirds use grasses and other materials to build their unusual nests.

Insta-Lab

Breath of Life

Drop some elodea into a clear container of water. Put the container in a sunny spot. Now watch. What are those bubbles forming on the leaves? Where do they come from?

This animal knows that few predators will come into the briars after it. The briars help the animal survive.

Standards Wrap-Up and Lesson Review

What is interdependence?

In this lesson, you learned that many plants depend on animals for pollination and seed spreading, and animals depend on plants for food and shelter.

Science Content Standard in This Lesson

3.c *Students know* many plants depend on animals for pollination and seed dispersal, and animals depend on plants for food and shelter.

1. (Focus Skill) **COMPARE AND CONTRAST** Draw and complete a graphic organizer to compare and contrast the ways plants help animals with the ways animals help plants. **3.c**

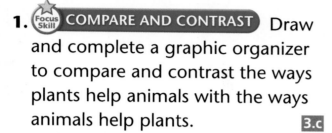

2. **SUMMARIZE** Write two sentences that tell what this lesson is mainly about. **3.c**

3. **DRAW CONCLUSIONS** Are you interdependent with any other living things? Explain. **3.c**

4. **VOCABULARY** Which statement is true about the relationship between honeybees and flowers?

   A Bees eat flowers.
   B Bees are pollinated by flowers.
   C Flowers are pollinated by bees.
   D Bees and flowers are pollinated by other animals. **3.c**

5. **Critical Thinking** How is the relationship between animals in a food chain different from the relationship between animals that are interdependent? **3.c**

6. **Investigate and Experiment** Acacia trees and ants are interdependent. If the ants and the trees could no longer depend on each other, what changes would result? **6.c**

7. Which of these have a mutually dependent relationship?
   A cats and dogs
   B cats and birds
   C dogs and fleas
   D dogs and their owners **3.c**

8. Could plants live without animals? Could animals live without plants? Explain your answers. **3.c**

The **Big** Idea

 Writing ELA—W.1.2

Write a Composition

Write several paragraphs explaining what, in your opinion, is the most important way plants help people. State your opinion in your introduction. In the next paragraphs, give facts and reasons for your opinion.

 Math NS 1.3

Round Whole Numbers

A bird called the Clark's nutcracker buries seeds to eat later. Last year a flock of these birds buried 33,034 seeds and later dug up 21,987 of them. How many seeds were left in the ground to sprout? Round your answer to the nearest thousand.

 Language Arts ELA—LC 1.3

Safe Homes

Animals often depend on other organisms for safe places to live. Illustrate an example of this kind of interdependence. Write a paragraph explaining how the form (shape) of each organism affects the relationship.

 For more links and activities, go to **www.hspscience.com**

▶ **DR. ASHANTI PYRTLE**

▶ Assistant Professor,
College of Marine Science,
University of South Florida

Ashanti Pyrtle

Are Earth's lakes, rivers, and oceans radioactive? That's what Ashanti Pyrtle is trying to find out. Pyrtle is a chemical oceanographer who studies radioactive pollution. Some of this pollution came from tests of nuclear weapons in the 1960s. Some of it is waste from making nuclear weapons.

Nuclear pollution washes off the land and into the water. Pyrtle is learning how it spreads through lakes, rivers, and oceans. Her findings will help if there is a nuclear accident. She is also testing ways to clean up this pollution.

Pyrtle wants to know exactly how nuclear pollution affects the living things in an environment. Scientists already know that it can harm fish. It can also harm the living things that eat fish—including people. Preventing nuclear pollution is very important.

 Think and Write

❶ What kinds of ecosystems are most likely to be affected by nuclear pollution? `3.a`

❷ Pyrtle does a lot of work on the East Coast of the United States. How could studying and cleaning up nuclear pollution on the East Coast help ecosystems in California? `3.a`

Wangari Maathai

Can ordinary people help the environment? Wangari Maathai knows that they can. She was the first woman in East and Central Africa to earn a doctorate degree. Maathai works to protect both Kenya's forests and its people's rights. She is best known for starting the Green Belt Movement.

▶ **DR. WANGARI MAATHAI**

▶ Assistant Minister for the Environment and Natural Resources, Kenya

In Africa, too many trees have been cut for wood and fuel. This has harmed the environment. In 1977, Maathai began organizing groups of women to plant new trees. Maathai's organization became known as the Green Belt Movement. At least 30 million new trees are growing in Kenya because of what the women did. Other African nations are starting their own Green Belt Movements.

The new forests provide shelter for many living things. They also show the people who plant and protect them how they can change their world. The women work to improve the environment. At the same time, they improve their own lives.

✏️ Think and Write

❶ Why do you think the leaders of the Green Belt Movement carefully choose the kinds of trees they plant? `3.b`

❷ How do more forests lead to more animals for Kenya? `3.c`

In 2004, Wangari Maathai received the Nobel Peace Prize for bringing people together to plant millions of trees.

253

Science Content

3.d *Students know* that most microorganisms do not cause disease and that many are beneficial.

Investigation and Experimentation

6.f Follow a set of written instructions for a scientific investigation.

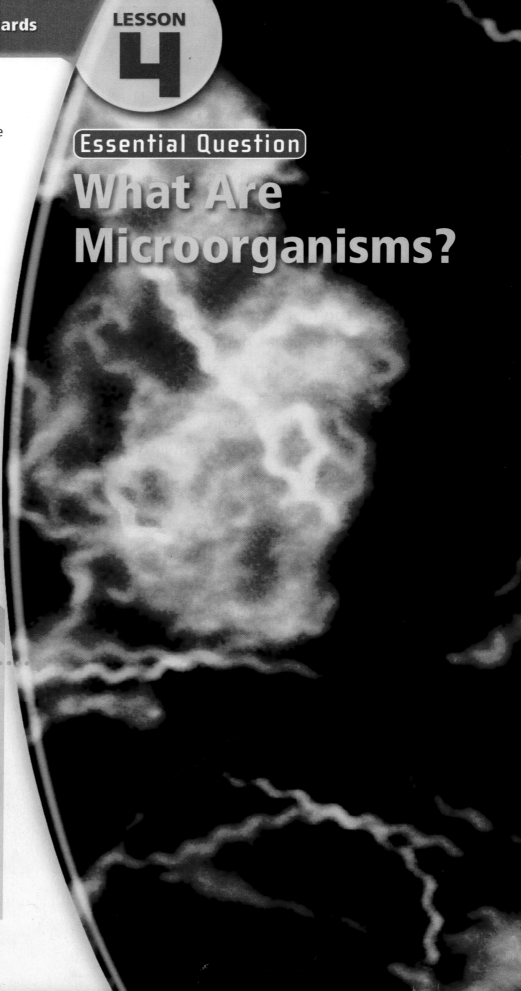

LESSON
4

Essential Question

What Are Microorganisms?

California Fast Fact

Extreme Bacteria

These microorganisms live deep in Mono Lake in California. The dark mud at the bottom of this lake has no oxygen in it. The water is three times as salty as the ocean. Yet these microorganisms are able to grow and meet their needs here.

254

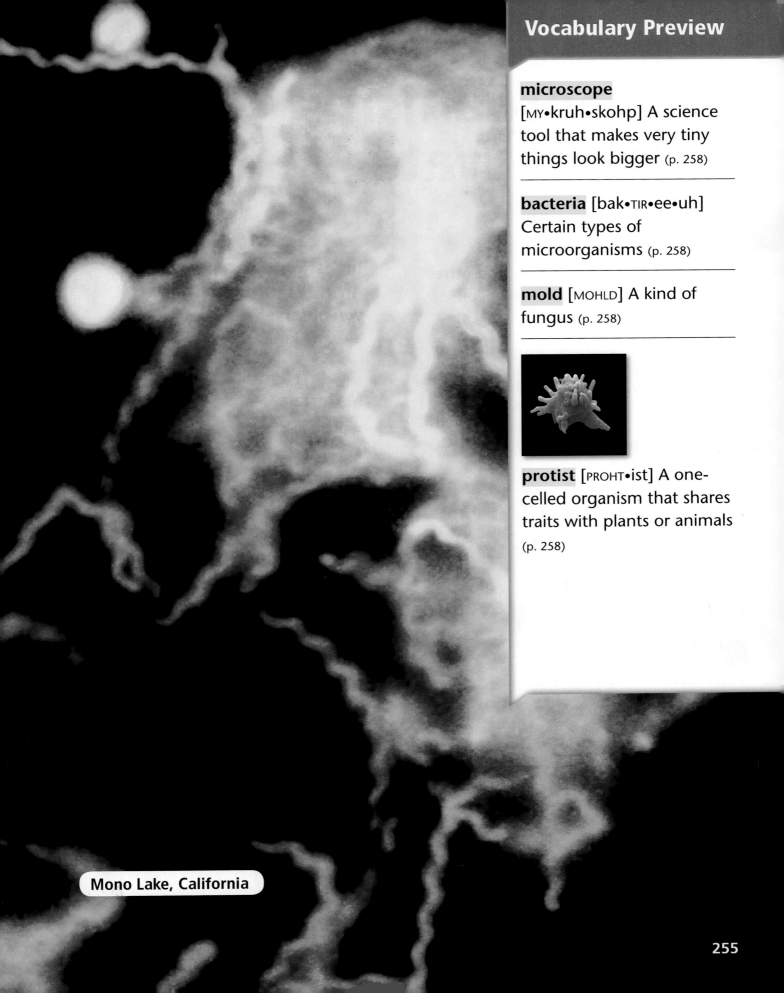

microscope
[MY•kruh•skohp] A science tool that makes very tiny things look bigger (p. 258)

bacteria [bak•TIR•ee•uh] Certain types of microorganisms (p. 258)

mold [MOHLD] A kind of fungus (p. 258)

protist [PROHT•ist] A one-celled organism that shares traits with plants or animals (p. 258)

Mono Lake, California

Microorganisms in Pond Water

Start with Questions

There are more bacteria and other microorganisms all around you than you might think!

- Where might you find bacteria?

- Could you find them in a pond?

Investigate to find out. Then read to find out more.

Yogurt can contain as many as 1 billion bacteria per gram!

Prepare to Investigate

Investigation Skill Tip
An inference is based on what you observe and what you already know.

Materials

- pond or creek water
- hay
- soap
- clear jar and lid
- pipette
- slides and slide covers
- microscope

Make an Observation Chart

Sample	Observations
Week 1	
Week 2 Top	
Week 2 Middle	
Week 2 Bottom	

Follow This Procedure

CAUTION: Always wash your hands thoroughly with soap after handling pond or creek water.

1 Put some water and hay in the jar.

2 With the pipette, put a sample of the water on a slide. Add a slide cover. Then use the microscope to look for living things in the water. Record and draw what you observe.

3 Cover the jar loosely. Wait a week. Then make slides of three more water samples, taken from the top, middle, and bottom of the jar. Label the slides *top, middle,* and *bottom.*

4 Observe the three samples under the microscope. Record and draw what you observe.

Step 2

Step 3

Draw Conclusions

1. Compare your drawings from Step 4 with the one from Step 2. What changes do you notice?

2. **Standards Link** Are there microorganisms in pond water? How many kinds did you find? How many other kinds, if any, did your classmates find? **3.d**

3. **Investigation Skill** What can you **infer** about the role of the hay in this investigation?

Independent Inquiry

Follow Written Steps in an Investigation

Think about the steps in this investigation. What step would you add, take away, or rewrite to make it easier for a younger person to complete the investigation? **6.f**

Write the steps you would take to continue this investigation. What might you add to the jar? When would you take new samples? Carry out your plan.

VOCABULARY
microscope p. 258
bacteria p. 258
mold p. 258
protist p. 258

SCIENCE CONCEPTS
▶ how helpful and harmful microorganisms affect people and the environment

Focus Skill CAUSE AND EFFECT
Look for ways microorganisms affect your life.

cause → effect

Kinds of Microorganisms

Microorganisms are living things that are too small to see without a microscope. In the investigation, you used a **microscope** to magnify things, or make them look bigger.

The environment contains thousands of kinds of microorganisms. Most have only one cell.

Bacteria are microorganisms. There are more bacteria on Earth than all other living things together. Bacteria may be shaped like rods, spirals, or balls.

Yeasts and **molds** are fungi that are microorganisms. Fungi look a little like plants, but they can't make their own food. Fungi are decomposers.

Protists are also microorganisms. There are about 80,000 kinds of protists. Some, such as algae, make their own food. Others, such as protozoans (proht•uh•ZOH•uhnz), hunt for food, as animals do.

Some microorganisms are harmful. The bacteria *Salmonella* and *E. coli* can make you very sick. They grow on raw

You probably have some of this kind of bacteria, called staph, on your skin right now. Staph bacteria can cause annoying pimples or boils. They can also cause serious infections of the blood, bones, and lungs.

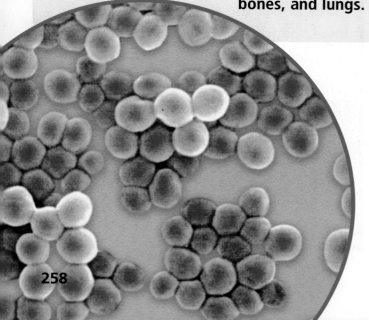

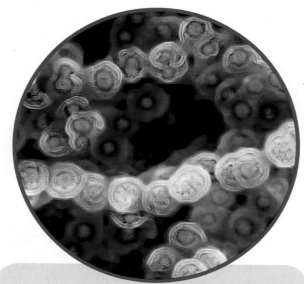

Strep bacteria can be a serious health threat. They cause illness in newborn babies. They can also harm pregnant women, children, older adults, and adults who have certain other illnesses.

This kind of algae can suddenly "bloom," or grow very quickly. People call this reddish water a red tide, though it has nothing to do with tides. Some algae in a red tide contain a poison that can kill fish.

chicken and other meats, raw eggs, and other raw foods. Cooking kills them. Harmful bacteria also grow on cooked food that is left out of the refrigerator for two hours or longer.

Harmful fungi can kill crops. They can also rot wood, spoil food, and cause several kinds of skin diseases, including athlete's foot.

Focus Skill **CAUSE AND EFFECT** Name two effects of harmful microorganisms.

Ringworm infection on skin

The organism that causes ringworm is a fungus, not a worm. Ringworm spreads easily and grows best on warm, moist skin.

Helpful Microorganisms

Many more microorganisms help people than harm them! Without the phytoplankton in the ocean, we wouldn't have enough oxygen to breathe. Other microorganisms make important medicines such as penicillin and streptomycin (strep•tuh•MY•sin). These medicines kill bacteria that cause diseases.

Some microorganisms remove harmful bacteria from wastewater at water treatment plants. Others help clean up oil spills.

Certain bacteria in our digestive systems help break down the foods we eat. Without them, we could not use the nutrients in the food. Without other microorganisms, we would have fewer foods to eat. Bacteria turn milk into yogurt. They also help produce certain kinds of cheese. Yeast makes bread rise.

Phytoplankton is the main food for tiny fish, which are eaten by bigger fish. Without phytoplankton, there would be few fish that we could eat. Certain fungi help plants take in nutrients from the soil. Without nutrients, the plants

Phytoplankton (fyt•oh•PLANGK•tuhn) is made up of tiny protists that float on the surface of the ocean. These protists use photosynthesis to make their own food. They also release oxygen. Phytoplankton produces at least half of the oxygen in the air you breathe.

Penicillin (pen·ih·SIL·in) is a substance made by a mold. It kills harmful bacteria. First used during World War II, it prevented thousands of deaths from infection.

The blue coloring in this cheese is actually mold. This mold, which is related to penicillin, is safe to eat.

Bakers add yeast to bread dough. To grow, the yeast feeds on sugar in the dough. This process releases bubbles of carbon dioxide that cause the dough to rise.

wouldn't grow well, if at all. There would be fewer plants. This would mean less food for people and other animals.

Microorganisms cause dead things to decay. Without them, Earth would be covered with dead plants and animals. We depend on microorganisms in all of these ways to survive.

Focus Skill CAUSE AND EFFECT If all the helpful microorganisms disappeared, what would be five effects?

Insta-Lab

Bubble, Bubble

Mix together 1 packet of active dry yeast, 1 cup of slightly warm water, and 2 tablespoons of sugar. Then watch what happens. What are the bubbles? How do they relate to the tiny holes you see in a slice of bread?

Standards Wrap-Up and Lesson Review

What are microorganisms?

In this lesson, you learned that most microorganisms don't cause disease and that many help people. For example, yeast is what makes bread rise.

Science Content Standard in this Lesson

3.d *Students know* that most microorganisms do not cause disease and that many are beneficial.

1. 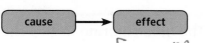 **CAUSE AND EFFECT** Draw and complete a graphic organizer to show the effects of microorganisms in your life. **3.d**

cause	→	effect

5 . main idea

2. **SUMMARIZE** Write two sentences to summarize this lesson. **3.d**

3. **DRAW CONCLUSIONS** How can decay caused by microorganisms be both helpful and harmful? **3.d**

4. **VOCABULARY** What kind of microorganism makes up phytoplankton?

   A protists
   B fungi
   C bacteria
   D yeasts **3.d**

5. **Critical Thinking** Why do you think many people believe that all microorganisms are harmful? **3.d**

6. **Investigate and Experiment** In an investigation, why is it important to follow the written steps carefully? **6.f**

7. Which statement is **not** true?
   A Microorganisms cause diseases.
   B Microorganisms cure diseases.
   C Microorganisms have different shapes.
   D Microorganisms all have two or more cells. **3.d**

8. Explain four ways in which we depend on microorganisms. **3.d**

The **Big** Idea

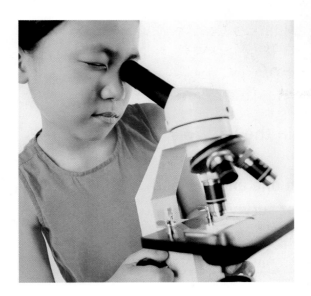

Writing

 ELA—W.2.3

Write a Report

Write a newspaper article about the discovery of a new microorganism. Explain whether it is harmful or helpful. Include quotes from imaginary experts in your article.

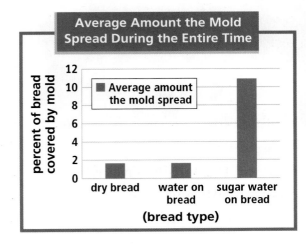

Average Amount the Mold Spread During the Entire Time

 ## Math SDAP 1.3

Use Data

This graph shows how mold grew on different kinds of bread. What conclusions can you draw from this graph? What do you think mold eats?

 ## Health

Does It Work?

Store shelves offer many kinds of antibacterial soap. Do some research to find out whether these soaps will kill bacteria and prevent disease. Are there any reasons not to use antibacterial soap? Write a paragraph that summarizes what you learned.

 For more links and activities, go to www.hspscience.com

Wrap-Up

▶ Visual Summary

Tell how each picture helps explain the **Big Idea**.

The Big Idea Living things depend on one another and on their environment for survival.

3.a, 3.b

Surviving in an Ecosystem
Cactus plants survive well in this dry, hot desert. They have adaptations for a dry climate. A maple tree would die quickly here.

3.c

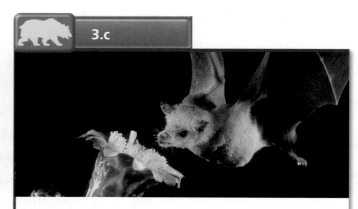

Depending on Each Other
This cactus and this bat, like many other pairs of plants and animals, depend on each other to survive.

3.d

Helpful Microorganisms
We could not survive without some microorganisms. Those in phytoplankton release most of the oxygen we breathe.

Show What You Know

Unit Writing Activity

Write a Persuasive Letter

Learn how your community could protect the honeybees in your environment. Perhaps people could start doing things to attract the bees or stop doing things that harm them. Then write a persuasive letter to the editor of your local newspaper. Explain ways in which we depend on honeybees, and try to persuade your readers to help them.

Unit Project

Yum! Microorganisms in Food!!

Set up a cafeteria display of some foods people eat that depend on microorganisms. You might include bread, cakes, cheeses, and yogurt. Label each kind of food. The label should explain the role microorganisms play in producing the food. You might offer people a taste of some of the foods— but be sure to ask them if they're allergic to anything! Think of a catchy title for your display. The display should make clear that many microorganisms are helpful.

Vocabulary Review

Use the terms below to complete the sentences. The page numbers tell you where to look in the unit if you need help.

ecosystem p. 212   **ecology** p. 218

biome p. 216   **mold** p. 258

adaptation p. 228   **bacteria** p. 258

accommodation p. 229

relationship p. 245

1. Migration is an example of an _accommodation_.   `3.b`

2. The study of ecosystems is known as _ecology_.   `3.a`

3. A large area of land with the same climate and living things is called a _biome_.   `3.a`

4. An animal that learns a new way to find food shows _adaptation_.   `3.b`

5. The living and nonliving things in a pond form an _ecosystem_.   `3.a`

6. One kind of fungus is a _mold_.   `3.d`

7. _Bacteria_ can both cause diseases and be used to cure them.   `3.d`

8. Plants and animals that help each other have a _relationship_.   `3.c`

Check Understanding

Choose the best answer for each question.

9. CAUSE AND EFFECT What always happens when an environment changes?

A Some plants die, but animals adapt.

B Some animals die, but plants adapt.

C Some plants and animals adapt.

D The plants and animals die.   `3.b`

10. MAIN IDEA AND DETAILS What is shown in this photo?   `3.c`

A a population   C migration

B a biome   D interdependence

11. What is one adaptation that helps cactus plants survive in their environment?   `3.b`

A They have no leaves or stems.

B They have a waxy coating.

C They hibernate.

D They don't need water.

Use the image below to answer Questions 12 and 13. **3.a**

12. What does this picture show?
   A microorganisms
   B ecology
   C an ecosystem
   D a population

13. How is this kind of environment different from all other environments? **3.a**
   A It has more kinds of living things.
   B It has fewer kinds of living things.
   C It has no nonliving parts.
   D It has no living things.

14. Which of these is a way that animals help plants?
   A Squirrels live in trees.
   B Birds make nests with grasses.
   C Anemones protect clownfish.
   D Bats drink nectar from flowers. **3.c**

15. Which of these is **not** caused by microorganisms? **3.d**
   A decay   C making oxygen
   B disease   D pollination

16. Which behavior is an accommodation? **3.b**
   A butterflies migrating
   B pigeons living in parks
   C bats hibernating
   D rabbits turning white in winter

Investigation Skills

17. This graph shows the kinds of insects and animals that pollinate plants. What observation can you make? What conclusion can you draw? **3.c** **6.a**

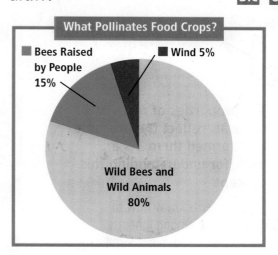

What Pollinates Food Crops?

Bees Raised by People 15%
Wind 5%
Wild Bees and Wild Animals 80%

18. A scientist found that one field has 100 fewer mice than it had a year ago. Should this scientist conclude that the population of this mouse is smaller throughout this ecosystem? Explain. **3.a** **6.d**

Critical Thinking

19. The roots of some plants, such as water lilies, grow underwater. What would happen if you moved a bean plant, which generally grows in moist soil, to the bottom of a deep lake?

The **Big** Idea

20. Why might the use of antibacterial soap, designed to kill microorganisms, be harmful? **3.d**

267

4 Rocks and Minerals

California Standards in this Unit

4 The properties of rocks and minerals reflect the processes that formed them. As a basis for understanding this concept:

4.a *Students know* how to differentiate among igneous, sedimentary, and metamorphic rocks by referring to their properties and methods of formation (the rock cycle).

4.b *Students know* how to identify common rock-forming minerals (including quartz, calcite, feldspar, mica, and hornblende) and ore minerals by using a table of diagnostic properties.

This unit also includes these Investigation and Experimentation Standards: **6.a** **6.c** **6.f**

What's the Big Idea?

You can tell a lot about how a rock or mineral formed by studying its properties.

Essential Questions

Pacific Coast Highway

Dear Anna,

I'm having a great time at my aunt's house. The drive here was fun because we went along the Pacific Coast Highway. We saw a lot of cool rocks along the sides of the road. The rock layers looked as if they'd been squashed and folded together. You've really got to see them!

See you later!
Marisa

What caused the rocks that Marisa described to look squashed? Have you ever seen rocks like that? How do you think the way they looked relates to the **Big Idea?**

Unit Inquiry

Growing Crystals

Some minerals form as water evaporates. What do you think affects how the crystals grow? Plan and carry out an investigation to find out.

Science Content

4.b *Students know* how to identify common rock-forming minerals (including quartz, calcite, feldspar, mica, and hornblende) and ore minerals by using a table of diagnostic properties.

Investigation and Experimentation

6.f Follow a set of written instructions for a scientific investigation.

Essential Question

How Are Minerals Identified?

California Fast Fact

Mega Minerals

Black Chasm Cavern, near Volcano, California, is one of the best places in the world to see rare mineral crystal forms called *helictites.* Some of the crystals are shown here. They formed when water containing dissolved minerals dripped slowly into the caves and evaporated. Over time, just the minerals were left behind.

Black Chasm Cavern near Volcano, California

mineral [MIN•er•uhl]
A nonliving solid that occurs naturally and has a repeating structure (p. 274)

streak [STREEK] The mark left by a mineral when it is rubbed across a rough white tile (p. 276)

luster [LUHS•ter] The brightness and reflecting quality of the surface of a mineral (p. 278)

cleavage [KLEEV•ij] The way that some minerals break into pieces with regular shapes (p. 278)

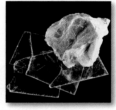

fracture [FRAK•cher] A way that minerals break when they do not cleave, or break into regular shapes (p. 279)

hardness [HARD•nis] A word describing how easily a mineral can be scratched (p. 280)

Mineral Properties

Start with Questions

You use minerals every day. You season your food with minerals. You drink out of cans made from minerals. And if you wear jewelry with gemstones, you are even wearing minerals!

- **What exactly is a mineral?**

- **What are some properties of minerals?**

Investigate to find out. Then read to find out more.

Prepare to Investigate

Investigation Skill Tip
When you classify, you sort objects into groups based on their properties.

Materials

- 6 labeled mineral samples
- hand lens
- steel nail
- streak plate
- glass plate
- pre-1983 penny

Make a Data Table

Sample	Color and Appearance	Streak Color	Scratches These	Is Scratched by These

benitoite crystal and cut, polished benitoite gemstone

Follow This Procedure

CAUTION: Be careful when working with the nail and the glass plate. Nails are sharp.

1 Use the hand lens to **observe** each mineral. Note the color of each mineral. **Record** your observations.

2 With each mineral, draw a line across the streak plate. What color is each mineral's streak? **Record** your observations.

3 Test the hardness of each mineral. Try to scratch each mineral with your fingernail, with the penny, and with the steel nail. Next, try to scratch the glass plate with each mineral. Finally, try to scratch each mineral with each of the other minerals. **Record** your observations.

4 **Classify** the minerals by using the properties you recorded: color, streak, and hardness. For each mineral, make a label that lists color and streak. Put the samples in order by hardness.

Step 2

Step 3

Draw Conclusions

1. How are the mineral samples different from one another?

2. **Standards Link** Which of the minerals you tested is the hardest? Explain your choice. `4.b`

3. **Investigation Skill** Scientists **classify** objects to make them easier to study. How do you think scientists **classify** minerals?

Independent Inquiry
Follow Written Instructions

Obtain five more mineral samples. Follow the instructions in this Investigate to record each mineral's color, streak, and hardness. Write step-by-step instructions to **classify** each of the five mineral samples according to the sample's properties. Exchange instructions with a partner. Test each other's instructions.

VOCABULARY
mineral p. 274
streak p. 276
luster p. 278
cleavage p. 278
fracture p. 279
hardness p. 280

SCIENCE CONCEPTS
► what minerals are
► how to identify minerals

MAIN IDEA AND DETAILS
Look for details about how minerals are identified.

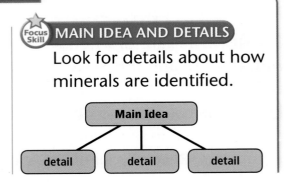

Minerals and How They Form

You've probably heard the word *mineral* before. Beautiful minerals such as diamonds and rubies are used in jewelry. What exactly is a mineral? A **mineral** is a naturally formed, nonliving solid that has a *crystalline* (KRIS•tuhl•in), or repeating, structure.

Minerals may form deposits deep within Earth. Diamonds form about 100 kilometers (60 mi) or more

underground. There, over time, high pressure and temperature turn carbon into its hard mineral form, diamond. Mineral crystals also form when melted rock, or magma, cools deep inside Earth.

Other minerals, such as calcite (CAL•syt), form deposits closer to Earth's surface. Calcite crystals can form on cave walls as dripping water evaporates. In some caves, calcite crystals are up to 7 meters (23 ft) long!

Calcite crystals also form from seawater. This happens when calcium combines with carbon and oxygen. Ocean animals take these materials from water to build shells. However, the shells are not minerals because animals made them.

Hot water underground is often rich in materials that make up minerals. When the water cools, mineral crystals form. Galena

◄ **The amethyst (AM•ih•thist) inside these geodes is a type of quartz. The purple color comes from tiny amounts of materials—such as iron—that are not found in clear quartz.**

When liquid water cools, it forms ice, which is made up of water crystals. When melted rock underneath Earth's surface cools slowly, the result can be mineral crystals. ▼

These feldspar crystals formed from melted rock that cooled slowly. ▶

Large amounts of magma take a long time to cool

Small amounts of magma cool quickly.

(guh•LEE•nuh), a mineral containing lead and sulfur, often forms in this way.

Minerals also form inside geodes (JEE•ohdz). Geodes are often round. They are usually dull in color on the outside, but the inside has crystals that may be bright. A geode may begin as a hole in mud or sand or as a buried animal shell. In time, the hole or shell fills with water and dissolved minerals. As the water evaporates, the minerals in it are left as crystals inside the geode.

MAIN IDEA AND DETAILS Where do minerals form?

Insta-Lab

Pass the Salt, Please

Examine some grains—or tiny pieces—of table salt with a hand lens. Focus on just one grain. Describe its shape. Why would you expect all grains of table salt to have the same structure?

Mineral Color

Some minerals are found in many different colors. Here are five colors of quartz.

amethyst

rose quartz

citrine (SIH•treen)

clear quartz

smoky quartz

Color and Streak

You may already be familiar with several kinds of minerals. Quartz, rubies, and salt are all minerals. Some metals are found as minerals. Copper, silver, and gold are examples. More than 3000 different minerals have been found on Earth. How do scientists identify all these minerals? They use the minerals' *properties,* or characteristics.

One property of minerals that's easy to see is color. Minerals come in a rainbow of colors, but color alone cannot be used to identify a mineral. Some minerals, such as quartz, seem to have many different colors. Pure quartz is clear, however. Some quartz contains small amounts of substances. These substances can make the quartz look pink, purple, gray, or orange.

Minerals change color in other ways, too. For example, pyrite, or fool's gold, has a gold color, but it turns black. This happens when it's exposed to air and rain for a long time.

A mineral can have different colors, so scientists often use other properties to identify it. **Streak** is the color of the powder left behind when a mineral is rubbed against a streak plate. A streak plate is a rough white tile.

Often the streak is the same color as the mineral. However, for some minerals, streak and color do not match.

For example, hematite—iron ore—can be black, dark brown, or silvery. Its streak, though, is always reddish brown. Pyrite is shiny and golden, but its streak can be either greenish black or brownish black.

Streak is usually a better property than color for identifying minerals. That's because, unlike color, streak doesn't often vary. For example, all colors of quartz make the same streak—white.

MAIN IDEA AND DETAILS What are some ways in which the same mineral can be different colors?

Mineral Streak

Compare the colors of the samples to the colors of their streaks

sulfur

galena

hematite

magnetite

▲ Sulfur, magnetite (MAG•nuh•tyt), hematite (HEE•muh•tyt), and galena all have different streaks.

◄ The colors of these two pieces of hematite are different, but their streaks are the same.

hematite

Luster, Cleavage, and Fracture

The way that a mineral's surface reflects light is a property called **luster**. Many minerals have a *metallic* luster. Think of how light reflects off metals such as gold, silver, and copper—that's metallic luster. Pyrite has a metallic luster. Some minerals have a *nonmetallic* luster. The luster of a nonmetallic mineral is described as glassy, silky, waxy, pearly, earthy, or resinous (plastic-like). Examples of different lusters are shown below.

Another property used to identify a mineral is the way the mineral breaks. Different minerals break in different ways. Some minerals have **cleavage**, the property of splitting along a smooth, flat

Mineral Luster

Luster is the way a mineral reflects light. The word for each type of luster describes objects you have seen.

▲ Gypsum (JIP•suhm) has a glassy, silky, or pearly luster.

▼ Pyrite (PY•ryt) has a metallic luster.

▲ Kaolinite (KAY•uh•luh•nyt) has an earthy luster.

◄ Wulfenite (WUL•fuhn•yt) has a resinous or greasy luster.

Talc has a greasy luster. ▶

▲ Artinite (AR•tin•yt) has a shiny luster.

▼ Topaz (TOH•paz) has a glassy luster.

Mineral Cleavage and Fracture

Cleavage and fracture both describe what can happen when a mineral is broken into pieces.

▼ Olivine (AHL•uh•veen) has a curved fracture.

▲ Halite (HAY•lyt) has a cubic cleavage.

▲ Mica (MY•kuh) shows good cleavage. It breaks easily into flat sheets.

surface. Diamond is one kind of mineral that has cleavage. A diamond will always break along flat surfaces in four different directions. Hornblende is another mineral that has easy, regular cleavage. Hornblende breaks along flat surfaces that form 60- and 120-degree angles.

Some minerals do not break along flat surfaces. Instead, they fracture. **Fracture** is the property of breaking unevenly or along a curved surface. Talc is a type of mineral that fractures to form rough clumps. Quartz fractures to form curved surfaces. Some minerals have both fracture and cleavage.

Focus Skill MAIN IDEA AND DETAILS

How would you describe the two main ways that minerals fracture?

Geologists use a special hammer to collect rock samples for study. ▼

Hardness

An important property of minerals is hardness. **Hardness** is a mineral's ability to scratch other materials or be scratched by other materials.

A scale called the *Mohs hardness scale* ranks minerals from 1 to 10 according to their hardness. Talc, the softest mineral, is ranked 1. Diamond, the hardest mineral, is ranked 10.

A mineral can scratch another mineral if its hardness value is greater than or equal to the other mineral's hardness value. Look at the values at the bottom of these pages. For example, gypsum has a hardness of 2. One piece of gypsum can scratch another piece of gypsum. Gypsum can also scratch talc, but gypsum cannot scratch calcite. Calcite has a hardness of 3.

The Mohs scale is easy to use. If you know the hardness of several minerals, you can use these minerals to find the hardness of an unknown mineral.

The table on the next page is called a *table of diagnostic properties.* It lists minerals and their properties. You can use it to identify minerals. First, you note the properties of the mineral sample that you want to identify. Then, you look for properties on the table that match your sample. When all of the properties match, you've identified your mineral sample.

(Focus Skill) MAIN IDEA AND DETAILS How can you find the hardness of a mineral?

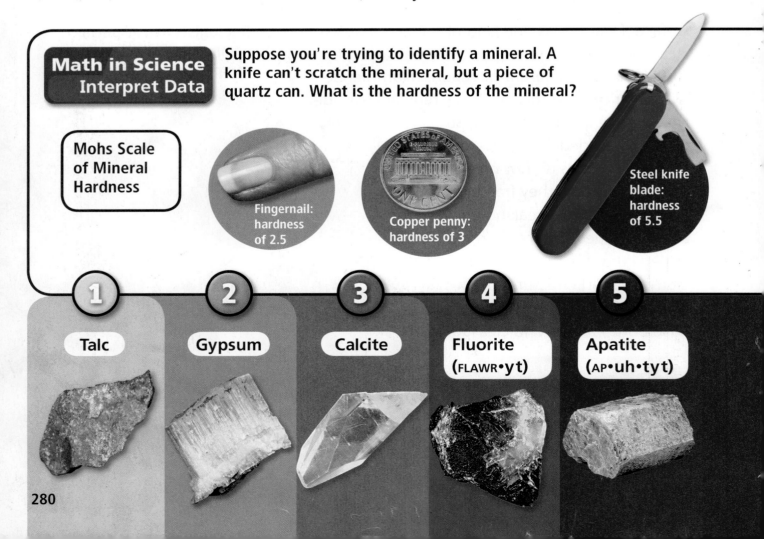

**Math in Science
Interpret Data**

Suppose you're trying to identify a mineral. A knife can't scratch the mineral, but a piece of quartz can. What is the hardness of the mineral?

Mohs Scale of Mineral Hardness

Fingernail: hardness of 2.5

Copper penny: hardness of 3

Steel knife blade: hardness of 5.5

1 — Talc

2 — Gypsum

3 — Calcite

4 — Fluorite (FLAWR•yt)

5 — Apatite (AP•uh•tyt)

280

Diagnostic Properties of Minerals

Mineral	Hardness	Luster	Streak	Color	Cleavage/Fracture
calcite	3	glassy	colorless or white	colorless, white, or various other colors	easy cleavage and curved fracture
copper	2.5–3	metallic	copper orange	copper-orange to dark red	jagged fracture
feldspar	6–6.5	glassy	colorless or white	gray, green, and white	easy cleavage and curved fracture
fluorite	4	glassy	colorless	colorless, white, or various colors	easy cleavage in eight directions
galena	2.5	metallic	gray to black	gray	cubic cleavage
gold	2.5–3	metallic	yellow	gold	jagged fracture
gypsum	2	pearly	white	colorless, gray, white, or brown	easy cleavage and curved fracture
hematite	6	metallic or earthy	reddish brown	black, dark brown, or silvery	curved fracture
hornblende	5–6	glassy or earthy	gray to white	green to black	easy cleavage and jagged fracture
magnetite	6	metallic or earthy	black	black	curved fracture
mica	2–3	pearly	white	silver gray, black, various colors	easy cleavage along one surface
pyrite	6.5	metallic	greenish black	light brassy yellow, black	curved fracture
quartz	7	glassy	colorless	colorless, various colors	curved fracture
talc	1	waxy	white	white, greenish	irregular fracture
topaz	8	glassy	colorless	colorless, white, pink, yellow, blue	easy cleavage and curved fracture

Glass: hardness of 6

6 Orthoclase (ORTH•oh•klays)

7 Quartz

8 Topaz

9 Ruby

10 Diamond

Standards Wrap-Up and Lesson Review

What are minerals?

In this lesson, you learned how to identify some common minerals by using their properties.

Science Content Standard in this Lesson

4.b *Students know* how to identify common rock-forming minerals (including quartz, calcite, feldspar, mica, and hornblende) and ore minerals by using a table of diagnostic properties.

1. **MAIN IDEA AND DETAILS** Draw and complete a graphic organizer to summarize the lesson's main idea and details that support it. **4.b**

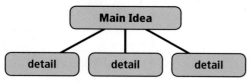

2. **SUMMARIZE** Use the graphic organizer to write a lesson summary. **4.b**

3. **DRAW CONCLUSIONS** Suppose you have two mineral samples with the same hardness. What other mineral properties could you use to decide whether the two samples are the same mineral? **4.b**

4. **VOCABULARY** Which of the following mineral properties can be expressed by a number?

A color   C luster
B hardness   D streak   **4.b**

5. **Critical Thinking** Some people think a gem is a diamond if it scratches glass. Is this a good way to identify a diamond? Explain your answer. **4.b**

6. **Investigation Skill** Write a set of instructions on how to classify a mineral by using hardness. **6.f**

7. If you hit a mineral sample with a hammer, which property are you testing?
A cleavage/fracture
B hardness
C luster
D streak   **4.b**

8. How is the hardness of a diamond related to the way it was formed? **4.b**

The Big Idea

 ## Writing   ELA—W 2.3

Write a Composition

Suppose you're a scientist who has discovered a new mineral. Write two paragraphs describing where you found it, how the mineral was formed, and how you will use the mineral's properties to identify it. Give your mineral a name.

 ## Math   MG 3.6

Model Geometric Figures

Use paper, cardboard, or other material to make a model of a mineral crystal. Start by drawing a pattern for crystal faces that will make a three-dimensional model when the pattern is cut and folded.

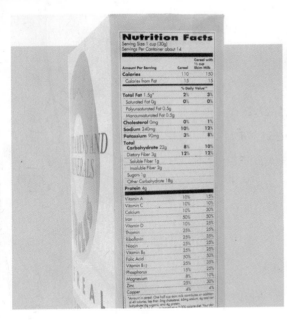

 ## Health

Eat Your Minerals

Some minerals, such as iron and halite, are important to your health. Research five minerals that are needed in a healthful diet. Put together a one-day meal plan that would provide a person with healthful amounts of these minerals.

 For more links and activities, go to **www.hspscience.com**

California State Mining and Mineral Museum

It was cold and clear at the American River near Coloma, California, on the morning of January 24, 1848. A work crew was heading out to build a mill on the river. They didn't know that they were about to find a few tiny specks of a mineral that would change history. Their discovery started one of the largest human migrations ever. What mineral caused more than half a million people to move to California in the 1840s and 1850s? Gold!

Mining platform at California State Mining and Mineral Museum

The California Gold Rush

The discovery of gold in the American River led to the California Gold Rush. People from all over the world moved to California to look for gold. Gold was not only found in rivers and streams, but also in mines, along with quartz and other minerals.

As more mines were started, California's mineral wealth became more and more evident. California was rich not only in gold, but also in gemstones. California is still the biggest producer of natural gemstones in the United States.

From a Mine to a Museum

So, where can you go to see some of California's gold and gemstones? The California State Mining and Mineral Museum, in Mariposa, is a great start. The museum is home to the California State Mineral Collection, which includes more than 13,000 minerals, rocks, and related items. One impressive mineral on display is the Fricot Nugget—a 5700-g (12.5-lb) chunk of gold!

The museum also has displays about mining. For example, the Mining Tunnel shows visitors what an underground miner's life was like during the Gold Rush. The next time you would like to dig deeper into California's history, head to the California State Mining and Mineral Museum.

Part of the museum's mineral collection

✎ Think and Write

1 Why is knowing about mineral properties important to miners?

4.b

2 What was one major effect of the California Gold Rush on California's history?

California Standards in This Lesson

Science Content

4.a *Students know* how to differentiate among igneous, sedimentary, and metamorphic rocks by referring to their properties and methods of formation (the rock cycle).

Investigation and Experimentation

6.a Differentiate observation from inference (interpretation) and know scientists' explanations come partly from what they observe and partly from how they interpret their observations.

California Fast Fact

A Mountain of Glass

Medicine Lake Volcano is the largest volcano in the Cascade Mountains. Its lava is spread out over 2000 square kilometers (770 sq mi). That's more than $1\frac{1}{2}$ times the size of Los Angeles! Glass Mountain is part of Medicine Lake Volcano. It gets its name from the volcanic glass it's made of.

LESSON 2

Essential Question

How Are Rocks Identified?

286

Glass Mountain near Dunmuir, California

rock [RAHK] A naturally occurring solid made of one or more minerals (p. 290)

igneous rock [IG•nee•uhs] Rock that forms when melted rock cools (p. 292)

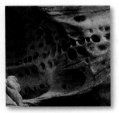

sedimentary rock [sed•uh•MEN•tuh•ree] Rock that forms from sand, mud, and other eroded materials (p. 294)

metamorphic rock [met•uh•MAWR•fik] Rock that has been changed through temperature and pressure without being melted (p. 296)

287

Identifying Rocks

Start with Questions

You probably see rocks every day. Rocks are used to build things such as homes, monuments, and garden paths.

- What exactly are rocks?

- Why is one rock different from another?

Investigate to find out. Then read to find out more.

Prepare to Investigate

Investigation Skill Tip
When you make an inference, you make a guess based on what you observe.

Materials

- 5 labeled rock samples
- hand lens
- dropper
- safety goggles
- vinegar
- paper plate

Make a Data Table

Sample	Picture	Texture	Observations

Follow This Procedure

CAUTION: Put on safety goggles.

1. Copy the table on page 288. In the column labeled *Picture,* make a drawing of each rock.

2. Use the hand lens to **observe** the color or colors of each rock. In the table, **record** your observations.

3. **Observe** any grains, or pieces, making up the rock. Under *Texture* in the table, **record** your observations.

4. Put the rocks on the paper plate. Use the dropper to gently put a few drops of vinegar on each rock. Vinegar makes bubbles form on rocks that contain the mineral calcite. **Observe** the results, and **record** your findings.

5. **Classify** the rocks into two groups so that the rocks in each group have similar properties.

Step 2

Step 4

Draw Conclusions

1. What properties did you use to classify the rocks?

2. **Standard Link** Ask at least two other students how they classified their rocks. Compare these classification systems. 4.a

3. **Investigation Skill** Scientists use their observations to make inferences about how rocks form. Choose one of the rocks, and **infer** how it might have formed.

Independent Inquiry

Interpret Observations

Use your observations from the Investigate to **infer** the best property to use to identify rocks. Try to **classify** five more rock samples according to the property you chose. Was it easy to classify the rocks by using the property? Was your inference correct? 6.a

VOCABULARY
rock p. 290
igneous rock p. 292
sedimentary rock p. 294
metamorphic rock p. 296

SCIENCE CONCEPTS
▶ how to tell the difference between types of rocks
▶ how different types of rocks form

 COMPARE AND CONTRAST
Look for ways in which rocks are similar to and different from each other.

| alike | different |

Rocks and Classification

What are mountains, valleys, hills, beaches, and the ocean floor all made of? Rocks! Rocks are found everywhere on Earth. You've probably seen many different kinds of rocks. All of them have one thing in common—minerals. A **rock** is a natural solid made of one or more minerals. In fact, you can think of most rocks as mineral mixtures.

Not all rocks contain the same kinds of minerals. Because of this, you can identify a rock by finding out which minerals it contains. For example, limestone is made up mostly of the mineral calcite. Limestone may contain small amounts of other minerals, too. Different rock types might contain the same minerals but in different proportions. They might also contain different minerals. Compare the minerals in the rocks shown on this page. How are they alike?

Both of these rocks contain the minerals hornblende and feldspar but in different amounts. Each rock also contains at least one mineral not found in the other rock. ▶

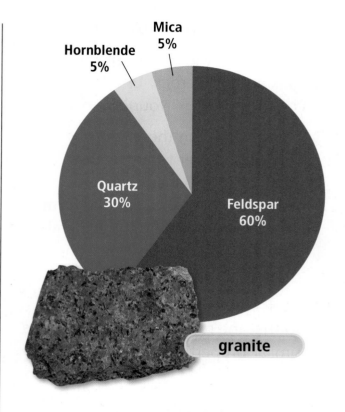

Hornblende 5%
Mica 5%
Quartz 30%
Feldspar 60%

granite

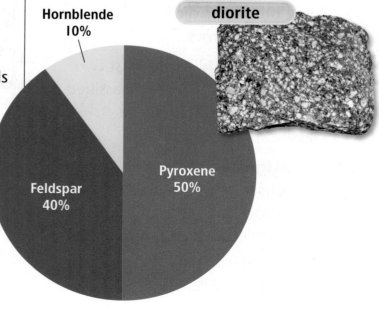

diorite

Hornblende 10%
Feldspar 40%
Pyroxene 50%

Rock Texture

Fine-grained rocks, like this siltstone, have very small grains. The grains touch but do not interlock.

Medium-grained rocks, like this sandstone, have a texture that is between the textures of fine-grained rocks and coarse-grained rocks.

Coarse-grained rocks, like this conglomerate (kuhn•GLAHM•er•it), have large rounded grains that can be the size of pebbles.

The size and shape of a rock's grains affect the rock's *texture.* Texture is a property you can use to classify rocks. You described the textures of the rocks in the Investigate. Some rocks, such as siltstone and sandstone, are alike except for their textures. Siltstone has small grains. Sandstone has medium grains. The different textures help scientists tell these rocks apart.

 **COMPARE AND CONTRAST** What is the difference between fine-grained rocks and coarse-grained rocks?

Igneous Rock

Rocks are classified into one of three groups, depending on how they form. One group is called **igneous rock**, which forms when melted rock cools and hardens. Igneous rock can form underground or on Earth's surface. Most igneous rocks are hard and do not have layers. Unlike sedimentary rock, the particles that make up igneous rock interlock tightly.

Igneous rocks themselves can be grouped by how they form. Igneous rocks that form underground look different from igneous rocks that form on Earth's surface. That's because melted rock cools much more slowly underground than on Earth's surface.

Crystals in Igneous Rock

Pumice, obsidian, and rhyolite are igneous rocks that form at or near Earth's surface. Pumice and rhyolite have very small mineral crystals. Obsidian hardens too quickly for any crystals to form—it is a glass.

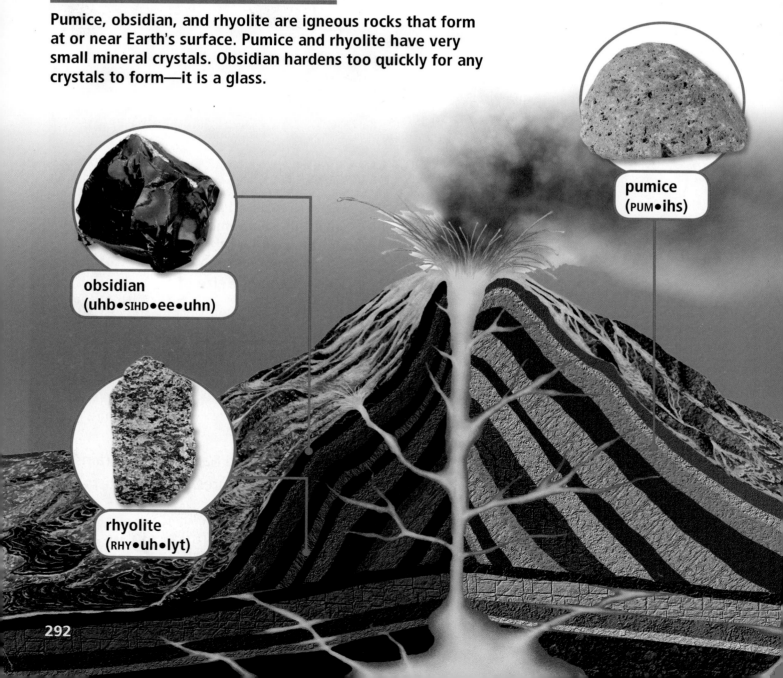

pumice
(PUM•ihs)

obsidian
(uhb•SIHD•ee•uhn)

rhyolite
(RHY•uh•lyt)

When melted rock cools slowly, mineral crystals have time to grow. Because of this, igneous rocks that form underground tend to have large crystals.

When melted rock cools quickly, it hardens before mineral crystals can grow large. As a result, igneous rocks that form above ground have small crystals or no crystals at all.

Igneous rocks also differ in another way. They are classified by how much of the substance silica they contain. Silica (SIL•ih•kuh) is found in many forms. Quartz is almost pure silica. Granite is an igneous rock that contains quartz. Because it contains a lot of quartz, granite is rich in silica. Such rocks tend to be light in color.

Some igneous rocks form from melted rock that does not have as much silica in it. These rocks are mostly made up of other minerals. For example, gabbro and basalt (buh•SAWLT) contain a lot of hornblende and minerals that contain iron. These minerals make the rocks dark in color.

Focus Skill **COMPARE AND CONTRAST** How is granite different from basalt?

Granite, diorite, and gabbro all form underneath Earth's surface. Because of this, they all have large mineral crystals. The main difference between these rocks is the minerals they contain. ▼

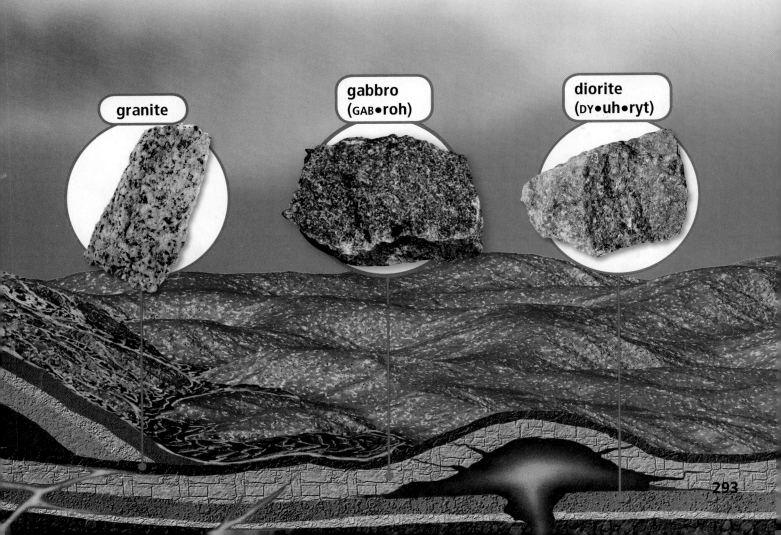

granite

gabbro (GAB•roh)

diorite (DY•uh•ryt)

Sedimentary Rock

Picture a rock at the top of a hill. Every spring, rain falls on the rock. The rain dissolves some of the rock's minerals. In the summer, heat causes the rock to crack. Small pieces flake off. Fall comes, and dust blown by the wind scratches the rock's surface. In the winter, water seeps into cracks in the rock and freezes. The ice expands and breaks off more pieces of the rock. This rock is slowly being worn away.

What happens to all these little pieces of rock, called *sediment*, that have broken off? Water and wind carry away the sediment. Then it drops in another place.

Over time, sediment piles up, one layer on top of another. The top layers push down on the bottom layers and press water out of them. Some minerals that were in the water may be left behind. They can form a kind of glue, or cement. The cement makes the pieces of sediment stick together. **Sedimentary rock** is made up of this stuck-together sediment. The sediment pieces do not interlock tightly.

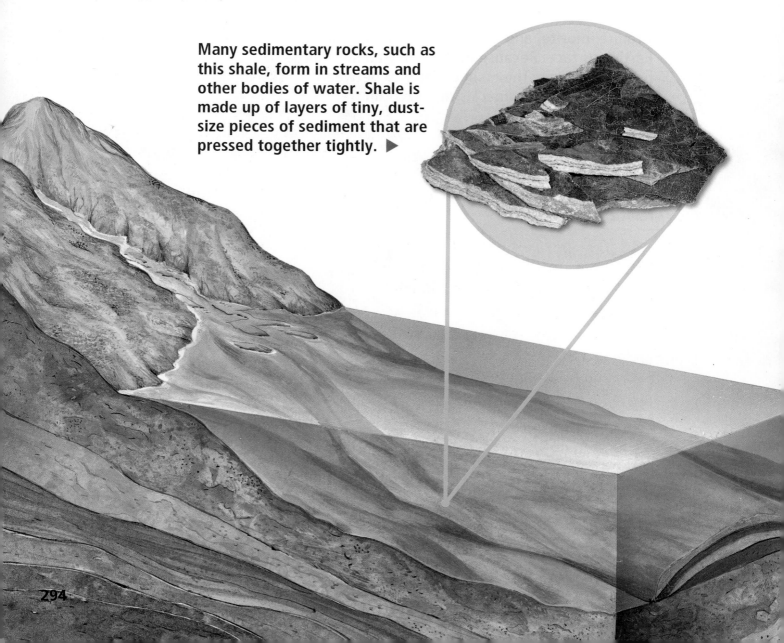

Many sedimentary rocks, such as this shale, form in streams and other bodies of water. Shale is made up of layers of tiny, dust-size pieces of sediment that are pressed together tightly. ▶

Types of Sedimentary Rocks

Like limestone, chert forms from the remains of living things. Chert is rich in silica and often forms on the ocean floor.

Sandstone is a sedimentary rock made up of sediment pieces the size of sand grains.

Coal forms from the remains of plants. As the plant matter is buried under layers of sediment, it is pushed together. Water and gases are pressed out.

Limestone is a sedimentary rock that usually forms in oceans, sometimes from seashells. The shells contain the substance that forms calcite.

Sedimentary rocks can form from any kind of rock that is worn down. They can contain sediment of any size. Some sedimentary rocks may also contain shells or other remains of living things. Some sedimentary rocks form when water that is rich in minerals evaporates.

Because sedimentary rock is formed from small pieces of other rock that have been "glued" together, this type of rock is often softer than other types. Most sedimentary rocks show layers.

 **COMPARE AND CONTRAST** How are limestone, chert, and coal similar?

Insta-Lab

Make a Sedimentary Rock

Put small pebbles, shells, and particles of sand and soil in a paper cup. Cover the "sediment" with glue. When the glue hardens, tear the cup away. How is this similar to the way a sedimentary rock forms?

Metamorphic Rock

Rock that is changed by high temperature and pressure without being melted is called **metamorphic rock**. Most metamorphic rocks are very hard. Many metamorphic rocks have mineral crystals that are lined up or arranged in stripes or bands. High temperature softens mineral crystals. Then high pressure locks them together. Sometimes the crystals flow into stripes.

To understand how pressure can change a rock, suppose a handful of small clay pellets are loosely gathered into a ball. Someone places several heavy books on the ball. What will happen? The clay will become a dense, flat sheet.

Now suppose the clay ball is a rock deep inside Earth. The weight of everything above the rock squashes it. The rock is also very hot, because temperature rises as you go deeper inside Earth. The high temperature makes the rock soft. So the rock, like the clay, changes shape. It becomes denser. It also may form layers and folds.

Metamorphic rocks form in other places, too. They form deep under the ocean floor, where there is a lot of pressure. They also form near volcanoes, where the temperature is high. The picture on these pages shows how different metamorphic rocks form.

 COMPARE AND CONTRAST What is similar about all places where metamorphic rocks form?

How Metamorphic Rocks Form

With enough pressure and temperature, both sedimentary rock and igneous rock can be changed into metamorphic rock. Even metamorphic rock can be changed into other kinds of metamorphic rock. These changes usually take a long time.

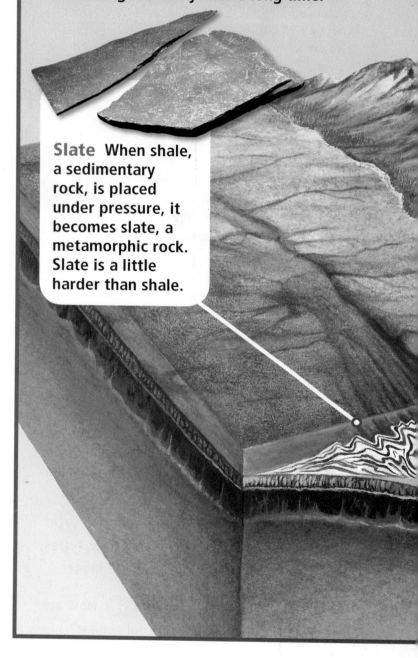

Slate When shale, a sedimentary rock, is placed under pressure, it becomes slate, a metamorphic rock. Slate is a little harder than shale.

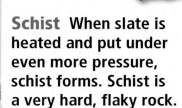

Schist When slate is heated and put under even more pressure, schist forms. Schist is a very hard, flaky rock.

Gneiss (NYS) When the temperature and pressure that formed schist increase, schist changes and forms gneiss. Sometimes, pressure folds gneiss into bands.

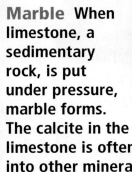

Marble When limestone, a sedimentary rock, is put under pressure, marble forms. The calcite in the limestone is often changed into other minerals in the marble. The minerals are pressed closer together, making marble denser and harder than limestone.

Essential Question

How Are Rocks Identified?

In this lesson, you learned some of the properties of igneous, sedimentary, and metamorphic rocks. These properties can tell you how the rocks formed.

Science Content Standard in This Lesson

4.a *Students know* how to differentiate among igneous, sedimentary, and metamorphic rocks by referring to their properties and methods of formation (the rock cycle).

1.  **COMPARE AND CONTRAST** Draw and complete a graphic organizer that compares and contrasts the three types of rock. **4.a**

   alike —— different

2. **SUMMARIZE** Use the lesson vocabulary terms to write a summary of this lesson. **4.a**

3. **DRAW CONCLUSIONS** Why are shells and other remains of living things not found in igneous rock? **4.a**

4. **VOCABULARY** What type of rock forms when sediment piles up?
   A igneous
   B melted
   C metamorphic
   D sedimentary **4.a**

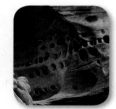

5. **Critical Thinking** How does the cooling rate of melted rock affect the texture of igneous rock? **4.a**

6. **Investigate and Experiment** Explain what scientists can observe about a rock that would help them infer how the rock formed. **6.a**

7. How are rocks classified into three types?
   A by hardness
   B by how they form
   C by crystal size
   D by texture **4.a**

8. You find a rock with large, tightly joined crystals. The rock shows no signs of layering. What type of rock have you most likely found? Where was the rock most likely formed? Explain how you know. **4.a**

 The **Big** Idea

Writing ELA—W 2.3

Write a Report

Research the origins of the words *igneous*, *sedimentary*, and *metamorphic*. Write a short paragraph that explains the meanings of the parts of these words.

9÷3 Math NS 1.7

Identify Fractions

The table shows the fraction of quartz in different types of rock. Draw a circle to represent each rock. In the circle, color the fraction of the rock that is quartz.

Type of Rock	Fraction of the Rock Made Up of Quartz
Granite	$\frac{1}{3}$
Sandstone	$\frac{1}{2}$
Quartzite	$\frac{9}{10}$

Art VPA—A 2.7

Make a Mosaic

Use different kinds of rocks to make a mosaic. Make a picture by contrasting light-colored rocks with dark-colored rocks. Try to use the properties of the rocks in your mosaic to identify them.

 For more links and activities, go to **www.hspscience.com**

Karen Chin

▶ **DR. KAREN CHIN**

▶ **Dinosaur scientist**

▶ The world's leading expert on dinosaur coprolites (fossilized animal droppings)

Many sedimentary rocks contain *fossils,* or traces of past life. As sediments pile up, the remains of animals often get buried. The remains can harden and become rock. Many things can be fossilized—even an animal's droppings! That's where Dr. Karen Chin comes in. Dr. Chin is the world's top expert on dinosaur dung.

Dr. Chin analyzed one of the largest pieces of dino dung ever found—44 cm long! It was left by a *Tyrannosaurus rex* (tuh•ran•uh•SAWR•uhs REKS), or *T. rex.* Dr. Chin studied the fossil to find out what the dinosaur had eaten. She found that the *T. rex* had snacked on another dinosaur called a *Triceratops* (try•SER•uh•tahps). A close look at the bone fragments showed that the *Triceratops* was young. It was only as big as a cow.

coprolite

✎ Think and Write

❶ What do you think Dr. Chin could learn by studying the dung of a plant-eating dinosaur?

❷ Why do you think almost all fossils are found in sedimentary rock? 4.a

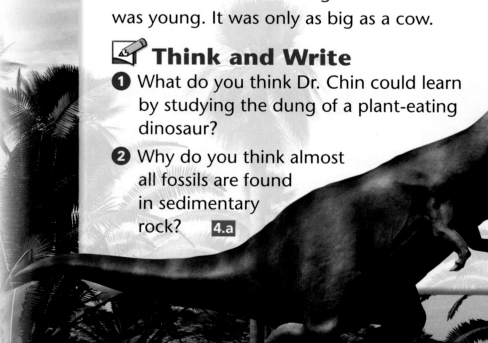

Tyrannosaurus rex

Robert Verish

About 25 years ago, Robert Verish was hiking through the Mojave Desert. Two strange-looking rocks caught his eye. Their color and texture were very different from other nearby rocks. Verish took the rocks home to add to his rock collection.

Years went by before Verish looked more closely at the rocks. He noticed that the rocks seemed to have a burned crust. He began to think that the rocks were not normal Earth rocks. Instead, he thought they were meteorites (MEET•ee•uhr•yts). *Meteorites* are rocks from space.

▶ **MR. ROBERT VERISH**

▶ **Rock Hunter**

▶ Discovered one of only 34 known Mars meteorites

Verish took samples of the rocks to the University of California in Los Angeles. Scientists analyzed the samples. Verish was right! The rocks were meteorites. They weren't just any kind of meteorite, though. They were from Mars. Verish's rocks were only the second Martian meteorites ever found in the United States. One of Verish's meteorites is now displayed at the Natural History Museum in Los Angeles.

Think and Write

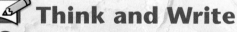

1 What observation led Verish to collect the meteorites?

2 Why do you think a rock from Mars would be different from an Earth rock? 4.b

One of Verish's Mars meteorites

The Eberswalde Delta on Mars

Science Content

4.a *Students know* how to differentiate among igneous, sedimentary, and metamorphic rocks by referring to their properties and methods of formation (the rock cycle).

Investigation and Experimentation

6.c Formulate and justify predictions based on cause-and-effect relationships.

California Fast Fact

Disappearing Act

At Pinnacles National Monument, about 500 columns of rock rise as high as 365 meters (1200 ft) into the air. These rocks are all that remain of an ancient volcano. How did a huge volcanic mountain become just scattered columns of rock? The mountain was worn away by winds and rain over a period of 23 million years.

LESSON

3

Essential Question

What Is the Rock Cycle?

Pinnacles National Monument near Soledad, California

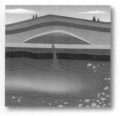

magma [MAG•muh] Molten rock that is beneath Earth's surface (p. 306)

lava [LAH•vuh] Molten rock that is on Earth's surface (p. 306)

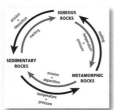

rock cycle [RAHK SY•kuhl] An endless process in which rocks are changed from one type to another by weathering, erosion, and high pressure and temperature (p. 308)

weathering: The process of wearing away rock

Erosiml Procen of carring away sedimen from their source

Deasitionl proces setting down sedent of

Modeling Changes in Rock

Start with Questions

You may have seen round, smooth pebbles on a beach or in a stream.

- How did the pebbles become round and smooth?

- In what other ways can rocks change?

Investigate to find out. Then read to find out more.

Prepare to Investigate

Investigation Skill Tip

A model is a simpler way to show something that is very large, small, or complex. You can understand how something works by studying the model rather than the real thing. Using a model can also help you understand a process that happens too slowly in nature for people to observe.

Materials

- clay of 3 different colors
- metric ruler
- 2 sheets of wax paper
- plastic foam pellets
- dowel
- 2 blocks of wood

Make a Data Table

Step Number	What the Model Looks Like
4	
5	
6	

Follow This Procedure

1. Use clay of one color to **make a model** of a layer of sediment about 12 cm square and 2 cm thick. Place the clay on wax paper.

2. Use clay of another color to make 5 to 10 2-cm pellets. Place them and the foam pellets on the model.

3. Use the third color of clay to make a second layer of sediment. Place it over the pellet layer.

4. Place a sheet of wax paper on top of the model. Press gently to form a model of sedimentary rock.

5. Roll the dowel to apply pressure to the top of the model. Next, place the wooden blocks at the sides of the model. Then, press the model into a new shape. The model now represents a different type of rock.

6. Now **use the model** to show how rock can change again from one type of rock into another. Make drawings to show all the changes.

Draw Conclusions

1. What new type of rock did the model represent in Step 5?

2. **Standards Link** How might high pressure and temperature affect igneous rock? `4.a`

3. **Investigation Skill** How might **using models** help scientists study the ways rocks are formed?

Step 2

Step 5

Independent Inquiry — **Make Predictions**

Design and **use a model** that can help you **predict** how rocks in certain areas might change over time. Think of cause-and-effect relationships that tell how rocks are changed. For example, water causes rocks to wear down. You might predict that a rock in a river will wear down faster than a rock on dry land. `6.c`

VOCABULARY
magma p. 306
lava p. 306
rock cycle p. 308

SCIENCE CONCEPTS

▶ how rocks change over time

▶ how rocks move through the rock cycle

Focus Skill CAUSE AND EFFECT

Look for processes that cause rocks to change.

cause ➞ effect

Processes That Change Rocks

Molten, or melted, rock under Earth's surface is called **magma**. In some places in the world, magma rises up to the surface through cracks in Earth's crust. If the magma erupts onto Earth's surface, a volcano forms.

The magma that flows out of a volcano onto Earth's surface is called **lava**. Molten lava cools and hardens to form igneous rock. That's not the end of the story for the newly formed rock. On Earth, rock is constantly being formed and worn away.

Igneous rock, like all rocks on Earth's surface, may be exposed to running water, ice, wind, and sunlight. All these things wear away rocks into sediment. The process of wearing away rocks is called *weathering*. Rocks that contain soft minerals are weathered much faster than rocks that contain hard minerals.

Weathering is only one process that changes rocks on Earth's surface. Wind

Rock that has been worn down by wind and water is rounded and cracked.

As soon as molten lava cools and forms igneous rock, the rock begins to wear away.

The Colorado River erodes sediment from upstream areas and moves it downstream. Some of the sediment is deposited at the river's mouth, forming a delta, a piece of new land.

and running water move sediment from one place to another. The process of carrying sediment away from its source is called *erosion* (ee•ROH•zhuhn).

After sediment is eroded, it can be deposited, or set down. This is called *deposition* (deh•puh•ZISH•uhn). If the pieces of sediment are pressed together and cemented, sedimentary rock forms.

High pressure and temperature, which form metamorphic rock, are common deep inside Earth. High pressure and temperature are also caused where large rock masses push against each other. One such place is where mountains are forming. Rock layers in mountain ranges often look folded, broken, and tilted. This shows that the rocks have been through many changes.

CAUSE AND EFFECT What causes igneous rock to be changed into sedimentary rock?

People cut this rock to make a road. You can see how the rock layers were bent and folded as the mountain was formed. ▶

307

The Rock Cycle

Weathering, erosion, deposition, heat, and pressure can all change rocks. Together, these processes make up the rock cycle. The **rock cycle** is the endless process in which rocks are changed from one type to another.

The rock cycle never stops—rocks are constantly changing. This usually doesn't happen quickly. Rocks change into other kinds of rocks over thousands or even millions of years. The Science Up Close feature on this page shows the different paths that rocks can follow in the rock cycle. Study the feature to see how the rock cycle works.

The ways rocks form affect their properties in the rock cycle. Igneous rocks have tightly interlocking mineral grains. Sedimentary rocks have loosely interlocking grains. Metamorphic rocks look as if they've been heated and squeezed.

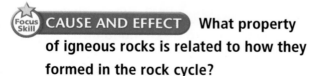 **CAUSE AND EFFECT** What property of igneous rocks is related to how they formed in the rock cycle?

Soil and the Rock Cycle

Soil is always forming. This is part of the rock cycle. Pick up a handful of soil, and look at it with a hand lens. What do you see? What type of rock might be formed from layers of soil?

The Rock Cycle

Much as you recycle aluminum cans and waste paper, processes on Earth recycle rocks through the rock cycle.

Igneous Rock
Weathering and erosion can change granite, an igneous rock, into sandstone, a sedimentary rock. High pressure and temperature can change granite into a metamorphic rock. With high enough temperature, granite can melt, then cool and harden into new igneous rock.

For more links and animations, go to **www.hspscience.com**

Sedimentary Rock

High temperature and pressure can change sandstone, a sedimentary rock, into gneiss, a metamorphic rock. If sandstone becomes molten magma, the magma can cool to form an igneous rock. If sandstone is weathered and eroded, it can form a new sedimentary rock.

Metamorphic Rock

Gneiss, a metamorphic rock, can be weathered, eroded, deposited, and cemented into a sedimentary rock. If a metamorphic rock melts and then hardens again, it will become an igneous rock. With high pressure and temperature, a metamorphic rock can become a different kind of metamorphic rock.

Standards Wrap-Up and Lesson Review

What Is the Rock Cycle?

In this lesson, you learned how properties of rocks are related to they way they formed in the rock cycle.

Science Content Standard in This Lesson

4.a *Students know* how to differentiate among igneous, sedimentary, and metamorphic rocks by referring to their properties and methods of formation (the rock cycle).

1. (**Focus Skill**) **CAUSE AND EFFECT** Draw and complete a graphic organizer that shows three causes and their effects that are parts of the rock cycle. **4.a**

   cause → effect

2. **SUMMARIZE** Write a paragraph that summarizes this lesson. Begin with this sentence: *The rock cycle works slowly and never stops.* **4.a**

3. **DRAW CONCLUSIONS** How might igneous rock become metamorphic rock? **4.a**

4. **VOCABULARY** Define the term *rock cycle* in your own words without using the word *cycle*. **4.a**

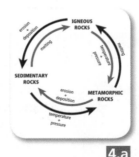

5. **Critical Thinking** Identify and describe a part of the rock cycle that you might see. **4.a**

6. **Investigate and Experiment** Suppose that sedimentary rock, deep under the ocean floor, is buried under hundreds of tons of sediment. What do you predict will happen to the rock?

   A It will be eroded.

   B It will be weathered quickly.

   C It will become granite.

   D It will become metamorphic rock. **6.c**

7. Which of these does **not** play a big role in the rock cycle?

   A lava

   B insects

   C minerals

   D sediment **4.a**

8. You find a rock that looks as if it is made of pieces of other rocks. What type of rock have you most likely found? Explain your answer. **4.a**

The **Big** Idea

 Language Arts ELA—W 2.1

Write a Report

Choose one type of rock in the rock cycle. Write a step-by-step explanation of how that type of rock changes into other types of rock.

Assayer's balance

 Math MR 1.1

Measure Mass

Collect several rock samples that are about the same size. Use a balance to find the mass of each sample. Explain why rocks that are the same size may have different masses. Apply what you know about the rock cycle to your answer.

California Capitol

 Art VPA—A 4.3

Rock Structure

Research a monument, building, piece of art, or some other structure that is made out of rock. Write a report about the rock structure. Discuss in your report how the type of rock relates to the structure's meaning or purpose.

 For more links and activities, go to **www.hspscience.com**

KEEPING AN EYE ON MARS

You probably already know that there are many satellites orbiting Earth. In fact, there are over 4,000 satellites soaring around the planet every day! People use these satellites in many ways. They are used to forecast the weather, broadcast TV shows, and send phone calls. Did you know that Earth is not the only planet that people have put satellites around? NASA has sent satellites to other planets in our solar system, including Mars.

This is an artist's idea of what *Mars Global Surveyor* looks like as it orbits Mars.

A Mission to Mars

In 1996, NASA launched the Mars Global Surveyor (MGS). The MGS's mission was to take detailed pictures of Mars's surface. To do this, the MGS was equipped with a special camera called the Mars Orbiter Camera (MOC). MOC was built by scientists at the California Institute of Technology and Malin Space Science Systems.

Mars in Focus

It took almost a year for the MGS to get to Mars. When it began to orbit, MOC began taking shot after shot of Mars's surface. It took pictures that probably are dried-out riverbeds, very old hot springs, and minerals that formed from evaporating water. These all support the hypothesis that Mars once had surface water.

MOC also took pictures of sand dunes on Mars. However, the sand dunes kept changing. This showed that Mars's sand dunes are active. Wind is still blowing the dunes around. Back on Earth, geologists can analyze the dune images. The data help them estimate how fast the rocks are being eroded on Mars's surface.

A View of Earth

In 2001, the MGS's mission was over. However, the satellite was still working well. NASA decided to keep using it. Today, MOC continues to photograph Mars. Every day, Malin Space Science Systems operates the camera from its offices in San Diego, California. The company then makes the images available to scientists around the world. In 2003, MOC took a one special photo— the first picture of Earth ever taken from another planet!

✎ Think and Write

❶ What evidence supports the idea that there was once water on Mars?

❷ Do you think rocks would weather faster on Earth or Mars? Explain your answer.

Changes in these dune pictures showed geologists that Mars's dunes were still undergoing erosion and deposition.

For more links and activities, go to www.hspscience.com

313

Wrap-Up

▶ Visual Summary

Tell how each picture helps explain the **Big Idea**.

The Big Idea You can tell a lot about how a rock or mineral formed by studying its properties.

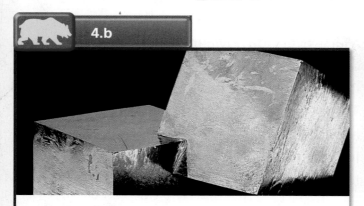

4.b

Mineral Properties

Minerals form in different ways. Because of this, they show many differences in their properties of hardness, streak, and luster.

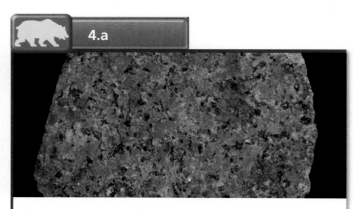

4.a

Igneous Rocks

Igneous rocks like this form from melted rock. They have large mineral crystals if they cool slowly.

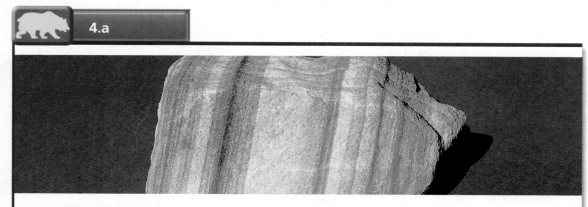

4.a

Sedimentary and Metamorphic Rocks

Sedimentary rocks often form when sediment builds up in layers. High temperature and pressure can change them to metamorphic rocks.

Show What You Know

Write a Report

Choose a mineral that is found in different colors or in crystal formations. Use library resources to find out more about the mineral. Then write a report. First, describe all of the variations of that mineral. Next, discuss the different ways the mineral can form. Finally, relate the mineral's process of formation to its properties.

Unit Project

Signs of the Rock Cycle

Look for evidence that a stage of the rock cycle is taking place in the area where you live. Start by finding a rock formation or a group of rocks. Draw or take a picture of the rock. Use the rock's properties to determine whether it is igneous, sedimentary, or metamorphic. Then write a brief report. Describe how you think the rock formed. What does the rock tell you about the geology of your area?

Vocabulary Review

Use the terms below to complete the sentences. The page numbers tell you where to look in the unit if you need help.

mineral p. 274

streak p. 276

luster p. 278

hardness p. 280

sedimentary rock p. 294

metamorphic rock p. 296

magma p. 306

rock cycle p. 308

1. Igneous rock forms when _magma_ cools. **4.a**

2. A rock that has been changed by high temperature and pressure is a _meta_. **4.a**

3. Quartz and galena are each an example of a _miner_. **4.b**

4. One type of rock changes into another type during the _rock cy_. **4.a**

5. A rock that forms from small pieces of other rock is a _sed_. **4.a**

6. A mineral's ability to scratch another mineral is its _hardness_. **4.b**

7. The color of the line that results when you rub a mineral across a white tile is the mineral's _st_. **4.b**

8. The way a mineral reflects light is its _____. **4.b**

Check Understanding

Choose the best answer.

9. **MAIN IDEA AND DETAILS** A mineral can be scratched by a penny but not by a fingernail. How hard is the mineral? **4.b**
   A 2.5 or less   **C** 3 to 4
   B 2 to 3   **D** 4 or more

10. Which of the following mineral properties is the **least** reliable to use when identifying a mineral? **4.b**
   A color   **C** luster
   B hardness   **D** streak

11. Which property is shown by the mineral below? **4.b**

   A cleavage   **C** hardness
   B fracture   **D** streak

12. What type of rock is shown below? `4.a`

A conglomerate rock
B igneous rock
C metamorphic rock
D sedimentary rock

13. What type of rock is shown below? `4.a`

A igneous rock
B metamorphic rock
C sedimentary rock
D volcanic rock

14. Which type of rock would most likely have interlocking mineral crystals and no sign of layers? `4.a`
A igneous rock
B metamorphic rock
C mineral rock
D sedimentary rock

15. **CAUSE AND EFFECT** Which could cause an igneous rock to change into a sedimentary rock? `4.a`
A great pressure
B high temperatures
C stretching
D weathering

16. You find an igneous rock with no visible mineral crystals. Where did this rock most likely form? `4.a`
A in a cave
B under the ocean floor
C on Earth's surface
D deep underground

Investigation Skills

17. Explain some ways in which minerals are classified. `4.b`

18. What are you looking for when you compare rocks? `4.a`

Critical Thinking

19. Examine the two samples. Explain how and where each rock probably formed. Tell how they could be related through the rock cycle. `4.a`

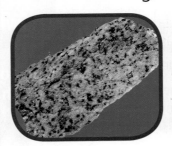

20. Why is most metamorphic rock harder than the sedimentary rock from which it formed?

The **Big Idea**

Waves, Wind Water, and Ice

What's the Big Idea?

Waves, wind, water, and ice shape and reshape Earth's land surface.

Essential Questions

Dear Chris,

I had a great day today! My dad and I drove along the coast on Route 101, north of Arcata. From the road, you can see amazing rock formations. There are rocks that look like towers rising out of the ocean. Here's a picture I took. I wish I could live there!

I'll give you a call when I get home and tell you all about it.

Your friend,
Andy

Think of the things that change or wear down rock and soil. How do they change the landscape around you? How do you think this relates to the **Big Idea?**

Unit Inquiry

Streams and Erosion

People who live near water often have to consider how erosion might effect the land around them. How might a stream table help them predict the effects of a stream? Plan and conduct an experiment to find out.

Science Content

5.a *Students know* that some changes in the Earth are due to slow processes such as erosion, and some changes are due to rapid processes such as landslides, volcanic eruptions, and earthquakes.

Investigation and Experimentation

6.a Differentiate observation from inference (interpretation) and know scientists' explanations come partly from what they observe and partly from how they interpret their observations.

6.d Conduct multiple trials to test a prediction and draw conclusions about the relationships between predictions and results.

California Fast Fact

Mountain Peaks

The Sierra Nevada range has the highest mountain peaks in North America, except for those in Alaska. Its steep mountains plunge dramatically into the deep valleys between them. Some of these drops and valleys were formed thousands of years ago by huge sheets of ice that scraped over the land.

LESSON

1

Essential Question

What Causes Changes to Earth's Surface?

Sierra Nevada range, California

earthquake
[ERTH•kwayk]
The shaking
of Earth's
surface
caused by movement of
rock in the crust (p. 324)

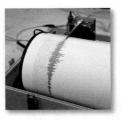

landslide
[LAND•slyd]
The sudden
movement
downhill of
rock and soil (p. 324)

creep [KREEP]
The slow
movement
of soil
or rock
downhill (p. 325)

volcano [vahl•KAY•noh] A
mountain that forms as
molten rock flows through
a crack onto Earth's surface
(p. 326)

lava [LAH•vuh] Molten rock
on Earth's surface that
flows from a volcano (p. 326)

dune [DOON] A large
mound of sand piled by
wind (p. 328)

Model a Glacier

Start with Questions

Glaciers, huge blocks of ice, have shaped much of Earth's land surface.

- How did glaciers shape the land?

- What other processes shape Earth's landforms?

Investigate to find out. Then read to find out more.

Prepare to Investigate

Investigation Skill Tip
Scientists use their observations to infer what the results of an investigation mean.

Materials

- paper cup
- sand and small pebbles
- water
- towel
- bar of soap

Make an Observation Chart

✔	Task	Sketch Observations
	Construct model glacier	
	Model effects of glacier	
	Record observations	

Follow This Procedure

1 Fill the paper cup halfway with sand and pebbles. Then add water to fill the cup. Place the cup in a freezer for about 90 minutes.

2 Remove the cup from the freezer, using a towel to protect your hand. Tear the paper cup off the ice.

3 Rub the model glacier over the soap. **Record** your observations.

Draw Conclusions

1. What did you **observe**?

2. **Standards Link** Interpret your results. Are these changes fast or slow changes? **5.a**

3. **Investigation Skill** Scientists often **infer** facts from observations. From your observations, what can you **infer** about how the movement of glaciers affects Earth's surface? Explain. **6.a**

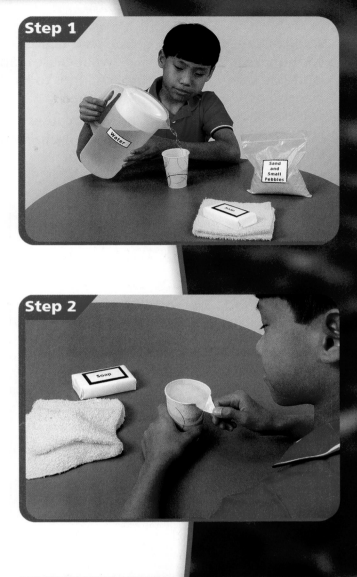

Step 1

Step 2

Independent Inquiry | **Develop an Experiment**

Think about the results of your investigation. Is there another activity you could perform to see if you get the same results? Develop another experiment that tests your results from the Investigate.

Identify variables from your new experiment. Which is the control variable? Which is the dependent variable? **6.d**

VOCABULARY
earthquake p. 324
landslide p. 324
creep p. 325
volcano p. 326
lava p. 326
dune p. 328

SCIENCE CONCEPTS
▶ what causes rapid changes to Earth's surface
▶ what causes slow changes to Earth's surface

COMPARE AND CONTRAST
Fill in the chart to show fast and slow changes to Earth's surface.

alike —— different

Earthquakes and Landslides

On January 17, 1994, at a crack in Earth's crust, the ground under Los Angeles shifted. The result was the huge Northridge earthquake. An **earthquake** is the shaking of Earth's surface. It is caused by the movement of rock in the crust along a fault, or large break.

In just seconds, the earthquake greatly changed Earth's surface. Huge cracks opened. Pieces of the ground tilted up. A nearby mountain rose several inches. As the ground shook, buildings broke and fell to the ground.

Earthquakes and some other natural disasters can cause very fast changes to Earth's surface.

Landslides cause fast changes. A **landslide** is the sudden movement of rock and soil down a hill. Soil and rock can slide down a hill rapidly—and without warning. Have you ever seen a picture of a house hanging over the edge of a cliff? The soil below it has fallen away. The house looks as if it will fall at any minute. This is the result of a landslide.

Landslides leave piles of soil and rock at the bottom of a hill. They leave holes

◀ **These rows of crops have been shifted by an earthquake. The ground on the sides of the fault moved in opposite directions.**

in the hill where soil has fallen away. Landslides and earthquakes cause fast changes to Earth's surface.

In contrast, **creep** is the very slow movement of soil downhill. Creep is so slow that you cannot see it happen. Over months or years, creep tilts fence posts and tips power poles. It even breaks roads. Over time, creep can flatten what was once a hill.

Focus Skill **COMPARE AND CONTRAST** What is the difference between a landslide and creep?

The curves of these tree trunks were caused by creep. Creep first tilted the tree trunks downward. Then the trunks curved upward as the trees grew toward the sun.

In a landslide, rock and dirt can slide downhill at more than 160 kilometers (100 mi) per hour.

Volcanoes

On May 18, 1980, Mount St. Helens, a volcano in the state of Washington, erupted. The huge explosion blew the top off the mountain. The force of the blast knocked down trees around the mountain. Ash rose 19 kilometers (12 mi) into the air. The ash fell on farms and towns hundreds of kilometers away.

Mount St. Helens is one of hundreds of volcanoes on Earth. A **volcano** is a mountain that forms as lava flows from a crack in Earth's surface. **Lava** is melted rock at Earth's surface.

Some volcanoes have forceful and violent eruptions, as Mount St. Helens did. These eruptions quickly change Earth's surface. Hot rock, ash, and lava rain down on the nearby land. Huge clouds of superhot steam flow down the sides of the volcano, burning forests and killing wildlife. Ash may cover the ground for miles around. The land around the volcano can look like the surface of the moon.

Other volcanoes erupt quietly. Hot lava flows out of the volcano and over the surrounding land. It may cover buildings, roads, and plants. As it cools, it hardens into new rock.

After more than 100 years of being quiet, Mount St. Helens erupted with a blast in the spring of 1980.

▲ **The 1980 eruption changed the shape of Mount St. Helens. The top 400 meters (1,350 ft) of the mountain were blown away. The ground around the mountain was burned, as were the plants that grew there.**

▲ **More than 20 years after the eruption, life has returned to an area that was covered with gray ash and lava. Many new bushes and young trees have already grown. In another 100 years, a young forest will surround the mountain**

When volcanoes erupt, they often cause harmful changes. However, they can cause helpful ones, too. The ash that falls from a volcanic eruption has many nutrients in it. It can break down into rich soil that makes good farmland.

Volcanoes on the sea floor can form new land. Over time, the lava released from these undersea cracks in Earth's crust forms huge mountains. The tops of these mountains can rise above the ocean surface as islands. The islands of Hawai`i are the tops of volcanoes on the ocean floor.

Focus Skill COMPARE AND CONTRAST In what two ways can volcanoes erupt?

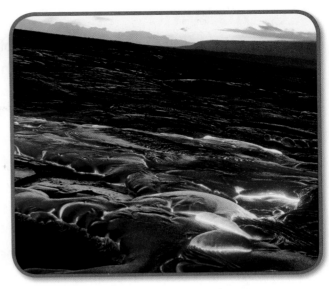

▲ **Red-hot, glowing lava flows down the sides of Kīlauea volcano, in Hawai`i.**

▲ **Kīlauea's lava moves toward the ocean nearby. When it hits the cool water, it cools and hardens. The black lava adds new land to the coast of Hawai`i, forming unusual black sand beaches.**

Mount Shasta is the largest volcano in the California section of the Cascade Range. Shasta has not erupted for hundreds of years—but it could

Ice and Wind

During the last ice age, huge sheets of ice called *glaciers* covered much of Earth. They slowly moved, scraping the land beneath them. You saw this process at work in the investigation.

The movement of ice slowly shaped many landforms we see today. Ice-age glaciers once filled many valleys. They scraped the bottoms and sides of the valleys as they moved. They widened the valleys, making them U-shaped.

Glaciers also scooped holes in Earth. These holes later filled with water from the melting ice and became lakes. Glaciers, which move like conveyor belts, also pushed soil and rock from place to place. When the glaciers melted, ridges of soil and rock were left behind.

Wind can change Earth's surface, too. Desert sand is dry and loose, and it blows easily. A **dune** forms when wind blows sand into a mound. Dunes are common desert landforms.

◀ This is desert pavement in Death Valley, California. Wind blows away the fine, sandy soil, leaving large rocks and pebbles behind.

Wind moves sand in deserts. It can build huge sand dunes that may reach a length of 20 meters (656 ft).

A glacier once filled this wide valley. The glacier pushed a mound of rock and soil in front of it as it moved. When the glacier melted, it left this ridge of rock and soil.

▲ A huge sheet of ice scraped over this rock thousands of years ago, leaving these grooves in it.

Wind can also remove sand and soil. *Desert pavement* is a layer of hard ground covered with large pebbles and gravel. It forms when wind blows away the fine sand, leaving only rocks and stones on the hard ground.

Around the world, the wind shapes, polishes, and breaks down rock. It picks up sand and slams it into rock surfaces. This sandblasting makes pits in rock and carves desert rocks into unusual shapes.

COMPARE AND CONTRAST How are dunes and desert pavement alike? How are they different?

Insta-Lab

Dune in a Box

Put two cupfuls of sand into a shoe box. Hold the straw in one spot about one inch above the sand. Blow steadily through the straw for about 10 seconds. Observe the pattern in the sand. What does it look like?

Standards Wrap-Up and Lesson Review

Essential Question

What causes changes to Earth's surface?

In this lesson, you learned that earthquakes, landslides, and volcanoes can cause fast changes to Earth's surface. You also learned that creep, volcanoes, wind, and ice can cause slow changes to Earth's surface.

Science Content Standard in This Lesson

5.a *Students know* that some changes in the Earth are due to slow processes such as erosion, and some changes are due to rapid processes such as landslides, volcanic eruptions, and earthquakes.

1. **COMPARE AND CONTRAST** Draw and complete this graphic organizer to compare and contrast creep and landslides. **5.a**

2. **SUMMARIZE** Write a summary of this lesson. Begin with this sentence: *Changes to Earth's surface can be fast or slow.* **5.a**

3. **DRAW CONCLUSIONS** Scientists study some volcanoes to find out when they might erupt. Why is this important? **5.a**

4. **VOCABULARY** How are the terms *volcano* and *lava* related? **5.a**

5. **Critical Thinking** Why would you not expect to find dunes in an area that gets a lot of rainfall? **5.a**

6. **Investigate and Experiment** Why is it important to conduct multiple trials to test predictions? **6.d**

7. Which of these causes slow changes to Earth's surface?
   A volcano
   B creep
   C earthquake
   D landslide **5.a**

8. Which of these landforms is caused by moving ice?
   A dunes
   B beaches
   C desert pavement
   D U-shaped valleys **5.a**

The **Big Idea**

 Writing ELA—W 1.1

Write a Composition

Look at photographs of Yosemite Valley provided by your teacher. The movement of glaciers shaped it. Write a letter to a friend describing the landforms as if you are an explorer seeing them for the first time.

 Math SDAP 1.1

Organize Data

What are the five largest glaciers in the United States? Look in an encyclopedia to find out. Then list their names in a table, from the smallest to the largest glacier.

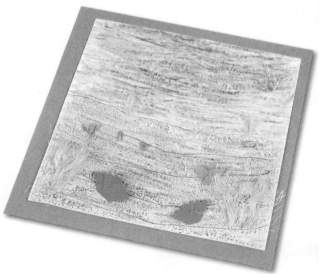

 Art VPA—VA 5.3

Make a Poster

Make a poster that shows a California landform. Use pictures and words that will make people want to visit it. The poster should describe the landform, explain how it formed, and tell why it's worth seeing.

 For more links and activities, go to **www.hspscience.com**

▶ **RICHARD HOBLITT**

▶ **Volcanologist**

▶ Hawai`i Volcanoes Observatory of the United States Geological Survey

Richard Hoblitt

Richard Hoblitt knows a lot about volcanoes. That's because he studies them for a living. He is a volcanologist (vahl•kuh•NAHL•uh•jist).

Dr. Hoblitt actually works on an active volcano. He is on the staff of the Hawai`i Volcanoes Observatory (HVO). Each of the islands of Hawai`i is a volcano sitting on the ocean floor.

At HVO, Hoblitt monitors active volcanoes, such as Kīlauea (kee•low•AY•uh). This Hawaiian volcano has erupted nonstop for many years. Hoblitt also studies the dangers the volcanoes present for people nearby. The scientists at HVO can then warn the public if their instruments tell them a volcano is about to erupt.

Before coming to Hawai`i, Dr. Hoblitt worked at the Cascades Volcano Observatory in the state of Washington. There, he studied the volcanoes of the Cascade Range of Washington, Oregon, and California. One of those volcanoes is Mount St. Helens.

The volcanoes of Hawai`i and those of the Cascades are different. But Dr. Hoblitt finds all volcanoes fascinating—no matter where they are.

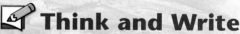 **Think and Write**

❶ What does Dr. Hoblitt study?

❷ How does Dr. Hoblitt help people by doing his job?

5.a

Inés Cifuentes

Inés Cifuentes really knows how to shake things up. She has studied earthquakes and how to predict them. Now she's working to improve science education for children.

Dr. Cifuentes started out studying earthquakes in South America. She set up seismographs in rural areas and collected data.

▶ **INÉS CIFUENTES**

▶ **Seismologist**
▶ Science Educator

Collecting that data helped prepare her for researching the Chilean earthquake of 1960—the largest earthquake ever recorded. It measured 9.5 on the Richter scale and lasted for almost 5 minutes.

Before the Chilean earthquake, a strange event had been recorded on seismographs at the California Institute of Technology. Dr. Cifuentes's work showed that there was a link between that event and the huge Chilean earthquake. Understanding the link has helped other scientists predict earthquakes.

Now Dr. Cifuentes works in the Washington, D.C., area to help science teachers improve their classes. She works with elementary school students, too. Inés Cifuentes wants to teach people that learning about science is a way to increase their opportunities in life.

Think and Write

❶ What kind of quick changes to Earth's surface does Inés Cifuentes study?

5.a

❷ What does Dr. Cifuentes hope to teach people about science?

Damage from Chilean earthquake of 1960

Science Content

5.b *Students know* natural processes including freezing and thawing, and the growth of roots causes rocks to break down into smaller pieces.

Investigation and Experimentation

6.c Formulate and justify predictions based on cause-and-effect relationships.

6.f Follow a set of written instructions for a scientific investigation.

LESSON 2

Essential Question

What Causes Weathering?

California Fast Fact

Volcanic Dome

These pieces of granite were once magma deep inside Earth. Over thousands of years, water, wind, and glaciers uncovered the granite. Their continued action split it into pieces. In time, the entire rock will be worn down.

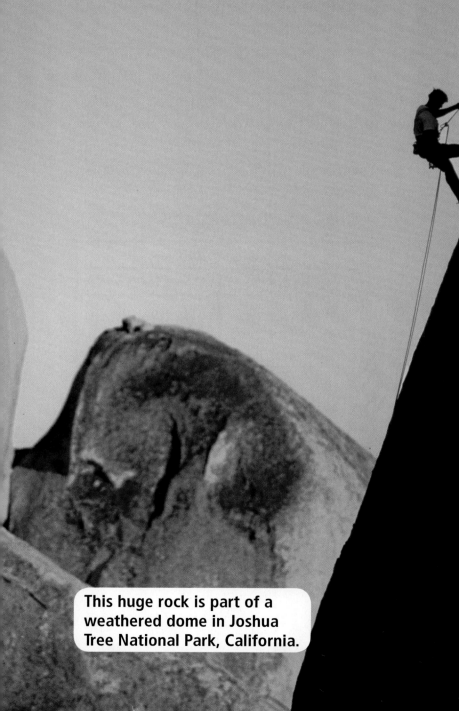

This huge rock is part of a weathered dome in Joshua Tree National Park, California.

weathering
[WETH•er•ing]
Process that breaks down rock (p. 338)

soil [SOYL] A mixture of weathered rock, remains of dead organisms, water, and air (p. 338)

mechanical weathering
[muh•KAN•ih•kuhl WETH•er•ing]
Process by which rocks are broken down through physical methods (p. 338)
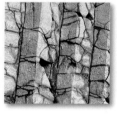

chemical weathering
[KEM•ih•kuhl WETH•er•ing]
Process by which the chemical makeup of a rock is changed and the rock is broken down (p. 340)

Soda Pop!

Start with Questions

Nothing on Earth lasts forever. Even the strongest rocks and mountains are worn down.

- What causes rock to break down?

- What happens to rock that has been broken down?

Investigate to find out. Then read to find out more.

Prepare to Investigate

Investigation Skill Tip
When you predict the results of an experiment, write your prediction in terms of cause and effect.

Materials

- goggles
- unopened can of soda
- freezer

Make an Observation Chart

Possible Predictions	
Cause	Effect
Because the can was frozen . . .	

Follow This Procedure

CAUTION: Put on goggles before removing the can from the freezer.

❶ Sketch your can.

❷ Place the can in the freezer. **Predict** the effect that freezing will have on the can. After an hour, remove the can of soda from the freezer.

❸ **Observe** any changes in the can. Sketch the can again.

Draw Conclusions

1. How did the soda can change?

2. Standards Link What effect did you predict freezing would have on the can? Why? `6.c`

3. Investigation Skill Scientists make predictions and inferences based on cause-and-effect relationships. What effect do you infer freezing has on rocks? `6.c`

Step 1

Step 2

Independent Inquiry ▸ Change Variables

Change one variable—the substance that is frozen—and rewrite the procedure to match. Follow the new instructions to find out if the results are the same.

Design an experiment to test how another cause affects a soda can. `6.f`

VOCABULARY
weathering p. 338
soil p. 338
mechanical weathering p. 338
chemical weathering p. 340

SCIENCE CONCEPTS
▶ what mechanical weathering is
▶ what chemical weathering is

CAUSE AND EFFECT
Use the graphic organizer to show the two types of weathering.

cause ⟶ effect

Mechanical Weathering

Weathering is the part of the rock cycle in which rocks break down into smaller pieces, called sediment. The sediment may then form new rock or may help form soil. **Soil** is a mixture of weathered rock, the remains of dead organisms, water, and air.

Mechanical weathering physically breaks rock into smaller pieces. Ice, water, wind, and temperature can all weather rock mechanically. All these are *physical changes*.

Water runs into cracks in rocks and freezes. Remember, water expands as it freezes. As a result, the rock cracks more, and pieces break off. Ice also cracks sidewalks and causes potholes in roads.

Moving water and wind break down rocks by *abrasion,* or scraping. Sediment carried by a river grinds against rock. Wind carries sand. Over time, the scraping action of sediment and sand can cause rocks to crack or break.

Changes in temperature also cause weathering. Rocks get a little bigger when heated and get a little smaller when cooled. Repeated heating and cooling weakens some rocks, causing them to crack or break.

▼ **Water in the form of ice can break down rock and concrete.**

Water runs into a crack.

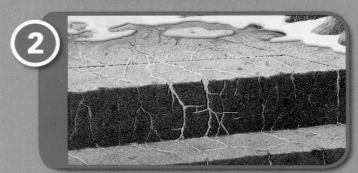

The water freezes and becomes ice. Frozen water takes up more space than liquid water. It pushes against the sides of the crack.

The crack becomes wider and breaks the rock. This is a physical change.

338

Living things cause weathering, too. Plant roots split rock around them as the roots grow. Animals loosen soil and break rocks by digging.

 **CAUSE AND EFFECT** How does abrasion cause rocks to break down?

Insta-Lab

Scrape a Rock

Rub a piece of chalk with a piece of rock. Observe what happens to the chalk. How is this similar to what happens in weathering?

◀ Roots often grow into cracks in rock. As the roots get larger, they split the rock into smaller pieces.

◀ A mushroom rock, like the one shown here, has this shape because the wind blew sand around the bottom of the rock, wearing it away.

The type of weathering shown below is called *exfoliation* (eks•foh•lee•AY•shuhn). Pieces of the rock's surface separate and fall off in sheets. Surfaces formed this way look as if layers have been peeled away.

Chemical Weathering

Chemical weathering changes the chemical makeup of rock. Water and gases in the air cause most chemical weathering. Rain mixes with carbon dioxide in the air. The result is rain that is slightly acid. Acid rain easily weathers soft rocks, such as limestone, rock salt, and calcite.

Oxygen in the air also causes chemical weathering. It combines with minerals in rocks. Some rocks, such as those with iron in them, break down as a result.

When iron mixes with oxygen, it forms iron oxide, or rust.

Mechanical and chemical agents often work together to speed up weathering. For example, first a rock is mechanically weathered into pieces. Then chemical weathering can act on more surfaces and a greater area. In another example, as chemical weathering forms rust, it weakens a rock. It is then easier for mechanical weathering to break the rock into pieces.

Many other things affect the rate at which rock weathers. One is the type

Water can wear away bits of surface rock. A chemical change has turned the surface of this rock brown. Iron oxide, or rust, breaks down the outer layer of some kinds of rock. ▼

Lichens grow on rocks in harsh environments, such as deserts and cold Arctic regions. Lichens get nutrients from the rocks on which they grow. This often weakens the rock.

▲ **This tombstone is made of marble. Chemical weathering softens and breaks down rocks such as marble and limestone. Writing and art on old marble tombstones can be worn away.**

of rock. Granite, for example, resists chemical weathering. Other rocks, such as marble, break down more easily.

Climate has an effect as well. Warm, wet conditions speed up chemical weathering. Cold and dryness slow these processes.

Focus Skill CAUSE AND EFFECT How does chemical weathering cause changes in rock?

Science Up Close

Formation of a Sinkhole

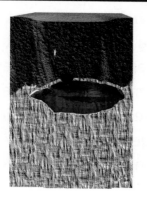

1 Rain soaks into the ground. The rainwater eats away limestone rock under the surface. Water carries away the dissolved rock. A small opening forms.

2 The opening in the rock becomes larger as time passes.

3 Rock and soil that covered the underground opening cave in. A sinkhole forms on the surface. Do you think this process happens quickly or slowly? Explain.

Sinkholes are often the result of chemical weathering. This 15-story-deep sinkhole formed several years ago in Florida.

For more links and animations, go to **www.hspscience.com**

Standards Wrap-Up and Lesson Review

Essential Question

What causes weathering?

In this lesson, you learned that Earth's surface can be weathered, or broken down. Ice, plants and animals, freezing, thawing, and abrasion cause mechanical weathering. The mixing of water and gases in the air can cause chemical weathering.

Science Content Standard in This Lesson

5.b *Students know* natural processes including freezing and thawing, and the growth of roots causes rocks to break down into smaller pieces.

1.  **CAUSE AND EFFECT** What are the causes of mechanical weathering? What are the effects? **5.b**

2. **SUMMARIZE** Use the lesson vocabulary terms to write a summary of this lesson. **5.b**

3. **DRAW CONCLUSIONS** What type of weathering do you think is most common in the Mojave Desert of California? **5.b**

4. **VOCABULARY** What is the connection between weathering and soil? **5.b**

5. **Critical Thinking** If weathering were to stop, how would this affect the rock cycle? **5.b**

6. **Investigate and Experiment** The leaders of a city want to set up a new monument in a park. They can make it of marble or granite. Which monument do you predict would last longer in a hot, rainy climate? Explain. **6.c**

7. Which of these is a chemical weathering process?
   A roots growing into rock
   B heating and cooling of rock
   C the formation of rust on rock
   D ice expanding in cracks in rock **5.b**

8. Ice reshapes Earth's surface through
   A mechanical weathering.
   B exfoliation.
   C chemical weathering.
   D oxidation. **5.b**

 The **Big Idea**

 Writing ELA—W 1.3

Write a Report

Write a paragraph that explains the difference between mechanical weathering and chemical weathering. Include examples.

9÷3 **Math** NS 2.1

Solve Problems

Rock in a certain area weathers at the rate of 1 mm each year. How much has the rock weathered during your lifetime?

 Social Studies HSS 4.4.2

Gold Rush Report

Gold was discovered on the American River in the 1840s. Find out what part weathering played in the discovery of the gold. Write a report, and share with the class what you find.

 For more links and activities, go to **www.hspscience.com**

Big Sur

Much of California's coast is developed, or used for buildings. It is covered with houses, beach resorts, and businesses. In contrast, most of Big Sur is still natural and wild. Highway 1 winds through beautiful scenery along the coastal cliffs and canyons of Big Sur. To enjoy this beauty, more than 1.5 million people travel through Big Sur on Highway 1 each year.

At times, however, travel along the Big Sur coast becomes difficult or even impossible. Parts of the coast road sometimes slide into the ocean. What's going on in Big Sur?

Coastal mountains meet the Pacific Ocean in Big Sur.

The Mountains and the Sea

Big Sur is the part of California's coast between Carmel and San Simeon. The land of Big Sur is beautiful and rugged. The Santa Lucia Mountains plunge into the Pacific Ocean, forming high, steep cliffs along the coast.

It was difficult to build a highway along this wild coast. Coastal erosion has made it even more difficult to keep the highway open.

An Eroding Coastline

Along parts of the California coast, wide beaches protect the cliffs behind them from the pounding ocean waves. This is not the case in Big Sur. The mountains here drop straight down into deep water close to shore. Because of this, waves hit the coastal cliffs hard, especially during winter storms. Waves eat away about 18 centimeters (7 in.) of cliff rock in Big Sur each year.

Heavy rainfall also loosens soil in the cliffs, causing landslides to dump tons of soil onto Highway 1. They can even carry pieces of the highway down into the sea.

The road has been rebuilt many times. New vegetation has been planted to hold the soil in place. Still, the ocean will continue to wear away the cliffs of Big Sur. The coast will keep changing.

✍️ Think and Write

1. Explain the process of erosion in Big Sur. `5.c`
2. How do you think planting vegetation on cliffs helps reduce erosion in Big Sur? `5.c`

LESSON 3

Science Content

5.a *Students know* that some changes in the Earth are due to slow processes such as erosion, and some changes are due to rapid processes such as landslides, volcanic eruptions, and earthquakes.

5.c *Students know* moving water erodes landforms, reshaping the land by taking it away from some places, and depositing it as pebbles, sand, silt and mud in other places (weathering, transport, deposition).

Investigation and Experimentation

6.c Formulate and justify predictions based on cause-and-effect relationships.

6.f Follow a set of written instructions for a scientific investigation.

California Fast Fact

Rock Island

An undersea mountain range runs 100 kilometers (60 mi) from Anacapa Island to San Miguel Island. The tops of these mountains form islands, including Anacapa. Ocean waves have battered Anacapa for thousands of years, carving the rock formations along its coast.

Essential Question

How Does Moving Water Shape the Land?

Rock formations of Anacapa Island, California

erosion [uh•ROH•zhuhn]
The process of moving sediment from one place to another (p. 350)

transport
[TRANS•port]
The movement of sediment from place to place by water (p. 350)

runoff
[RUN•off]
Water that flows over land without sinking in (p. 350)

deposition
[dep•uh•ZISH•uhn]
The dropping of sediment by rivers as they slow down (p. 351)

Make a Landform Model

Start with Questions

California's coast has beautiful cliffs hanging right over the ocean.

- Have you ever seen cliffs like these?

- Have you ever seen a huge rock that seems to rise from nowhere?

- What kinds of landforms do you see around you?

- How does water shape the land?

Investigate to find out. Then read to find out more.

Prepare to Investigate

Investigation Skill Tip
Scientists often observe an object in nature and then make a model of it to understand it better.

Materials
- paper
- pencil
- modeling clay
- heavy cardboard

Make an Observation Chart

Details of landform	Sketch of landform

Follow This Procedure

❶ Choose a landform in your area.

❷ **Observe** the landform's shape and size. Sketch it on paper.

❸ Use modeling clay and your sketch to **make a model** of the landform on a sheet of cardboard.

Draw Conclusions

1. Which type of landform did you **make a model** of with the clay?

2. **Standards Link** How do you think the landform might change in the future? What might cause the change? `5.a`

3. **Investigation Skill** You made a model to learn about an object in nature. What can you learn about the real landform by observing the model? `6.c`

Step 2

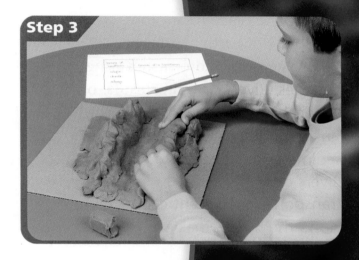

Step 3

Independent Inquiry

Extend the Investigate

Predict how different forms of weathering will affect your model. Then design and conduct an investigation about how a landform is affected by moving water and other forms of weathering. Write out procedures so others can follow your instructions. `6.c` `6.f`

VOCABULARY
erosion p. 350
runoff p. 350
transport p. 350
deposition p. 351

SCIENCE CONCEPTS
▶ how rivers change the land
▶ how ocean waves shape the land

Focus Skill **MAIN IDEA AND DETAILS**
Look for details about how water shapes landforms.

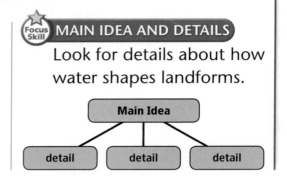

Rivers Shape the Land

What happens to sediment after weathering takes place? **Erosion** moves it from one place to another, changing the shape of Earth's surface.

Rivers erode landforms, causing changes. Rivers contain **runoff**, or water that flows over land without sinking in. Runoff **transports**, or moves, sediment from weathered rock to rivers. Rivers carry the sediment along. As it is transported, sediment causes abrasion along the banks, making the river wider.

Abrasion along the bottom causes the river to cut deeper, carving a valley. As the river flows faster, it carries sediment with larger pieces in it, causing more erosion.

▼ When a river enters a lake or an ocean, it slows down. It can then carry less sediment. The river drops most of the sediment to form a delta.

Palo Duro Canyon was carved by water. Weathering and erosion widen the valley and carry sediment to the river. The rushing river then deepens the valley as it carries the sediment away.

The shape of a valley depends on slope of the land over which the river runs. In steep areas, rivers rush downhill, cutting deeply into the land. This forms a narrow, V-shaped valley. It can also form a canyon, which is a deep valley with steep sides.

In flat areas, or areas with gentle slopes, rivers flow more slowly, so they do not cut deeply into the land. They may move in large curves. Their valleys are wide, with gently sloping sides and flat floors.

Slow-moving rivers cause less abrasion and more deposition. **Deposition** (dep•uh•ZISH•uhn) is the dropping of sediment by rivers as they slow down. This deposition forms landforms such as deltas at the mouths of rivers and point bars at curves along their banks.

Focus Skill **MAIN IDEA AND DETAILS** Why does a fast-flowing river cause more erosion than a slow-flowing river?

Weathering forms sediment that rivers carry. This river is full of sediment washed from nearby fields.

point bar

Math in Science
Interpret Data

Gravel (boulders, cobbles, *pebbles*) are the largest pieces of sediment. What are the smallest pieces of sediment?

SEDIMENT COMES IN ALL SIZES		
256 mm and up	BOULDERS	GRAVEL
64-256 mm	COBBLES	
2-64 mm	PEBBLES	
0.0625-2 mm	SAND	
0.002-0.0625 mm	SILT	
0.002 mm and under	CLAY	

Ocean Waves Shape the Land

Another cause of weathering and erosion is waves. Large ocean waves pound coastlines. Over time, this pounding breaks the rock into pieces.

Weathering along coasts can form unique landforms. If you have driven along the California coast, you have seen cliffs that drop into the sea. Tall rock towers and stone arches rise from the water. How do these form?

Waves crash into rocky pieces of land that extend into the water. They wear away the weakest part of the rock. When waves weather a hole through the bottom of a large rock, a *sea arch* forms. If the top of the arch breaks and falls, stone towers called *sea stacks* are left.

Waves and ocean currents also move sediment from some areas and drop it in others. This erosion and deposition of sand forms sand bars. Barrier islands are another result of deposition. Barrier

◀ The force of waves carved this sea arch. The hole at the center is an area where rock wore away first.

Waves hit cliffs such as these with great force. During storms, thousands of tons of water can smash into coastal rocks.

▲ Currents and waves deposit sand in shallow areas near the shore. Some deposits build up to form small, sandy islands.

islands are long, thin, sandy islands that form along a coast.

Deposition on coasts is what forms beaches. The waves and ocean currents pick up sediment from weathered cliffs. Rivers also drop sediment into the sea. The ocean deposits both types of sediment on the shore—as beach sand.

 **MAIN IDEA AND DETAILS** What is the source of beach sand?

Shaping Land

Fill half of a large plastic cup with soil. Hold it at an angle. Fill a second cup with water, and hold it about 7 cm above the first. Slowly pour a thin stream of water on the soil. What do you observe? What natural process does this model?

Essential Question

How Does Moving Water Shape the Land?

In this lesson, you learned that moving water erodes landforms, reshaping the land by taking it away from some places and depositing it in other places.

Science Content Standards in this Lesson

5.a *Students know* that some changes in the Earth are due to slow processes such as erosion, and some changes are due to rapid processes such as landslides, volcanic eruptions, and earthquakes.

5.c *Students know* moving water erodes landforms, reshaping the land by taking it away from some places, and depositing it as pebbles, sand, silt and mud in other places (weathering, transport, deposition).

---

1. **Focus Skill** **MAIN IDEA AND DETAILS** Use the graphic organizer to explain how moving water shapes land. **5.c**

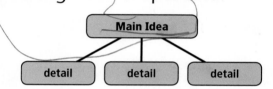

Main Idea

detail   detail   detail

2. SUMMARIZE Summarize this lesson in two sentences. *Five* **5.c**

3. DRAW CONCLUSIONS Deltas form where some rivers flow into the sea. Why do other rivers not form deltas? **5.a**

4. VOCABULARY Write a sentence that contains the words *runoff* and *transport*. **5.c**

5. Critical Thinking You see sea stacks near the shore. What

landform was probably there before them? What might the sea stacks look like in the future? **5.c**

6. Investigate and Experiment A dam is built across a river that carries a great amount of sediment to the sea. The dam now blocks the sediment. Predict what will happen to a beach near the river's mouth that formed mostly from river sediment? **6.c**

7. A fast-flowing river forms a
- **A** V-shaped valley.
- **B** sea stack.
- **C** barrier island.
- **D** delta. **5.a**

The Big Idea

8. Which of these is not formed mostly by the action of ocean waves?
- **A** sea stack
- **B** beach
- **C** delta
- **D** sea arch **5.c**

Writing ELA—W 2.1

Write a Narrative

Write the story of a grain of sediment that has been weathered from a mountain, transported to the sea by a river, and then deposited on a beach. Write it from the sediment's point of view. Share your story with the class.

9÷3 ### Math MR 1.2

Solve Problems

A layer of sedimentary rock is 5 meters thick. The layer was deposited at a rate of $\frac{1}{2}$ centimeter per year. How many years did it take to form? Break the problem into parts to solve it.

 ### Social Studies HSS 4.1.3

Make a Brochure

Design a tourist brochure that tells details about three different California landforms. Describe them in a way that will make people want to visit. Be sure to include a map!

 For more links and activities, go to **www.hspscience.com**

WIPEOUT! Splash

Simon Day is doing research on tsunamis (tsoo•NAH•meez) at University College in London, England. He believes that history's biggest tsunami will be caused by a future eruption of the Cumbre Vieja (KOOM•bray vee•AY•ha) volcano. Cumbre Vieja is in the Canary Islands, a group of islands in the Atlantic Ocean off the northwest coast of Africa.

Simon Day predicts that a volcanic eruption could cause a giant landslide on the unstable western side of the volcano, plopping a trillion tons of rock into the Atlantic. Such a big landslide would cause a tsunami that would travel a long distance at great speed.

Coastal Terrors

The landslide's impact would produce swells, large waves that radiate from their source until they hit land. Out at sea, the swells are harmless and hardly noticeable. As they approach land, however, they become monstrous. In shallow water, the swells bunch up and gain height. Coming ashore, a tsunami stikes coastal cities and shores with terrible destructive force.

Danger, Danger!

Simon Day and wave expert Steven Ward, of the University of California, recently worked together. They used a computer model to calculate the impact of a Cumbre Vieja tsunami. Their calculations show that the danger zones lie north, west, and south of the Canary Islands.

After 6 hours
After 3 hours
NORTH AMERICA
EUROPE
AFRICA
Epicenter of tsunami
ATLANTIC OCEAN
SOUTH AMERICA

Danger Zones
A tsunami caused by a giant Cumbre Vieja landslide would travel north, west, and south of the Canary Islands and strike coastal areas in Africa, South America, and North America.

The scientists calculate that on Africa's Western Sahara shore, waves would reach heights of 100 meters (328 feet)—higher than a 30-story building! Waves on the north coast of Brazil would be more than 40 meters (131 feet) high. Closer to home, Florida and the Caribbean would be hit with waves 50 meters (164 feet) high. These multiple disasters would occur just hours after a powerful landslide caused by Cumbre Vieja.

Think and Write

1 What changes to Earth's surface may cause tsunamis? `5.a`

2 How is technology used to study tsunamis? `5.a`

TSUNAMI OF 2004

- **On December 26, 2004, an earthquake at the bottom of the Indian Ocean caused a tsunami. The huge wave destroyed coastal areas from Thailand in Asia to Somalia in Africa.**
- **More than 250,000 people died, and millions were left homeless.**
- **This tsunami was one of the w... natural disasters in history.**

Find out more. Log on to www.hspscience.com

358

▶ Visual Summary

Tell how each picture helps explain the **Big Idea**.

The Big Idea Waves, wind, water, and ice shape and reshape Earth's land surface.

5.b

Weathering Breaks Down Rock

Mechanical weathering breaks rock physically. Chemical weathering weakens rock by changing its composition.

5.c

Erosion Transports Rock

Erosion by wind, running water, glaciers, and waves transports and deposits sediment.

5.a

Earth's Surface Changes

The changes caused by earthquakes and landslides are rapid. Changes such as those caused by wind and water are slow.

Show What You Know

Unit Writing Activity

Make a Picture Dictionary

Work with a partner. Design and write a picture dictionary for the processes in this unit that change Earth's surface. These include volcanic eruptions, landslides, wind, weathering, and earthquakes. For each process, write a short definition in your own words. Tell whether the process is slow or fast. Illustrate each dictionary entry with a small drawing or with a photo or an illustration cut from an old magazine.

Unit Project

Prepare a News Report

Work in a small group. Choose a process that has changed or is still changing Earth's surface in your area of California. Then film a television news report about the change. Include its effect on people and on the land. Have each person do a different task as you put the report together. Some people might do research. Others might write the script for the report. One or two people might like to be the reporters. Others might prefer to do the filming. Share your report with the rest of the class.

Vocabulary Review

Use the terms below to complete the sentences. The page numbers tell you where to look in the unit if you need help.

earthquake p. 324

landslide p. 324

volcano p. 326

lava p. 326

weathering p. 338

chemical weathering p. 340

runoff p. 350

deposition p. 351

1. A mountain that forms as lava flows through a crack onto Earth's surface is a _____. `5.a`

2. Hot melted rock from deep in Earth is _____. `5.a`

3. Changes to the chemical makeup of rock are caused by _____. `5.a`

4. Water that flows over Earth's surface without sinking in is _____. `5.c`

5. The shaking of Earth's surface caused by the movement of rocks in the crust is an _____. `5.a`

6. The dropping of sediment by rivers as they slow down is _____. `5.c`

7. The sudden movement of rock and soil down a slope is a _____. `5.a`

8. The breaking down of rock into smaller pieces is _____. `5.b`

Check Understanding

Choose the best answer.

9. **COMPARE AND CONTRAST** How is mechanical weathering different from chemical weathering? `5.a` `5.b`
   A It breaks down rock.
   B It helps form soil.
   C It changes what rocks are made of.
   D It changes rock only physically.

10. **MAIN IDEA AND DETAILS** Which of the following forms when rivers deposit sediment? `5.c`
    A sea stack   C delta
    B mountain   D dune

11. Which of the following is a slow type of change to the landscape? `5.a`
    A creep   C mudslide
    B landslide   D eruption

12. Which of these changes to Earth's surface is rapid? `5.a`
    A chemical weathering of rock
    B eruption of volcanoes
    C creep
    D deposition of a delta

13. Which process is shown by the illustration below? `5.c`

- **A** chemical weathering
- **B** deposition by water
- **C** weathering by wind
- **D** erosion by water

14. What effect is caused by the cycle of freezing and thawing? `5.b`
- **A** erosion by ice
- **B** chemical weathering
- **C** mechanical weathering
- **D** erosion by wind

15. What produced this landform? `5.a`

- **A** weathering by ice
- **B** erosion by ocean waves
- **C** erosion by water
- **D** erosion by wind

16. Which of these landforms is formed by rapidly flowing water? `5.c`
- **A** sea arches
- **B** dunes
- **C** V-shaped valleys
- **D** U-shaped valleys

Investigation Skills

17. A scientist writes an explanation of how a sea arch formed. Is that explanation based mostly on what she could **observe** or what she could **infer**? Explain your answer. `6.a`

18. A glacier moves through a narrow valley during an ice age. Then the climate warms and the ice melts. **Predict** how the shape of the valley will have changed. `6.c`

Critical Thinking

19. A swiftly flowing river carries the sediments listed in this table. Which sediments will the river deposit first when it slows down? Explain your answer. `5.c`

SEDIMENT COMES IN ALL SIZES		
256 mm and up	BOULDERS	
64-256 mm	COBBLES	GRAVEL
2-64 mm	PEBBLES	
0.0625-2 mm	SAND	
0.002-0.0625 mm	SILT	
0.002 mm and under	CLAY	

20. Why do you think ice causes fewer changes to Earth's surface today than running water?

The **Big Idea**

References

Contents

Your Skin

Your skin is your body's largest organ. It provides your body with a protective covering. It protects you from disease. It provides your sense of touch, which allows you to feel pressure, texture, temperature, and pain. Your skin also produces sweat to help control your body temperature. When you play hard or exercise, your body produces sweat, which cools you as it evaporates. The sweat from your skin also helps your body get rid of extra salt and other wastes.

▼ The skin is the body's largest organ.

Epidermis
Many layers of dead skin cells form the top of the epidermis. Cells in the lower part of the epidermis are always making new cells.

Pore
These tiny holes on the surface of your skin lead to your dermis.

Sweat Gland
Sweat glands produce sweat, which contains water, salt, and various wastes.

Oil Gland
Oil glands produce oil that keeps your skin soft and smooth.

Dermis
The dermis is much thicker than the epidermis. It is made up of tough, flexible fibers.

Hair Follicle
Each hair follicle has a muscle that can contract and make the hair "stand on end."

Fatty Tissue
This tissue layer beneath the dermis stores food, provides warmth, and attaches your skin to the bone and muscle below.

Caring for Your Skin

- To protect your skin and to keep it healthy, you should wash your body, including your hair and your nails, every day. This helps remove germs, excess oils and sweat, and dead cells from the epidermis, the outer layer of your skin. Because you touch many things during the day, you should wash your hands with soap and water frequently.

- If you get a cut or scratch, you should wash it right away and cover it with a sterile bandage to prevent infection and promote healing.

- Protect your skin from cuts and scrapes by wearing proper safety equipment when you play sports or skate, or when you're riding your bike or scooter.

Your digestive system is made up of connected organs. It breaks down the food you eat and disposes of the leftover wastes your body does not need.

Mouth to Stomach

Digestion begins when you chew your food. Chewing your food breaks it up and mixes it with saliva. When you swallow, the softened food travels down your esophagus to your stomach, where it is mixed with digestive juices. These are strong acids that continue the process of breaking your food down into the nutrients your body needs to stay healthy. Your stomach squeezes your food and turns it into a thick liquid.

Small Intestine and Liver

Your food leaves your stomach and goes into your small intestine. This organ is a long tube just below your stomach. Your liver is an organ that sends bile into your small intestine to help it digest the fats in the food. The walls of the small intestine are lined with millions of small, finger-shaped bumps called villi. Tiny blood vessels in these bumps absorb nutrients from the food as it moves through the small intestine.

Large Intestine

When the food has traveled all the way through your small intestine, it passes into your large intestine. This last organ of your digestive system absorbs water from the food. The remaining wastes are held there until you go to the bathroom.

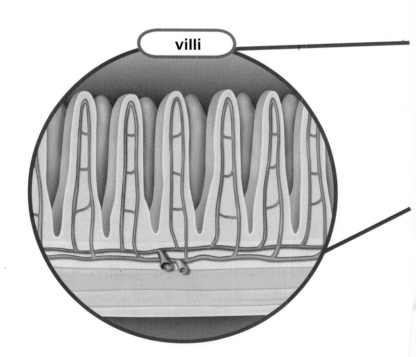

villi

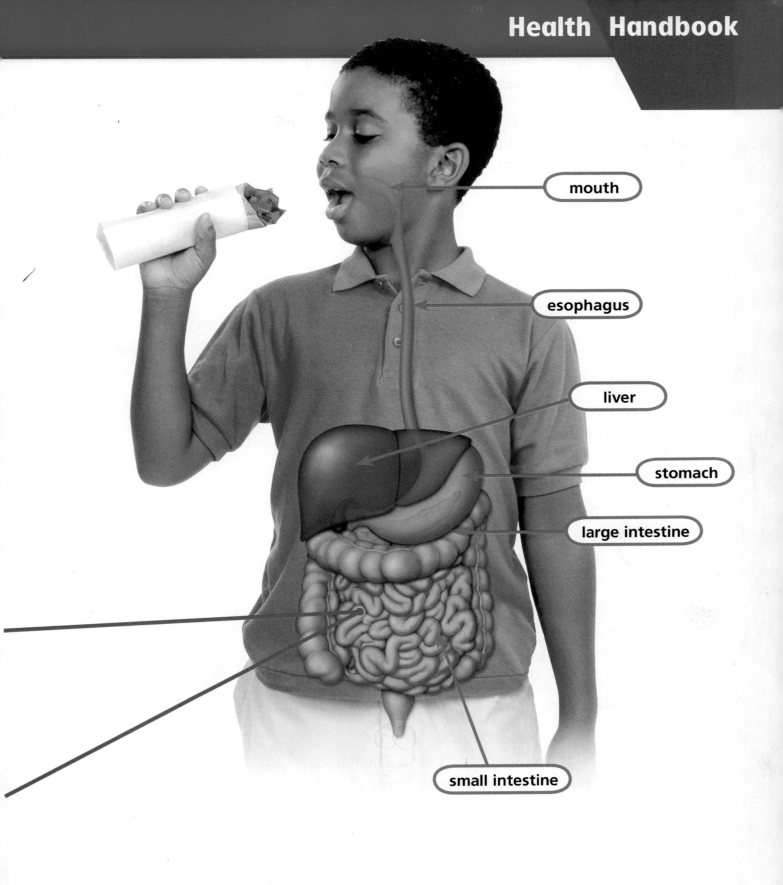

mouth

esophagus

liver

stomach

large intestine

small intestine

Your Circulatory System

Your circulatory system carries nutrients from the food you eat and oxygen from the air you breathe to every cell in your body. As your blood moves through your body, it helps your body fight infections, control your temperature, and remove wastes from your cells.

vein

heart

artery

Your Heart and Blood Vessels

Your heart is the organ that pumps your blood through your circulatory system. It is a strong muscle that beats all the time. As you exercise, it adjusts itself to beat faster to deliver the nutrients and oxygen your muscles need to work harder.

Blood from your heart is pumped first to your lungs, where it releases carbon dioxide and picks up oxygen. Your blood then travels back to your heart to be pumped through your arteries to every part of your body. The blood then returns to your heart through your veins, ready to be pumped out again.

Your Blood

The blood in your circulatory system is a mixture of fluids and specialized cells. The liquid part of your blood is called plasma. Plasma allows the cells in your blood to move through your blood vessels to every part of your body. It is also important in helping your body control your temperature.

Blood Cells

There are three main types of cells in your blood. Each type of cell in your circulatory system plays a special part in keeping your body healthy and fit.

Red blood cells are the most numerous cells in your blood. They carry oxygen from your lungs throughout your body. They also carry carbon dioxide from your cells back to your lungs so that you can breathe it out.

White blood cells help your body fight infections when you become ill.

Platelets help your body stop bleeding when you get a cut or other wound. Platelets clump together as soon as you start to bleed. The sticky clump of platelets traps red blood cells and forms a blood clot. The blood clot hardens to make a scab that seals the cut. Beneath the scab, your body begins healing the wound.

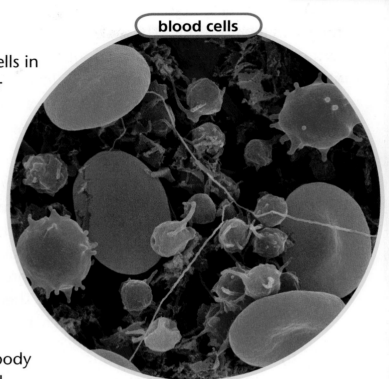

blood cells

Caring for Your Circulatory System

• Eat foods that are low in fat and high in fiber. Fiber helps take away substances that can cause fat to block your blood vessels.

• Eat foods high in iron to help your red blood cells carry oxygen.

• Drink plenty of water to help your body make enough blood.

• Avoid contact with another person's blood.

• Exercise regularly to keep your heart strong.

• Never smoke or chew tobacco.

Your Skeletal System

Your skeletal system includes all of the bones in your body. These strong, hard parts of your body protect your internal organs, help you move, and allow you to sit and to stand up straight.

Your skeletal system works with your muscular system to hold your body up and give it shape. It includes more than 200 bones of different shapes and sizes.

Your Skull

The wide, flat bones of your skull fit tightly together to protect your brain. The bones in the front of your skull give your face its shape.

Your Spine

Your spine, or backbone, is made up of nearly two dozen small, round bones. These bones fit together and connect your head to your pelvis. Each of these bones, or vertebrae (VER•tuh•bree), is shaped like a doughnut with a small, round hole in the center.

Your spinal cord is a bundle of nerves that carries information to and from your brain and the rest of your body. Your spinal cord runs from your brain down your back to your hips through the holes in your vertebrae. There are soft, flexible disks of cartilage between your vertebrae. This allows you to bend and twist your spine. Your spine, pelvis, and leg bones work together to allow you to stand, sit, and move.

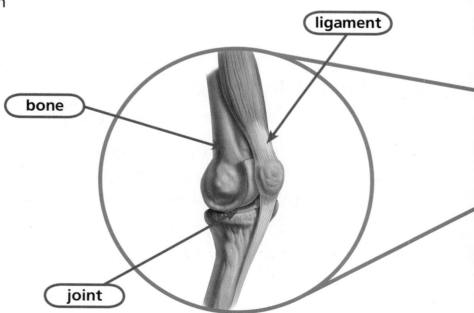

ligament

bone

joint

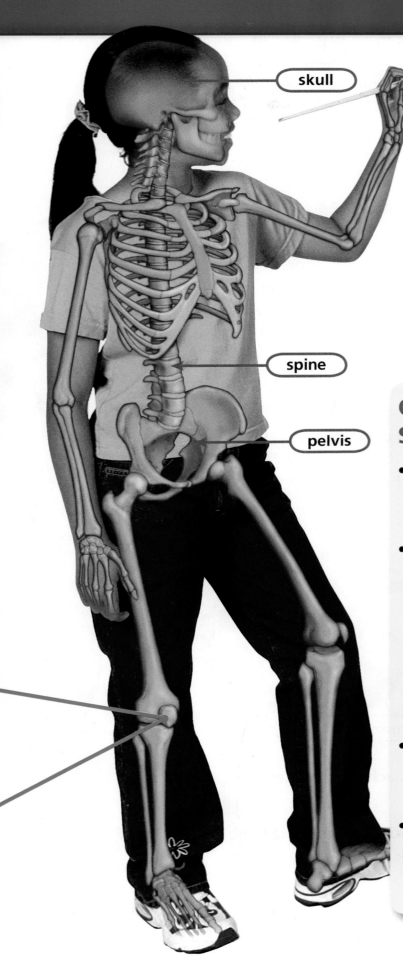

skull

spine

pelvis

Caring for Your Skeletal System

• Always wear a helmet and proper safety gear when you play sports, skate, or ride a bike or a scooter.

• Your bones are made mostly of calcium and other minerals. To keep your skeletal system strong and to help it grow, you should eat foods that are rich in calcium, such as milk, cheese, and yogurt. Dark green, leafy vegetables such as broccoli, spinach, and collard greens are also good sources of calcium.

• Exercise to help your bones stay strong and healthy. Get plenty of rest to help your bones grow.

• Stand and sit with good posture. Sitting slumped over puts strain on your muscles and on your bones.

Your Muscular System

A muscle is a body part that produces movement by contracting and relaxing. All of the muscles in your body make up the muscular system.

Voluntary and Involuntary Muscles

Voluntary Muscles are the muscles you use to move your arms and legs, your face, head, and fingers. You can make these muscles contract or relax to control the way your body moves.

Involuntary Muscles are responsible for movements you usually don't see or control. These muscles make up your heart, your stomach and other organs of your digestive system, and your diaphragm. Your heart beats and your diaphragm controls your breathing without your thinking about them. You cannot stop the action of these muscles.

How Muscles Help You Move

All muscles pull when they contract. Moving your body in more than one direction takes more than one muscle. To reach out with your arm or to pull it back, you use a pair of muscles. As one muscle contracts to stretch out your arm, the other muscle relaxes. As you pull your arm back, the muscles reverse their functions.

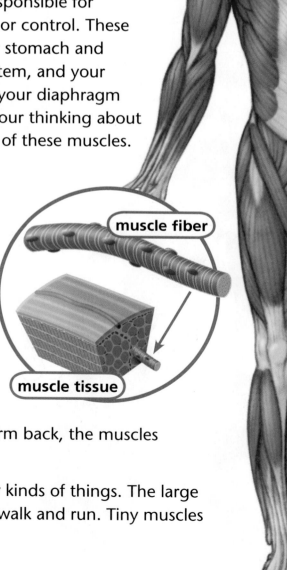

muscle fiber

muscle tissue

Your muscles let you do many kinds of things. The large muscles in your legs allow you to walk and run. Tiny muscles in your face allow you to smile.

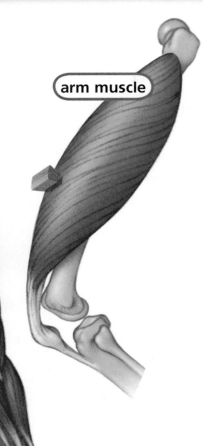

arm muscle

Your Muscles and Your Bones

The muscles that allow you to move your body work with your skeletal system. Muscles in your legs that allow you to kick a ball or ride a bicycle pull on the bones and joints of your legs and lower body. Your muscles are connected to your skeletal system by strong, cordlike tissues called tendons.

Your Achilles tendon just above your heel connects your calf muscles to your heel bone. When you contract those muscles, the tendon pulls on the heel bone and allows you to stand on your toes, jump, or push hard on your bicycle's pedals.

Caring for Your Muscular System

- Always stretch and warm your muscles up before exercising or playing sports. Do this by jogging or walking for at least ten minutes. This brings fresh blood and oxygen into your muscles and helps prevent injury or pain.

- Eat a balanced diet of foods to be sure your muscles have the nutrients they need to grow and remain strong.

- Drink plenty of water when you exercise or play sports. This helps your blood remove wastes from your muscles and helps you build endurance.

- Always cool down after you exercise. Walk or jog slowly for five or ten minutes to let your heartbeat slow and your breathing return to normal. This helps you avoid pain and stiffness after your muscles work hard.

- Stop exercising if you feel pain in your muscles.

- Get plenty of rest before and after you work your muscles hard. They need time to repair themselves and recover from working hard.

Your Senses

Your Eyes and Vision

Your eyes allow you to see light reflected by the things around you. This diagram shows how an eye works. Light enters through the clear outer surface called the cornea. It passes through the pupil. The lens bends the incoming light to focus it on the retina. The retina sends nerve signals along the optic nerve. Your brain uses the signals to form an image. This is what you "see."

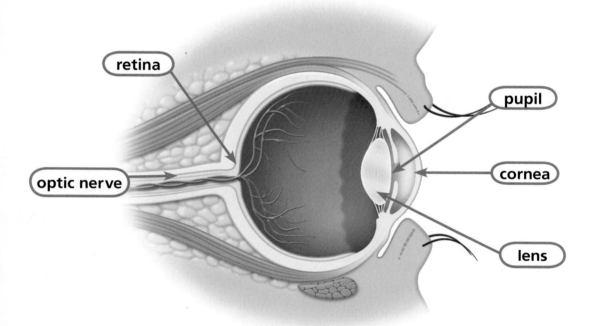

Caring for Your Eyes

- You should have a doctor check your eyesight every year. Tell your parents or your doctor if your vision becomes blurry or if you are having headaches or pain in your eyes.

- Never touch or rub your eyes.

- Protect your eyes by wearing safety goggles when you use tools or play sports.

- Wear swim goggles to protect your eyes from chlorine and other substances in the water.

- Wear sunglasses to protect your eyes from the sun's ultraviolet rays. Looking directly at the sun can damage your eyes permanently.

Your Ears and Hearing

Sounds travel through the air in waves. When those waves enter your ear, you hear a sound. This diagram shows the inside of your ear.

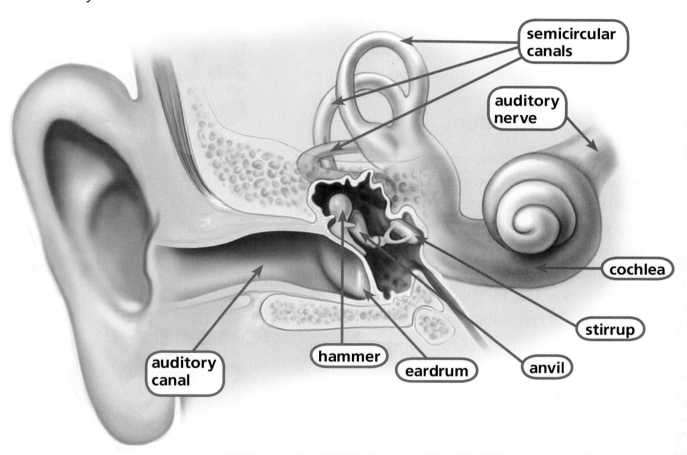

semicircular canals

auditory nerve

cochlea

stirrup

anvil

eardrum

hammer

auditory canal

Caring for Your Ears

- Never put anything in your ears.

- Wear a helmet that covers your ears when you play sports.

- Keep your ears warm in winter.

- Avoid loud sounds and listening to loud music.

- Have your ears checked by a doctor if they hurt or leak fluid or if you begin to have trouble hearing.

- Wear earplugs when you swim. Water in your ears can lead to infection.

Pathogens and Illness

You may know someone who had a cold or the flu this year. These illnesses are caused by germs called pathogens. Illnesses spread when pathogens move from one person to another.

Types of Pathogens

There are four kinds of pathogens—viruses, bacteria, fungi, and protozoans. Viruses are the smallest kind of pathogen. They are so small that they can be seen only with very powerful electron microscopes. Viruses cause many types of illness, including colds, the flu, and chicken pox. Viruses cannot reproduce by themselves. They must use living cells to reproduce.

Bacteria are tiny single-cell organisms that live in water, in the soil, and on almost all surfaces. Most bacteria can be seen only with a microscope. Not all bacteria cause illness. Your body needs some types of bacteria to work well.

The most common type of fungus infection is athlete's foot. This is a burning, itchy infection of the skin between the toes. Ringworm is another skin infection caused by a fungus. It causes itchy round patches to develop on the skin.

Protozoans are the fourth type of pathogen. They are single-cell organisms that are slightly larger than bacteria. They can cause disease when they grow in food or drinking water.

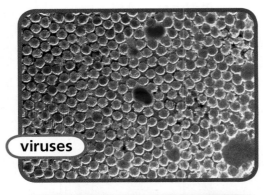

viruses

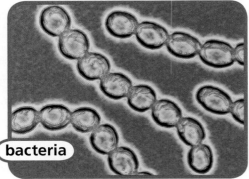

bacteria

fungi

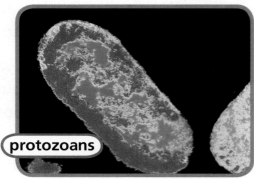

protozoans

Fighting Illness

Pathogens that can make you ill are everywhere. Following good health habits will prevent the spread of pathogens and protect you and others from the illnesses they can cause.

The best way to avoid spreading pathogens is to wash your hands with soap and water. This will remove germs from your skin. You should wash your hands often. Always wash them before and after eating, after handling animals, and after using the bathroom. Avoid touching your mouth, eyes, and nose. Never share cups or drinking straws. If you get a cut or scrape, pathogens can enter your body. It is important to wash cuts and scrapes carefully with soap and water. Then cover the injury with a sterile bandage to keep out germs.

When you are ill, you should avoid spreading pathogens to others. Cover your nose and mouth when you sneeze or cough. Don't share anything that has touched your mouth or nose. Stay home from school until an adult family member tells you that you are well enough to go back.

Even though pathogens are all around, most people become ill only once in a while. This is because the body has systems that protect it from pathogens. These defenses keep pathogens from entering your body.

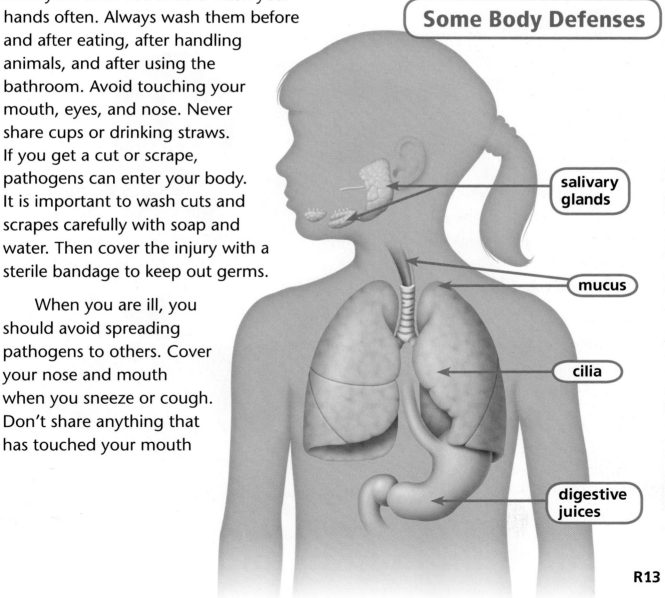

Some Body Defenses

- salivary glands
- mucus
- cilia
- digestive juices

Eat a Balanced Diet

Eating the foods your body needs to grow and fight illness is the most important thing you can do to stay healthy. A balanced diet of healthful foods gives your body energy. Your body's systems need nutrients to function properly and work together.

Choosing unhealthful foods can cause you to gain excess weight and to lack energy. Inactivity and poor food choices can lead to your becoming ill more frequently. Unhealthful foods can also cause you to develop noncommunicable diseases. Unlike communicable diseases, which are caused by germs, these illnesses occur because your body systems are not working properly.

Exercise Regularly

Exercise keeps your body healthy. Regular exercise helps your heart, lungs, and muscles stay strong. It helps your body digest food. It also helps your body fight disease. Exercising to keep your body strong also helps prevent injury when you play sports.

Exercise allows your body to rest more effectively. Getting enough sleep prepares your body for the next day. It allows your muscles and bones to grow and to recover from exercise. Getting the rest you need also helps keep your mind alert so you can learn well.

Identify the Main Idea and Details

Many of the lessons in this science book are written so that you can understand main ideas and the details that support them. You can use a graphic organizer like this one to show a main idea and details.

Main Idea: The most important idea of a selection

Detail: Information that tells more about the main idea

Detail: Information that tells more about the main idea

Detail: Information that tells more about the main idea

Tips for Identifying the Main Idea and Details

- To find the main idea, ask *What is this mostly about?*

- Remember that the main idea is not always stated in the first sentence of a passage.

- Look for details that answer questions such as *who, what, where, when, why,* and *how.* Use pictures as clues to help you.

Here is an example.

Main Idea

An environment that meets the needs of a living thing is called its habitat. Some habitats are as big as a whole forest. This is often true for birds that fly from place to place. Some habitats are very small. For example, fungi might grow only in certain places on a forest floor.

Detail

Here is what you could record in the graphic organizer.

Main Idea: An environment that meets the needs of a living thing is called its habitat.

Detail: Some habitats are as big as a whole forest.

Detail: A bird's habitat might be a whole forest.

Detail: Fungi might grow only in certain places on a forest floor.

More About Main Idea and Details

Sometimes the main idea is not stated at the beginning of a passage. If the main idea is not stated, it can be understood from the details. Look at the details in this graphic organizer. What do you think the main idea of the passage is?

Main Idea:

Detail: Green plants are the producers in a food chain. They make their own food.	**Detail:** Consumers make up the next level of a food chain. They eat plants and other living things for energy.	**Detail:** Decomposers are the next level. They feed on the wastes of consumers or on their remains.

A paragraph's main idea may be supported by details of different types. In the following paragraph, identify whether the details give reasons, examples, facts, steps, or descriptions.

A group of the same species living in the same place at the same time is called a population. A forest may have populations of several different kinds of trees. Trout may be one of several populations of fish in a stream. Deer may be one population among many in a meadow.

Skill Practice

Read the following paragraph. Use the Tips for Identifying the Main Idea and Details to answer the questions.

Animals do not get their energy directly from the sun. Many eat plants, which have used sunlight to make food. Animals that don't eat plants still depend on the energy of sunlight. They eat animals that have eaten plants. The sun is the main source of energy for all living things.

1. What is the main idea of the paragraph?

2. What supporting details give more information about the main idea?

3. What details answer any of the questions *who, what, where, when, why,* and *how?*

Compare and Contrast

Some lessons are written to help you see how things are alike or different. You can use a graphic organizer like this one to compare and contrast.

Topic: Name the two things you are comparing and contrasting.

Alike	**Different**
List ways the things are alike.	List ways the things are different.

Tips for Comparing and Contrasting

- To compare, ask *How are the people, places, objects, ideas, or events alike?*

- To contrast, ask *How are the people, places, objects, ideas, or events different?*

- When you compare, look for signal words and phrases such as *similar, alike, both, the same as, too,* and *also.*

- When you contrast, look for signal words and phrases such as *unlike, different, however, yet, while,* and *but.*

Here is an example.

Compare

Mars and Venus are the two planets closest to Earth. They are known as inner planets. Venus and Earth are about the same size, but Mars is a little smaller. Venus does not have any moons. However, Mars has two moons.

Contrast

Here is what you could record in the graphic organizer.

Topic: Mars and Venus

Alike	**Different**
Both are inner planets.	Mars is smaller than Venus.
Both are close to Earth.	Mars has two moons.

More About Compare and Contrast

You can better understand new information about things when you know how they are alike and how they are different. Use the graphic organizer from page R18 to sort the following items of information about Mars and Venus.

Mars	Venus
Mars is the fourth planet from the sun.	Venus is the second planet from the sun.
A year on Mars is 687 Earth days.	A year on Venus is 225 Earth days.
Mars has a diameter of 6794 kilometers.	Venus has a diameter of 12,104 kilometers.
The soil on Mars is a dark reddish-brown.	Venus is dry and has a thick atmosphere.

Sometimes a paragraph compares and contrasts more than one topic. In the following paragraph, one topic being compared and contrasted is underlined. Find the second topic being compared and contrasted.

Radio telescopes and optical telescopes are two types of telescopes that are used to observe objects in space. A radio telescope collects radio waves with a large, bowl-shaped antenna. An optical telescope collects light. There are two types of optical telescopes. A refracting telescope uses lenses to magnify an object. A reflecting telescope uses a curved mirror to magnify an object.

Skill Practice

Read the following paragraph. Use the Tips for Comparing and Contrasting to answer the questions.

Radio telescopes and optical telescopes work in the same way. However, optical telescopes collect and focus light, while radio telescopes collect and focus invisible radio waves. Radio waves are not affected by clouds and poor weather. Computers can make pictures from data collected by radio telescopes.

1. How are radio and optical telescopes alike and different?

2. What signal words can you find in the paragraph?

Cause and Effect

Focus Skill

Some of the lessons in this science book are written to help you understand why things happen. You can use a graphic organizer like this one to show cause and effect.

Cause
A cause is an action or event that makes something happen.

→

Effect
An effect is what happens as a result of an action or event.

Tips for Identifying Cause and Effect

- To find an effect, ask *What happened?*

- To find a cause, ask *Why did this happen?*

- Remember that actions and events can have more than one cause or effect.

- Look for signal words and phrases such as *because* and *as a result* to help you identify causes and effects.

Here is an example.

Cause

Effect

A pulley is a simple machine. It helps us do work. It is made up of a rope or chain and a wheel around which the rope fits. When you pull down on one end of the rope, the wheel turns and the other end of the rope moves up.

Here is what you could record in the graphic organizer.

Cause
One end of the rope in a pulley is pulled down.

→

Effect
The pulley wheel turns, and the other end of the rope moves up.

R20

More About Cause and Effect

Actions and events can have more than one cause or effect. For example, suppose the paragraph on page R20 included a sentence that said *The pulley can be used to raise an object.* You could then identify two effects of operating a pulley, as shown in this graphic organizer.

Cause
One end of the rope in a pulley is pulled down.

Effect
The pulley wheel turns, and the other end of the rope moves up.

Effect
An object is raised.

Some paragraphs contain more than one cause and effect. In the following paragraph, one cause and its effect are underlined. Find the second cause and its effect.

A fixed pulley and a movable pulley can be put together to make a compound machine. Using a fixed pulley changes the direction of your force. Adding a movable pulley increases your force.

Skill Practice

Read the following paragraph. Use the Tips for Identifying Cause and Effect to help you answer the questions.

A lever can be used to open a paint can. The outer rim of the can is used as the fulcrum. Your hand supplies the effort force. The force put out by the end of the lever that is under the lid is greater than the effort force. As a result, the lid is popped up.

1. What causes the paint can's lid to pop up?

2. What is the effect when an effort force is applied?

3. What signal phrase helped you identify the cause and effect in this paragraph?

 # Sequence

Some lessons in this science book are written to help you understand the order in which things happen. You can use a graphic organizer like this one to show a sequence.

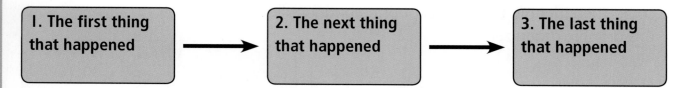

| 1. The first thing that happened | → | 2. The next thing that happened | → | 3. The last thing that happened |

Tips for Understanding a Sequence

- Pay attention to the order in which events happen.

- Recall dates and times to help you understand the sequence.

- Look for signal words such as *first, next, then, last,* and *finally.*

- Sometimes it is helpful to add your own time-order words to help you understand a sequence.

Here is an example.

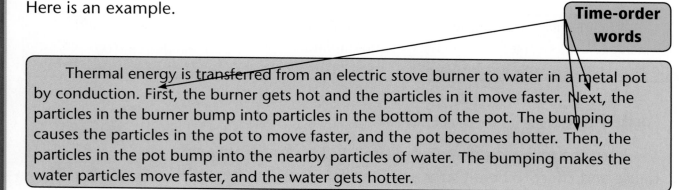

Time-order words

Thermal energy is transferred from an electric stove burner to water in a metal pot by conduction. First, the burner gets hot and the particles in it move faster. Next, the particles in the burner bump into particles in the bottom of the pot. The bumping causes the particles in the pot to move faster, and the pot becomes hotter. Then, the particles in the pot bump into the nearby particles of water. The bumping makes the water particles move faster, and the water gets hotter.

Here is what you could record in the graphic organizer.

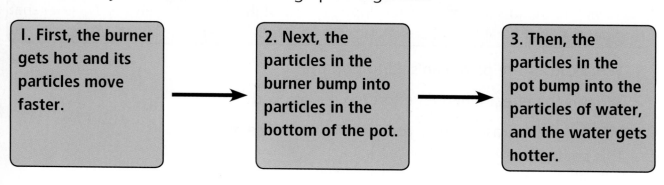

| 1. First, the burner gets hot and its particles move faster. | → | 2. Next, the particles in the burner bump into particles in the bottom of the pot. | → | 3. Then, the particles in the pot bump into the particles of water, and the water gets hotter. |

More About Sequence

Sometimes information is sequenced by time. For example, in an experiment to measure temperature change over time, a graphic organizer could sequence the steps of the procedure.

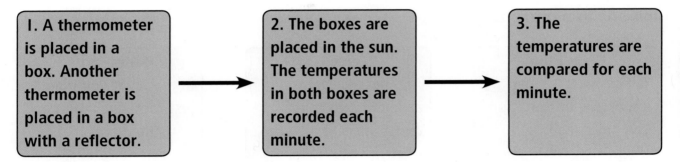

| 1. A thermometer is placed in a box. Another thermometer is placed in a box with a reflector. | → | 2. The boxes are placed in the sun. The temperatures in both boxes are recorded each minute. | → | 3. The temperatures are compared for each minute. |

When time-order words are not given, add your own words to help you understand the sequence. In the paragraph below, one time-order word has been included and underlined. What time-order words can you add to understand the paragraph's sequence?

> Convection is the transfer of thermal energy in a fluid, a liquid, or gas. As the fluid near a hot object gets hot, it expands. The hot fluid is forced up by the cooler, denser fluid around it. <u>Then</u>, as the hot fluid is forced up, it warms the fluid around it. It slowly cools as it sinks.

Skill Practice

Read the following paragraph. Use the Tips for Understanding a Sequence to answer the questions.

> Solar energy can be used to heat water in a home. First, solar panels are placed on the roof of a house. Next, the panels absorb infrared radiation from the sun. Then, the radiation heats the water as it flows through the panels.

1. What is the first thing that happens in the sequence?

2. How many steps are involved in the process?

3. What three signal words helped you identify the sequence in this paragraph?

Summarize

At the end of every lesson in this science book, you are asked to summarize. When you summarize, you use your own words to tell what something is about. In the lesson, you will find ideas for writing your summary. You can also use a graphic organizer like this one to summarize.

| **Main Idea:** Tell about the most important information you have read. | + | **Details:** Add details that answer important questions such as *who, what, where, when, why,* and *how*. | = | **Summary:** Retell what you have just read, including only the most important details. |

Tips for Summarizing

- To write a summary, first ask *What is the most important idea of the paragraph?*

- To add details, ask *who, what, when, where, why,* and *how*.

- Remember to use fewer words than the original.

- Tell the information in your own words.

Here and on the next page is an example.

Main Idea

Details

The water cycle is the constant recycling of water. As the sun warms the ocean, water particles leave the water and enter the air as water vapor. This is evaporation, the process of a liquid changing to a gas. Clouds form when water vapor condenses high in the atmosphere. Condensation occurs when the water vapor rises, cools, and changes from a gas to a liquid. When the drops are too large to stay up in the air, precipitation occurs as the water falls back to Earth.

Here is what you could record in the graphic organizer.

Main Idea:
The water cycle is the constant recycling of water.

+

Details:
Evaporation is the change from a liquid to a gas. Condensation is the change from a gas to a liquid. Precipitation is water that falls to Earth.

=

Summary:
The constant recycling of water is the water cycle. It includes evaporation, condensation, and precipitation.

More About Summarizing

Sometimes a paragraph has details that are not important enough to be included in a summary. The graphic organizer remains the same because those details are not important to understanding the paragraph's main idea.

Skill Practice

Read the following paragraph. Use the Tips for Summarizing to answer the questions.

> Tides are the changes in the ocean's water level each day. At high tide, much of the beach is covered with water. At low tide, waves break farther away from the shore and less of the beach is underwater. Every day most shorelines have two high tides and two low tides. High tides and low tides occur at regular times and are usually a little more than six hours apart.

1. If a friend asked you what this paragraph was about, what information would you include? What would you leave out?

2. What is the main idea of the paragraph?

3. Which two details would you include in a summary of the paragraph?

Draw Conclusions

At the end of each lesson in this science book, you are asked to draw conclusions. To draw conclusions, use the information that you have read and what you already know. Drawing conclusions can help you understand what you read. You can use a graphic organizer like this.

What I Read Use facts from the text to help you understand.	+	**What I Know** Use your own experience to help you understand.	=	**Conclusion:** Combine facts and details in the text with personal knowledge or experience.

Tips for Drawing Conclusions

• To draw conclusions, first ask *What information from the text do I need to think about?*

• Then ask *What do I know from my own experience that could help me draw a conclusion?*

• Ask yourself whether the conclusion you have drawn is valid, or makes sense.

Here is an example.

> Plants need air, nutrients, water, and light to live. A plant makes its own food by a process called photosynthesis. Photosynthesis takes place in the plant's leaves. In an experiment, a plant is placed in a dark room without any light. It is watered every day.

Text information

Here is what you could record in the graphic organizer.

What I Read A plant needs air, nutrients, water, and light to live.	+	**What I Know** Plants use light to make the food they need to live and grow.	=	**Conclusion:** The plant will die since it is not getting any light.

More About Drawing Conclusions

Sensible conclusions based on your experience and the facts you read are valid. For example, suppose the paragraph on page R26 included a sentence that said *After a day, the plant is removed from the dark room and placed in the sunlight.* You could then draw a different conclusion about the life of the plant.

What I Read		**What I Know**		**Conclusion:**
A plant needs air, nutrients, water, and light to live.	+	Plants use light to make the food they need to live and grow.	=	The plant will live.

Sometimes a paragraph might not contain enough information to draw a valid conclusion. Read the following paragraph. Think of one valid conclusion you could draw. Then think of one conclusion that would be invalid or wouldn't make sense.

Cacti are plants that are found in the desert. Sometimes it does not rain in the desert for months or even years. Cacti have thick stems. The roots of cactus plants grow just below the surface of the ground.

Skill Practice

Read the following paragraph. Use the Tips for Drawing Conclusions to answer the questions.

Animals behave in ways that help them meet their needs. Some animal behaviors are instincts, and some are learned. Tiger cubs learn to hunt by watching their mothers hunt and by playing with other tiger cubs. They are not born knowing exactly how to hunt.

1. What conclusion can you draw about a tiger cub that is separated from its mother and other tigers?

2. What information from your own experience helped you draw the conclusion?

3. What text information did you use to draw the conclusion?

Using Tables, Charts, and Graphs

As you do investigations in science, you collect, organize, display, and interpret data. Tables, charts, and graphs are good ways to organize and display data so that others can understand and interpret your data.

The tables, charts, and graphs in this Handbook will help you read and understand data. The Handbook will also help you choose the best ways to display data so that you can draw conclusions and make predictions.

Reading a Table

A scientist is studying the rainfall in Bangladesh. She wants to know which months are part of the monsoon season, or the time when the area receives the greatest amount of rainfall. The table shows the data she has collected.

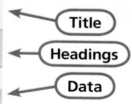

Monthly Rainfall in Chittagong, Bangladesh	
Month	Rainfall (inches)
January	1
February	2
March	3
April	6
May	10
June	21
July	23
August	10
September	13
October	7
November	2
December	1

Title
Headings
Data

How to Read a Table

1. **Look** at the title to learn what the table is about.

2. **Read** the headings to find out what information is given.

3. **Analyze** the data. Look for patterns.

4. **Draw conclusions.** When data is displayed in a graph, you are able to see patterns easily.

By studying the table, you can see how much rain fell during each month. If the scientist wanted to look for patterns, she might display the data in a graph.

Reading a Bar Graph

The data in this bar graph is the same as that in the table. A bar graph can be used to compare data about different events or groups.

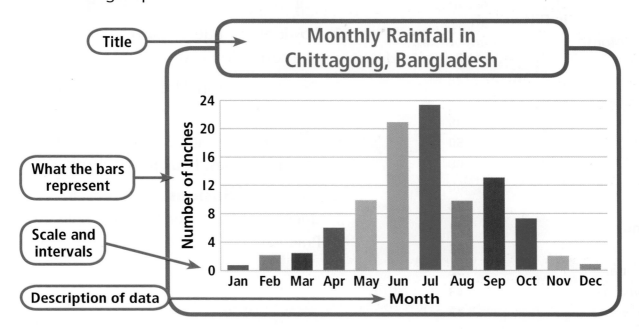

Title → **Monthly Rainfall in Chittagong, Bangladesh**

What the bars represent →

Scale and intervals →

Description of data →

How to Read a Bar Graph

1. **Look** at the title to learn what kind of information is shown.

2. **Read** the graph. Use the numbers and labels to guide you.

3. **Analyze** the data. Study the bars to compare the measurements. Look for patterns.

4. **Draw conclusions.** Ask yourself questions like the ones under Skills Practice.

Skills Practice

1. In which two months does Chittagong receive the most rainfall?

2. Which months have the same amounts of rainfall?

3. **Predict** During which months are the roads likely to be flooded?

4. How does the bar graph help you identify the monsoon season and the rainfall amounts?

5. Was the bar graph a good choice for displaying this data? Explain.

Reading a Line Graph

A scientist collected this data about temperatures in Pittsburgh, Pennsylvania.

| Average Temperatures in Pittsburgh ||
Month	Temperature (degrees Fahrenheit)
January	28
February	29
March	39
April	50
May	60
June	68
July	74
August	72
September	63
October	52
November	43
December	32

How to Read a Line Graph

1. **Look** at the title to learn what kind of information is shown.

2. **Read** the graph. Use the numbers and labels to guide you.

3. **Analyze** the data. Study the points along the lines. Look for patterns.

4. **Draw conclusions.** Ask yourself questions like the ones under Skills Practice.

Here is the same data displayed in a line graph. A line graph is used to show changes over time.

Title

What the points represent

Scale and intervals

Description of data

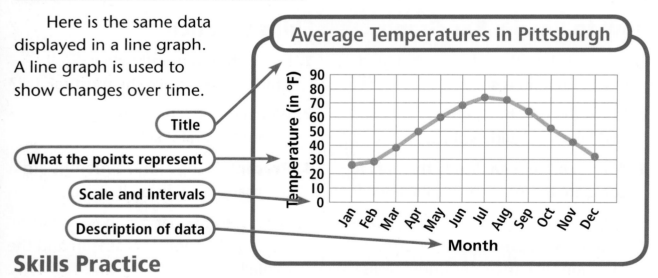

Average Temperatures in Pittsburgh

Skills Practice

1. In which three months are the temperatures the warmest in Pittsburgh?

2. **Predict** During which months are ponds in Pittsburgh likely to freeze?

3. Was the line graph a good choice for displaying this data? Explain.

Reading a Circle Graph

Some scientists counted 100 animals at a park. The scientists wanted to know which animal group had the most animals. They classified the animals by making a table. Here is their data.

Animal Groups at the Park	
Animal Group	**Number Observed**
Mammals	7
Insects	63
Birds	22
Reptiles	5
Amphibians	3

The circle graph shows the same data as the table. A circle graph can be used to show data as a whole made up of parts.

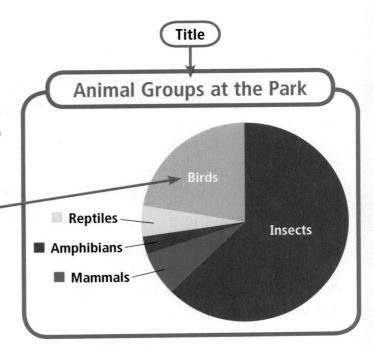

Title

Animal Groups at the Park

Label for a section

Birds

Reptiles

Amphibians

Mammals

Insects

How to Read a Circle Graph

1. **Look** at the title to learn what kind of information is shown.

2. **Read** the graph. Look at the label of each section to find out what information is shown.

3. **Analyze** the data. Compare the sizes of the sections to determine how they are related.

4. **Draw conclusions.** Ask yourself questions like the ones under Skills Practice.

Skills Practice

1. Which animal group had the most members? Which one had the fewest?

2. **Predict** If you visited a nearby park, would you expect to see more reptiles or more insects?

3. Was the circle graph a good choice for displaying this data? Explain.

Measurements

When you measure, you compare an object to a standard unit of measure. Scientists almost always use the units of the metric system.

Measuring Length and Capacity in Metric Units

When you measure length, you find the distance between two points. The table shows the metric units of **length** and how they are related.

Equivalent Measures
1 centimeter (cm) = 10 millimeters (mm)
1 decimeter (dm) = 10 centimeters (cm)
1 meter (m) = 1000 millimeters
1 meter = 10 decimeters
1 kilometer (km) = 1000 meters

You can use these comparisons to help you learn the size of each metric unit of length:

A **millimeter (mm)** is about the thickness of a dime.	A **centimeter (cm)** is about the width of your index finger.	A **decimeter (dm)** is about the width of an adult's hand.	A **meter (m)** is about the width of a door.
	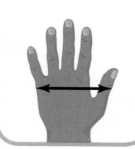		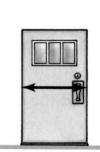

The following diagram shows how to multiply and divide to change to larger and smaller units.

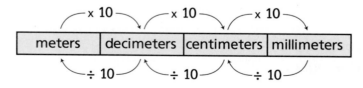

When you measure capacity, you find the amount a container can hold when it is filled. The images show the metric units of **capacity** and how they are related.

A **milliliter (mL)** is the amount of liquid that can fill one section of a dropper.

1 mL

A **liter (L)** is the amount of liquid that can fill a plastic water bottle.

1 L = 1000 mL

You can use multiplication to change liters to milliliters.

You can use division to change milliliters to liters.

2 L = _____ mL

Think: There are 1000 mL in 1 L.

2 L = 2 x 1000 = 2000 mL

So, 2 L = 2000 mL.

4000 mL = _____ L

Think: There are 1000 mL in 1 L.

4000 ÷ 1000 = 4

So, 4000 mL = 4 L.

Skills Practice

Complete. Tell whether you multiply or divide.

1. 3 L = _____ mL

2. 5000 mL = _____ L

3. 7000 mL = _____ L

4. 6 L = _____ mL

5. 500 dm = _____ cm

6. 4 m = _____ mm

7. 8 _____ = 80 cm

8. _____ m = 1400 cm

Measuring Mass

Matter is what everything is made of. **Mass** is the amount of matter that is in something. The metric units of mass are the gram (g) and the kilogram (kg). You can use these comparisons to help you understand the masses of some everyday objects:

A paper clip is about **1 gram** (g).

A slice of wheat bread is about **20 grams.**

A box of 12 crayons is about **100 grams.**

A large wedge of cheese is about **1 kilogram** (kg).

You can use multiplication to change kilograms to grams.

You can use division to change grams to kilograms.

2 kg = _____ g	4000 g = _____ kg
Think: There are 1000 g in 1 kg.	Think: There are 1000 g in 1 kg.
2 kg = 2 x 1000 = 2000 g	4000 ÷ 1000 = 4
So, 2 kg = 2000 g.	So, 4000 g = 4 kg.

Skills Practice

Complete. Tell whether you multiply or divide by 1000.

1. 5000 g = _____ kg

2. 3000 g = _____ kg

3. 4 kg = _____ g

4. 7 kg = _____ g

Measurement Systems

SI Measures (Metric)

Temperature
Ice melts at 0 degrees Celsius (°C).
Water freezes at 0°C.
Water boils at 100°C.

Length and Distance
1000 meters (m) =
             1 kilometer (km)
100 centimeters (cm) = 1 m
10 millimeters (mm) = 1 cm

Force
1 newton (N) = 1 kilogram x
  1 meter/second/second (kg-m/s^2)

Volume
1 cubic meter (m^3) =
          1 m x 1 m x 1 m
1 cubic centimeter (cm^3) =
       1 cm x 1 cm x 1 cm
1 liter (L) = 1000 milliliters (mL)
1 cm^3 = 1 mL

Area
1 square kilometer (km^2) =
          1 km x 1 km
1 hectare = 10,000 m^2

Mass
1000 grams (g) = 1 kilogram (kg)
1000 milligrams (mg) = 1 g
1000 kilograms = 1 metric ton

Rates
km/hr = kilometers per hour
m/sec = meters per second

Customary Measures

Temperature
Ice melts at 32 degrees
  Fahrenheit (°F).
Water freezes at 32°F.
Water boils at 212°F.

Length and Distance
12 inches (in.) = 1 foot (ft)
3 ft = 1 yard (yd)
5280 ft = 1 mile (mi)

Force
16 ounces (oz) = 1 pound (lb)
2000 pounds = 1 ton (T)

Volume of Fluids
2 cups (c) = 1 pint (pt)
2 pt = 1 quart (qt)
4 qt = 1 gallon (gal)

Area
1 square mile (mi^2) = 1 mi x 1 mi
1 acre = 4840 sq ft

Rates
mph = miles per hour
ft/sec = feet per second

Safety in Science

Doing investigations in science can be fun, but you need to be sure you do them safely. Here are some rules to follow.

1. **Think ahead.** Study the steps of the investigation so you know what to expect. If you have any questions, ask your teacher. Be sure that you understand all caution statements and safety reminders.

2. **Be neat.** Keep your work area clean. If you have long hair, pull it back so it doesn't get in the way. Roll or push up long sleeves to keep them away from your activity.

3. **Oops!** If you should spill or break something, or you get cut, tell your teacher right away.

4. **Watch your eyes.** Wear safety goggles anytime you are directed to do so. If you get anything in your eyes, tell your teacher right away.

5. **Yuck!** Never eat or drink anything during a science activity.

6. **Don't get shocked.** Be especially careful if an electric appliance is used. Be sure that electrical cords are in a safe place where you can't trip over them. Don't ever pull a plug out of an outlet by pulling on the cord.

7. **Keep it clean.** Always clean up when you have finished. Put everything away, and wipe your work area. Wash your hands.

Visit the Multimedia Science Glossary to see illustrations of these words and to hear them pronounced.
www.hspscience.com

Every entry in the glossary begins with a term and a *phonetic respelling*. A phonetic respelling writes the word the way it sounds, which can help you pronounce new or unfamiliar words. The definition of the term follows the respelling. An example of how to use the term in a sentence follows the definition.

If there is a page number in () at the end of the entry, it tells you where to find the term in your textbook. Many of these terms are highlighted in yellow in the chapter in your textbook. Most entries have an illustration to help you understand the term. The Pronunciation Key below will help you understand the respellings. Syllables are separated by a bullet (•). Small, uppercase letters show stressed syllables.

Pronunciation Key

Sound	As in	Phonetic Respelling	Sound	As in	Phonetic Respelling
a	bat	(BAT)	oh	over	(OH•ver)
ah	lock	(LAHK)	oo	pool	(POOL)
air	rare	(RAIR)	ow	out	(OWT)
ar	argue	(AR•gyoo)	oy	foil	(FOYL)
aw	law	(LAW)	s	cell	(SEL)
ay	face	(FAYS)		sit	(SIT)
ch	chapel	(CHAP•uhl)	sh	sheep	(SHEEP)
e	test	(TEST)	th	that	(THAT)
	metric	(MEH•trik)		thin	(THIN)
ee	eat	(EET)	u	pull	(PUL)
	feet	(FEET)	uh	medal	(MED•uhl)
	ski	(SKEE)		talent	(TAL•uhnt)
er	paper	(PAY•per)		pencil	(PEN•suhl)
	fern	(FERN)		onion	(UHN•yuhn)
eye	idea	(eye•DEE•uh)		playful	(PLAY•fuhl)
i	bit	(BIT)		dull	(DUHL)
ing	going	(GOH•ing)	y	yes	(YES)
k	card	(KARD)		ripe	(RYP)
	kite	(KYT)	z	bags	(BAGZ)
ngk	bank	(BANGK)	zh	treasure	(TREZH•er)

Multimedia Science Glossary: www.hspscience.com

A

accommodation
[uh•kahm•uh•DAY•shuhn] **A learned behavior that helps the individual members of a species survive:** Wearing gloves is an *accommodation* that helps people survive in cold climates. (229)

adaptation
[a•duhp•TAY•shuhn] **A body part or behavior that helps an organism survive:** This insect's stick-like body is an *adaptation* that makes it look like part of a tree. (228)

attract [uh•TRAKT] **To pull toward:** Magnets *attract* iron. (59)

axis [AKS•uhs] **A line at the side or bottom of a graph:** Most graphs have two *axes.* (34)

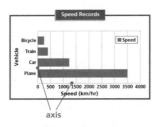

B

bacteria
[bak•TEER•ee•uh] **A certain type of microorganism:** Some *bacteria* can make you sick. (258)

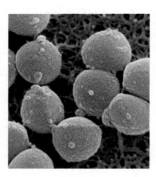

battery [BAT•uh•ree] **An energy storage device that uses chemical energy to produce a flow of electric current:** We use *batteries* to power some toys. (70)

biome [BY•ohm] **A large area that has a similar climate and similar ecosystems in all parts of it:** A deciduous forest is one kind of *biome.* (216)

boulder [BOHL•der] A large, rounded rock larger than 256 millimeters (10 in.) in diameter: *Boulders* are usually heavy and hard to move. (351)

bulb [BUHLB] A device made up of a glass globe, a filament, and metal, which produces heat and light when an electric current passes through it: Flashlights have light *bulbs* in them. (70)

 C

carnivore [KAR•nih•vawr] An animal that eats only other animals: *Carnivores* have sharp teeth to help them eat meat. (160)

chemical change [KEM•ih•kuhl CHAYNJ] A change that results in a new substance; chemical weathering involves chemical changes: Scientists can produce *chemical changes* in their laboratories. (340)

chemical weathering [KEM•ih•kuhl WETH•er•ing] A process by which the chemical makeup of a rock is changed and the rock is broken down: Water is involved in a lot of *chemical weathering.* (340)

cleavage [KLEEV•ij] The way some minerals break into pieces with regular shapes: Mica's *cleavage* is smooth, producing flat sheets. (278)

color [KUHL•er] A visual property used to identify minerals: The *color* of this mineral helps me identify quartz. (276)

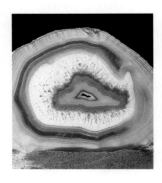

community
[kuh•MYOON•uh•tee]
All the populations of organisms living in an environment: A *community* has many kinds of living things. (214)

compass [KUHM•puhs] **A tool used to determine direction:** This *compass* is pointing north. (100)

competition [kahm•puh•TIH•shuhn] **The working of organisms to win limited resources:** A cold winter increases *competition* for food. (198)

consumer [kuhn•SOOM•er] **A living thing that can't make its own food and must eat other living things:** Animals are *consumers*. (158)

convert [kuhn•VERT] **To change:** Pressure *converts* igneous rock to metamorphic rock. (120)

cork [KAWRK] **The lightweight, spongy bark of a kind of oak tree:** You can push pins into the *cork* on a bulletin board. (97)

creep [KREEP] **The slow movement of soil or rock downhill:** *Creep* can put soil over mountain roads. (325)

D

decomposer [dee•kuhm•POH•zer] **A living thing that feeds on the wastes of plants and animals:** Mushrooms are one kind of *decomposer*. (170)

deposit [dee•PAHZ•it] **An amount of a mineral in a certain place:** Mines let people get to useful mineral *deposits* in the ground. (274)

deposition [deh•puh•ZIH•shuhn] **The dropping of sediment by rivers as they slow down:** Deltas are formed by *deposition.* (351)

dune [DOON] **A large mound of sand piled up by wind:** *Dunes* can move when the wind blows. (328)

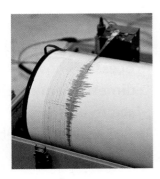

E

earthquake [ERTH•kwayk] **A shaking of Earth's surface, caused by movement of rock in the crust:** This seismograph is recording an *earthquake.* (324)

ecology [ee•KAHL•uh•jee] **The study of ecosystems:** *Ecology* helps us understand different ecosystems. (218)

ecosystem [EE•koh•sis•tuhm] **A community of living things and the community's physical environment:** A pond is one example of an *ecosystem.* (212)

electric charge [ee•LEK•trik CHARJ] **A basic property of the tiny particles that make up matter; it can be positive or negative:** Some particles of matter have *electric charge.* (58)

electric circuit [ee•LEK•trik SER•kit] **A continuous pathway that can carry an electric current:** The lights in your home are on an *electric circuit.* (72)

electric current

[ee•LEK•trik KER•uhnt] **A flow of electric charges:** *Electric current* flows through a circuit. (72)

electric field

[ee•LEK•trik FEELD] **The area around electric charges in which electric forces can act:** Strong static electric charges have large *electric fields.* (62)

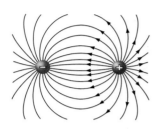

electric motor

[ee•LEK•trik MOHT•er] **A device that converts electricity to motion:** Some toys have *electric motors.* (124)

electricity

[ee•lek•TRIS•ih•tee] **The group of effects and properties that are related to electric charges and their interactions; also the form of energy carried by electric current:** Many things in your home run on *electricity.* (59, 120)

electromagnet

[ee•LEK•troh•mag•nuht] **A device made up of a current-carrying wire coil around an iron core:** You can make an *electromagnet* with a nail, some wire, and a battery. (111)

electron

[ee•LEK•trahn] **A subatomic particle with negative electric charge:** Most electric currents are a flow of *electrons.*

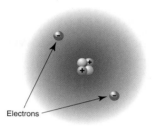

Electrons

energy conversion

[EN•er•jee kuhn•VER•zhuhn] **A changing of energy from one form to another:** Energy stations perform *energy conversions.* (123)

erosion

[ee•ROH•zhuhn] **The process of moving sediment from one place to another:** This gully was formed by *erosion.* (350)

estimate
[ES•tuh•muht]
A careful guess about the amount of something: When you can't measure something, you might make an *estimate*. (22)

experiment
[eks•PAIR•uh•muhnt]
A controlled test of a hypothesis: An *experiment* has controlled variables and a dependent variable. (23)

F

fault [FAWLT] **In Earth's crust, a break along which rocks can move:** The San Andreas *fault* is more than 1300 kilometers (800 mi) long. (324)

filament
[FIL•uh•muhnt]
The glowing wire coil inside a light bulb: You can see the glowing *filament* through the clear glass of this light bulb. (137)

food chain
[FOOD CHAYN] **A series of organisms that depend on one another for food:** A producer is at the bottom of every *food chain*. (184)

food web [FOOD WEB]
A group of food chains that overlap: *Food webs* show interdependence in ecosystems. (186)

fracture [FRAK•cher]
A way minerals break if they do not cleave, or break into regular shapes: Pieces of quartz are often rough because of its curved *fracture*. (279)

fungus [FUHN•guhs]
An organism that can't make food and can't move about: Mushrooms are a kind of *fungus*. (172)

G

generator
[JEN•uh•ray•ter]
A device that converts other forms of energy into electricity:
People use portable *generators* when the power is out. (126)

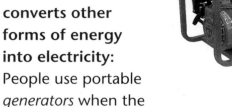

H

habitat [HAB•uh•tat]
An environment that meets the needs of an organism: Different living things need different *habitats.* (196)

hardness [HARD•nuhs]
The measure of how difficult it is for a mineral to be scratched: Minerals that can be scratched with a fingernail have a low *hardness.* (280)

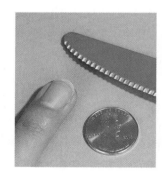

heat [HEET] **The form of energy related to the random motion of the atoms and molecules that make up matter:** These steel bars have been exposed to a lot of *heat.* (137)

herbivore
[HER•bih•vawr] **An animal that eats only plants or other producers:** Cows are *herbivores.* (160)

hypothesis
[hy•PAHTH•uh•sis]
A scientific explanation that can be tested:
Scientists carry out experiments to test their *hypotheses.* (23)

I

identify
[eye•DENT•uh•fy]
To recognize and give a scientific name to a sample:
Hardness and color can help you *identify* a mineral. (278)

igneous rock
[IG•nee•uhs] **Rock that forms when melted rock cools:** Granite is one kind of *igneous* rock. (292)

inference
[IN•fer•uhns] **An untested interpretation of observations:** *Inferences* can help you make hypotheses to test. (18)

insect [IN•sekt] **A type of animal that has three main body parts and six legs:** Ants are one kind of *insect.* (152)

insulate [IN•suh•layt] **To protect from electricity by covering with rubber or another material that does not carry current:** The red, blue, and green plastic *insulates* these wires. (140)

interdependence
[in•ter•dee•PEN•duhns] **The dependence of populations of organisms on one another for survival:** Healthy ecosystems show *interdependence* between many kinds of organism. (244)

interpret
[in•TER•pret] **To evaluate evidence or data to draw a conclusion:** Scientists *interpret* their results to explain what happened in their experiments. (32)

K

kinetic energy
[kih•NET•ik EN•er•jee] **The energy of motion:** When you move, you have *kinetic energy.* (120)

L

landslide [LAND•slyd] The sudden movement of rock and soil downhill: *Landslides* can be very dangerous. (324)

lava [LAH•vuh] Molten rock that flows from a volcano onto Earth's surface: *Lava* may flow quickly at first, but it slows down as it cools. (326)

light [LYT] A form of energy that can travel in waves through empty space: The sun produces *light* energy. (137)

lithification [lith•ih•fuh•KAY•shuhn] The process of becoming a rock: Sediment becomes rock through *lithification.*

living [LIV•ing] Made up of cells and able to react to surroundings and to reproduce: All animals are *living* things. (212)

luster [LUHS•ter] The brightness and reflecting quality of the surface of a mineral: Minerals with a metallic *luster* look shiny. (278)

M

magma [MAG•muh] Melted rock that is beneath Earth's surface: *Magma* sometimes hardens into solid rock underground. (306)

magnet [MAG•nuht] An object that attracts iron and some other metals: This *magnet* is strong enough to attract a paper clip even through three sheets of paper. (86)

magnetic field
[mag•NET•ik FEELD]
The space around a magnet in which magnetic forces can act: The metal filings show where the *magnetic field* is. (88)

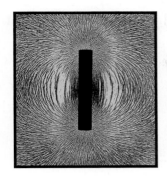

magnetic pole
[mag•NET•ik POHL]
One of the two areas on a magnet where it exerts the strongest force: Every magnet has two *magnetic poles.* (86)

mechanical weathering
[muh•KAN•ih•kuhl WETH•er•ing] A process by which rocks are broken down through physical methods: Wind and water cause a lot of *mechanical weathering.* (338)

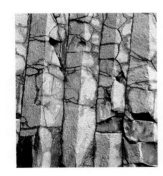

metamorphic rock
[met•uh•MAWR•fik]
Rock that has been changed through high temperature and pressure without being melted: Gneiss is one kind of *metamorphic* rock. (296)

microorganism
[my•kroh•AWR•guhn•iz•uhm] An organism that is too small to be seen with the unaided eye: This picture of a *microorganism* was taken with a microscope. (174)

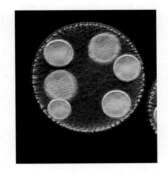

microscope
[MY•kruh•skohp]
A science tool that makes very tiny things look bigger: You might find this kind of *microscope* at your school. (8, 258)

mineral [MIN•uh•ruhl]
A nonliving solid that occurs naturally and has a repeating structure: Amethyst is a *mineral.* (274)

mold [MOHLD] **A kind of fungus:** Some kinds of *mold* help people make cheese. (258)

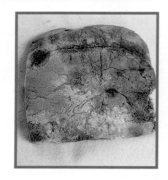

molten [MOHL•tuhn] **Melted, especially as rock or metal may be:** This *molten* gold is being poured into a mold. (306)

motion [MO•shuhn] **Any change in position:** This student is in *motion*. (120)

mud [MUHD] **A mix of water and fine sediment:** Some animals and even people use *mud* for building. (275)

mutually dependent [MYOO•choo•uhl•ee dee•PEN•duhnt] **Needing each other to survive:** Plants and animals are *mutually dependent*. (244)

N

needle [NEED•uhl] **The small, thin, magnetized pointer in a compass:** The *needle* of a compass points north. (99)

niche [NICH] **The role a living thing plays in its environment:** Every living thing has a *niche*. (197)

nonliving [nahn•LIV•ing] **Either not made of cells or made of cells but no longer alive:** A bicycle is a *nonliving* thing. (212)

north-seeking pole [NAWRTH•seek•ing POHL] **The pole of a magnet that moves to point to Earth's north magnetic pole:** The *north-seeking pole* of this magnet points north when the magnet is allowed to turn freely. (86)

nutrient [NOO•tree•uhnt] **A substance that a living thing must eat or absorb in order to survive:** Plants absorb *nutrients* from soil. (170)

O

observation [ahb•zer•VAY•shuhn] **Information that you gather with your senses:** You can make an *observation* with your eyes or ears. (18)

omnivore [AHM•nih•vawr] **An animal that eats both plants and other animals:** A bear is an *omnivore.* (160)

P

parallel circuit [PAIR•uhl•el SER•kit] **An electric circuit with two or more paths that current can follow:** If one bulb in a *parallel circuit* goes out, the others stay on. (76)

pebble [PEB•uhl] **A smooth, rounded rock that is about 4 to 75 millimeters (0.2 to 3 in.) in diameter:** You can hold several *pebbles* in your hand. (291, 351)

physical change
[FIZ•ih•kuhl CHAYNJ]
A change, such as mechanical weathering, that does not make a new substance: The freezing of water is a *physical change.* (338)

pollinate
[PAHL•uh•nayt]
To transfer pollen from a male part of a flower to a female part of a flower: Bees *pollinate* some flowers. (244)

population [pahp•yoo•LAY•shuhn]
All the individuals of one kind living in the same environment: Available resources limit animal *populations.* (212)

predator
[PRED•uh•ter] **A consumer that eats prey:** Cougars are *predators.* (184)

prediction
[pree•DIK•shuhn] **A statement of what will happen, based on observations and knowledge of cause-and-effect relationships:** Scientists make *predictions* based on what they already know and careful thought. (19)

prey [PRAY]
Consumers that are eaten by predators: Rabbits are one kind of *prey.* (184)

producer
[proh•DOO•ser] **A living thing, such as a plant, that can make its own food:** Grasses are *producers.* (158)

protist [PROH•tist] **A one-celled organism that may share traits with plants or animals:** An amoeba is a *protist*—it has only one cell. (258)

recycle [ree•sy•kuhl]
To use the material from an object to make new objects: You can *recycle* your plastic bottles. (170)

relationship
[rih•LAY•shuhn•ship]
A connection between organisms: Predators have a *relationship* with prey. (245)

repel [ree•PEL] **To push away:** The north-seeking poles of two magnets *repel* each other. (59)

resistance
[ree•ZIS•tuhns] **The measure of how much a material opposes the flow of electric current:** Most metals have low *resistance.* (78)

resources
[REE•sawr•suhz]
Useful things in the environment, such as air, food, water, and shelter, that animals need to survive: The amount of available *resources* changes with the seasons. (197)

rock [RAHK] **A naturally occurring solid made up of one or more minerals:** *Rocks* come in all shapes and sizes. (290)

rock cycle
[RAHK SY•kuhl] **An endless process in which rocks are changed from one type to another by weathering, erosion, heat, and pressure:** In the *rock cycle,* the same minerals may become different rocks. (308)

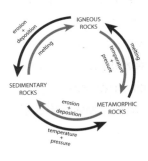

runoff [RUHN•awf]
Water that flows over land without sinking in: *Runoff* can cause erosion. (350)

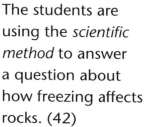

S

sand [SAND] Sediment whose pieces are smaller than pebbles and larger than the pieces in silt or clay, about 0.05 to 2 millimeters (0.002 to 0.08 in.) in diameter: When rocks are broken down into small pieces, they become *sand.* (295, 351)

scale [SKAYL] The set of lines on a graph that shows the sizes of the units on the graph: You label the *scale* to help people understand your graph. (33)

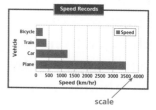

scale

scavenger [SKA•vuhn•jer]
A living thing that feeds on dead organisms: *Scavengers* have an important niche in an ecosystem. (171)

scientific method [sy•uhn•TIF•ik METH•uhd] A series of steps that scientists follow to test hypotheses and find out answers to their science questions: The students are using the *scientific method* to answer a question about how freezing affects rocks. (42)

sedimentary (rock) [sed•uh•MEN•ter•ee] Rock that forms from sand, mud, and other eroded materials: Sandstone is one kind of *sedimentary* rock. (294)

series circuit
[SEER•eez SER•kit] **An
electric circuit with
only one path that
current can follow:**
If one bulb in a *series
circuit* goes out,
the others also go
out. (74)

shock [SHAHK] **The
painful and possibly
dangerous result
of electric current
flowing through
the body:** You can
be badly hurt by an
electric shock. (61)

short circuit [SHAWRT
SER•kit] **A flaw in a
circuit that allows
a large current to
flow through where
it is not wanted:**
Short circuits can keep
electrical devices
from working. (79)

silt [SILT] **Sediment
whose pieces are
smaller than sand
and larger than
the pieces in clay,
about 0.002 to 0.05
millimeters (0.00008
to 0.002 in.) in
diameter:** You can
find *silt* at the bottom
of a river. (351)

soil [SOYL] **A mixture
of weathered
rock, bits of dead
organisms, water,
and air:** You can
grow plants in
soil. (338)

solar energy [SOHL•er
EN•er•jee] **Energy
released by the
sun:** *Solar energy*
can be changed to
electricity. (156)

south-seeking pole
[sowth•seek•ing pohl] **The pole of a magnet that moves to point to Earth's south magnetic pole:** The *south-seeking pole* of this magnet points south when the magnet is allowed to turn freely. (86)

spring scale
[spring skayl] **A tool that measures forces, such as weight:** You can find *spring scales* at some grocery stores. (11)

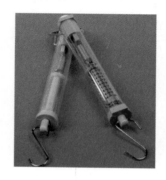

standard measure
[stan•derd mazh•er] **An accepted measurement:** A meter is a *standard measure* of length. (6)

static electricity
[stat•ik ee•lek•tris•ih•tee] **The buildup of electric charges in one place:** *Static electricity* might make your hair stand up. (59)

streak [streek] **The mark left by a mineral when it is rubbed across a rough, white tile:** This mineral leaves a brown *streak* on the tile. (276)

 T

transport
[trans•pawrt] **The movement of sediment from place to place by water:** *Transport* of sand in the river made those sandbars. (350)

V

variable
[VAIR•ee•uh•buhl] **A condition that can change in a scientific experiment:** You can control some *variables.* (24)

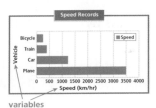
variables

volcano
[vahl•KAY•noh] **A mountain that forms as molten rock flows through a crack onto Earth's surface:** The lava from the *volcano* was thick and flowed slowly. (326)

W

weathering
[WETH•er•ing]
A process of breaking down rock: *Weathering* has formed a hole in this sandstone, making an arch. (338)

wire [WYR] **A long, thin piece of metal:** *Wires* can carry electricity. (140)

Index

GLOSSARY

R38 (*cl*) Buddy Mays/Corbis; **R38** (*tcr*) David Scharf/GettyImages; **R38** (*tl*) Paul Barton/zenfa/Corbis; **R39** (*tcr*) Bruce Cairns/Alamy; **R39** (*tr*) Corbis; **R39** (*tl*) Getty; **R39** (*br*) Mike Danton/Alamy Images; **R39** (*bcr*) Paul Silverman-Fundamental Photographs; **R40** (*tl*) Gabriela Staeble/zefa/Corbis; **R40** (*bcr*) Henry Westheim/Aalamy; **R40** (*bcl*) Stephen Alvarez/National Geographic/Getty Images; **R40** (*tcr*) W, Cody/Corbis; **R41** (*tcl*) Albrecht G. Schaefer/Corbis; **R41** (*tl*) Farrell Grehan; **R41** (*tcr*) Peter Weimann/Animals Animals/Earth Scenes; **R41** (*tl*) Tony Freeman/Photo Edit; **R41** (*bl*) Zephyr/Photo Researchers, Inc; **R42** (*br*) Alamy Images; **R43** (*bcl*) Lloyd Cluff/CORBIS; **R43** (*bcr*) Ric Ergenbright/CORBIS; **R44** (*tr*) D. Boschung/zefa/Corbis; **R44** (*br*) ER Degginger/Color-Pic, Inc.; **R44** (*tr*) Ingram Publishing/Alamy Images; **R45** (*br*) Ed Young/CORBIS; **R45** (*tr*) George D. Lepo/Corbis; **R45** (*bl*) Peter Arnold/gettyimages; **R45** (*bl*) Stock Connection Distribution/Alamy; **R46** (*bl*) Annie Griffiths Belt/National Geographic Image Collection; **R46** (*tl*) Jacques Jangoux/Getty; **R46** (*tcr*) Jose Manuel Sanchis Calvete/CORBIS;

R46 (*bcl*) K-P Wolf/Getty Images; **R46** (*tr*) Michelle Garrett/CORBIS; **R47** (*tcr*) Carolina Biological/GettyImages; **R47** (*tr*) Jon Sparks/Alamy Images; **R47** (*bl*) Nordicphotos/Alamy; **R47** (*tl*) Werner H. Muller/Corbis; **R48** (*tl*) Cat Gwynn/Getty Images; **R48** (*tcl*) Charles O'Rear/CORBIS; **R48** (*bcl*) Mike Brinson/Getty Images; **R48** (*tr*) Noble Proctor/Photo Researchers; **R49** (*br*) Jen Fong/Getty Images; **R50** (*tl*) Chuch Franklin/Alamy; **R50** (*br*) Dr Stanley Flegie/Getty Images; **R50** (*tr*) Getty Images; **R50** (*bl*) Joe McDonald/Corbis; **R50** (*bcl*) Karen Moskowitz/Getty Images; **R51** (*bl*) Mika/Zefa/Corbis; **R51** (*tcl*) Tom and Pat Leeson; **R51** (*tr*) W. Perry Conway/Corbis; **R52** (*tl*) Alamy RF; **R53** (*bl*) Douglas Fisher/Alamy

All other photos © Harcourt School Publishers. Harcourt Photos provided by the Harcourt Index, Harcourt IPR, and Harcourt photographers; Weronica Ankarorn, Eric Camden, Doug Dukane, Ken Kinzie, April Riehm, and Steve Williams.

Classification Black bears are omnivores. They prefer berries, nuts, and insects, but they will eat whatever is available.

Characteristics Adult black bears are 5 ½ to 6 feet tall.

CHARACTERISTICS Like you, black bears have five toes on each foot—except each toe has a 2 to 3 inch-long claw!

BEHAVIOR Bear cubs are taught to climb trees to avoid danger.

CHARACTERISTICS A bear's teeth grow continuously throughout its lifetime.